BASEBALL IN COLUMBIA

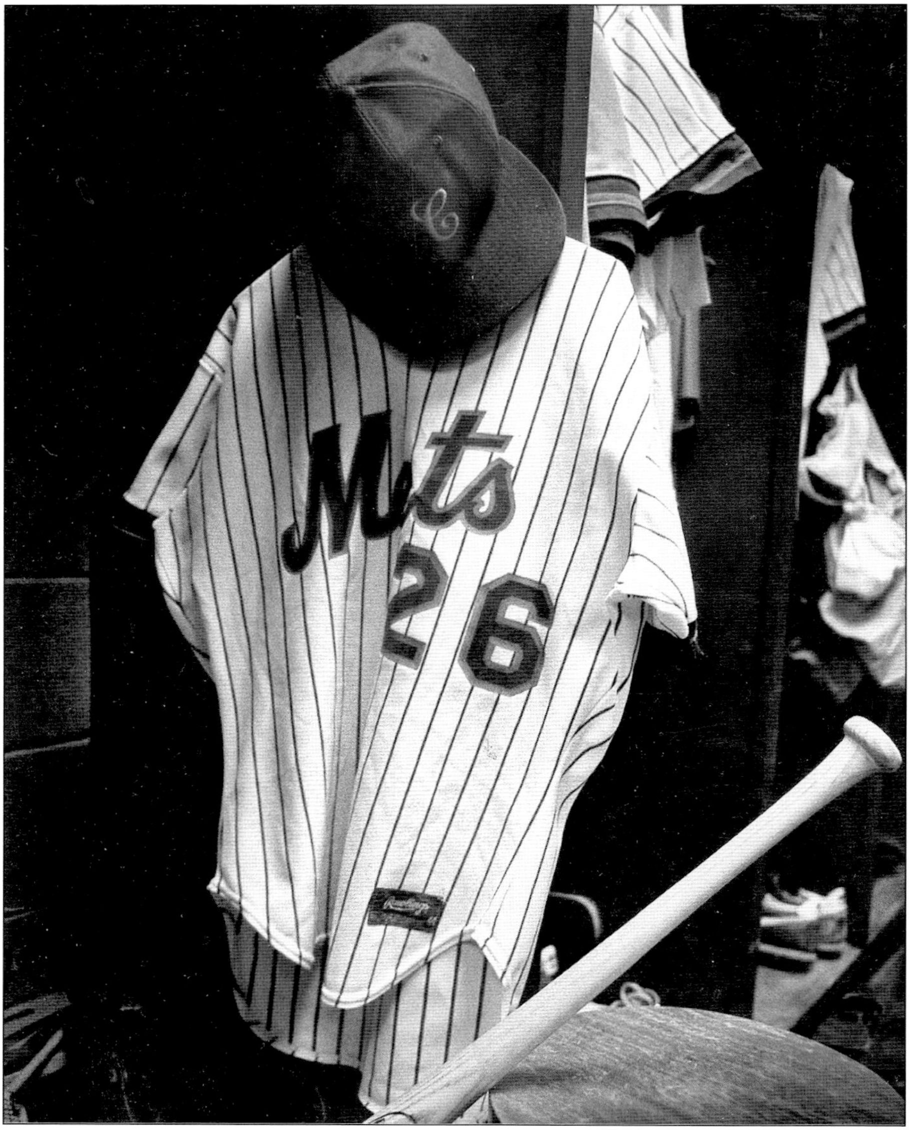

A Columbia Mets jersey hangs in a clubhouse locker. In more than a century of professional baseball in Columbia, no major league club fielded more teams in the city than the New York Mets. Every player and coach from the 1983 Columbia Mets through the 2004 Capital City Bombers belonged to the Mets organization. This affiliation is the longest-running connection in the South Atlantic League. (CCB.)

Front cover photo of 1928 Manager Joe Kelly is courtesy of the South Carolina State Museum.

Front cover photo of Preston Wilson and back cover photo of Capital City Stadium are from Capital City Bombers archives.

Background cover photo of 1941 Columbia Reds was donated by Sue Heath to the Capital City Bombers archives.

BASEBALL IN COLUMBIA

Mark Bryant

ARCADIA
PUBLISHING

ISBN 978-0-7385-1679-0

Published by Arcadia Publishing
Charleston, South Carolina

Printed in the United States of America

Library of Congress Catalog Card Number: 2004106067

For all general information contact Arcadia Publishing at:
Telephone 843-853-2070
Fax 843-853-0044
E-mail sales@arcadiapublishing.com
For customer service and orders:
Toll-Free 1-888-313-2665

Visit us on the Internet at www.arcadiapublishing.com

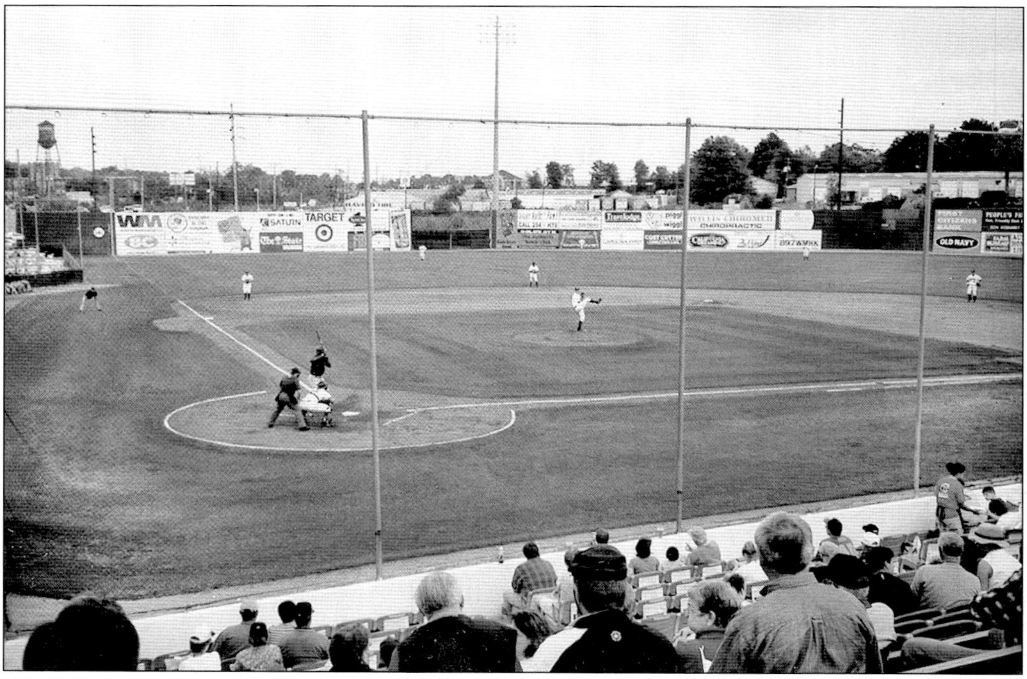

Fans watch a game at Columbia's ballpark in 2003. Whether you call it Dreyfuss Field, Capital City Park, Ouzts Field, or Capital City Stadium, the home of Columbia's professional baseball teams has been in the same place for quite a long time. Here we see the 21st-century version of the Capital City Bombers playing where the Comers, Sandlappers, Senators, Reds, Gems, and Mets had come and gone in previous decades. (CCB.)

Contents

ACKNOWLEDGMENTS

This book has been designed to give the reader a trip through the stages of baseball in Columbia, offering the chance to meet many of the players and other people who have shaped the game while also seeing the different directions it has taken. I apologize in advance if a favorite player or story did not make it to the final version of the book, as it would be impossible to cover every detail about Columbia baseball in a work of this format.

Obviously a project such as this one does not happen on its own. I owe so much to the people who have believed in this book and the people who have opened their memories and collections to making this possible. My thanks go out first to the Capital City Bombers and everyone who has worked alongside me over the many hot days and long nights at the ballpark. A special token of gratitude goes out to team president Rich Mozingo for allowing open access to team archives. I offer thanks to those who have donated to the team's collection over the years, including the windfall of Columbia Mets pictures from the files of the *Columbia Record* and the great work for the team by photographer Allen Sharpe. Fritz Hamer at the South Carolina State Museum provided great assistance for the pre-Depression years, as did the staff at the South Caroliniana Library at the University of South Carolina and the research of Lindsay Smith. I truly appreciate the help from the private collections of baseball fans Bob and Fran Somogyi, broadcasting legend Bob Fulton, Columbia Red Jim Kleckley, and antique dealer Mike Safran, along with Pat Reddick, Barbara Shealy, Flynn Bowie, and Michael Love. Thanks also to the cooperation from the Pittsburgh Pirates, Detroit Tigers, and New York Mets. At Arcadia Publishing, I want to acknowledge Laura New for putting the seed of this project in my mind and Barbie Langston for making it grow.

I owe my greatest thanks to my family for putting up with me during the creative process. My wife, Jeanne, may be the most understanding partner ever, putting up with my baseball life for most of our 10 years of marriage. I could never thank her enough. My son, Griffin, offers me inspiration with every smile on his two-year-old face. My parents instilled in me a passion for books and a passion for sports—what a perfect combination for this work. Lastly, I want to thank all my teachers over the years for giving me so much: particularly Mrs. Seeley in the second grade who told me, "You are

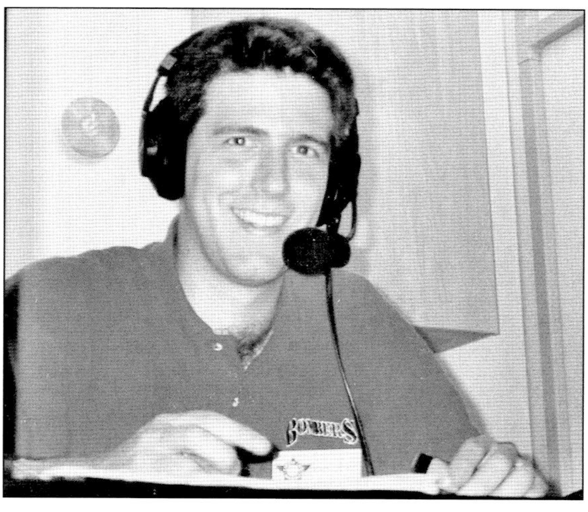

Author Mark Bryant served as the on-air "Voice of the Bombers" in his first three years with the team. Here he is on the job as "the radio guy" in Columbia during the 1998 season.

INTRODUCTION

Now that we have passed into the new millennium, baseball has become as much a metaphor as a sport in our lives. Its phrases have infiltrated our everyday speech to the degree that even someone who never goes to the ballpark can describe things in terms of "striking out" or "hitting a home run." Its status as the country's most popular sport has been challenged, but its role as the national pastime never has.

Why do we have such an ingrained connection to this game? Because baseball history has run parallel with American history: its great dates time-stamp our lives and its pivotal games define our moments. The successes and failures of baseball as a sport and a business often coincide with factors that have shaped our nation and its economy. Baseball intertwines with all those things that make us American.

Now let us look at the game from a local level. In many cases, a team becomes an integral part of a community, of who the people are and what they do. The citizens gather in one place with one common goal: root-root-root for the home team. Wins and losses mean something more than a number in the standings and players are more than just normal people because the city has its name on the results of the game. A team may operate like a private business, but part of each team will always belong to the town in which it plays. That is why fans always feel betrayed or heartbroken when teams move or fold.

The images and stories on the pages that follow take us on a bumpy journey through the relationship of one city and its baseball team over the years. In Columbia, South Carolina, it is not really the story of one team but of several teams that have come and gone. Such is the case for many cities in the minor leagues—and even a few in the majors. Although the path has not always been smooth, it has still produced many great teams and stellar players.

The game's 19th-century origins quickly blossomed into the organization of 20th-century minor league play, and Columbia was there from the beginning of the South Atlantic League (SAL) in 1904. Columbia's first true taste of on-field success came with the 1917 pennant, and the Columbia Comers did not want to let go—they ran the streak to four straight titles before falling. The Columbia teams lived a vagabond existence until finding a permanent location to play in 1927—that site, Dreyfuss Field, remained the home of Columbia baseball in 2004. Leon "Goose" Goslin and Lloyd "Little Poison" Waner, two future Hall-of-Famers, were among the legends of that period who took the field for the Columbia Comers. Unfortunately, the Great Depression snuffed out the first bright era of Columbia baseball: the Comers halted with the suspension of the league and did not return.

Although there were other efforts to revive the game, baseball did not truly spring back to life until the Columbia Reds came to town in 1938. The Reds provided a large number of talented players, managers, and teams for nearly two decades (with a hiatus taken for World War II). Ted Kluszewski, Johnny Temple, and Hall-of-Famer Frank Robinson were among the stars to play for the Columbia Reds. The 1950s in particular saw pennant-winning and title-contending squads in Columbia. But the Reds grew dissatisfied with Columbia attendance and decided to give Savannah a try. Businessman Julius Love and other prominent Columbians kept baseball alive by getting another team in for two years and then later convincing the Reds to return for two seasons, but it was not meant to last. The second bright period in Columbia baseball went dark.

Strangely enough, it took more than 20 years to see the national pastime return to South Carolina's capital city. Years of effort by community leaders brought the Columbia Mets to town. Although that franchise changed hands several times and even changed its name once, the same team remains in Columbia today. The Mets won the SAL title in 1986, bringing a championship to town for the first time in a generation. More titles arrived in 1991 and 1998, as the Mets continued to supply the team with quality players. From the arrival of the Columbia Mets in 1983 to the early part of the 2004 season, 99 players advanced from Columbia to play Major League Baseball.

When the Columbia Mets changed their name to the Capital City Bombers after 10 seasons, the change signified both a move forward and a look back. While the team took on the modern marketing approach of wearing its own name rather than relying on the parent club, the name that was chosen honored a significant event of Columbia's past: the training of the Doolittle Raiders for their attack on Japan following the devastation at Pearl Harbor. The Bombers still wore that name in 2004 with all the trappings of a modern team playing minor league baseball. Naturally, there have been fireworks, promotions, music, games, merchandise, silliness, and lots of extras at the ballpark. Nonetheless, at the heart of it all, the game has remained.

So despite the passage of wars, the fluctuation of the economy, the whims of teams and owners, and the evolution of a city, you still find baseball. Whether you believe that baseball is just a game or something more, you should visit the ballpark near you. You will get something out of it either way. Hopefully the same can be said of the journey taken in the pages that follow.

PHOTOGRAPH KEY:
Pictures from the archives of the Capital City Bombers are indicated by the letters CCB (with additional information if pictures were donated). All other images are individually credited.

ONE

The Very Early Days of Columbia Baseball

Newspaper accounts credit Columbia's first known baseball game as taking place in 1867, a time when the city was still trying to recover and rebuild from the devastation of the Civil War. Like many cities across America, the young sport of "base ball" began gaining momentum and popularity in Columbia over the years that followed. Organized leagues of teams on a local level came and went, with the strongest acknowledged versions of these leagues fielding teams in the 1890s before disbanding. When some forward-thinking businessmen conceived the South Atlantic League, Columbia was one of its charter cities. Professional baseball has been a part of the city's make-up ever since, although not on a continuous basis.

The original team owners reflected the growing nature of South Carolina's capital city by naming that first "Sally League" team the Skyscrapers, but that name quickly faded in favor of a more popular one in the area: the Gamecocks. Regardless of the name, Columbia was officially on the map of American baseball.

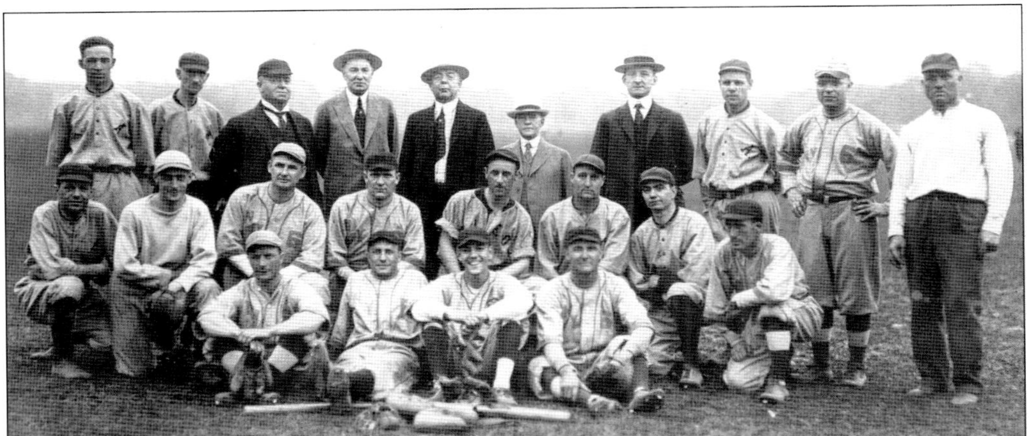

Printers League teams like this one formed the basis for the origins of organized baseball in many cities. Columbia found its first baseball teams in such a way: via unions, trade workers, or regional affiliations. Although such teams offered a quality version of the game that many in the community could rally around, genuine minor league ball remained a few years away. (Mulcahey family collection.)

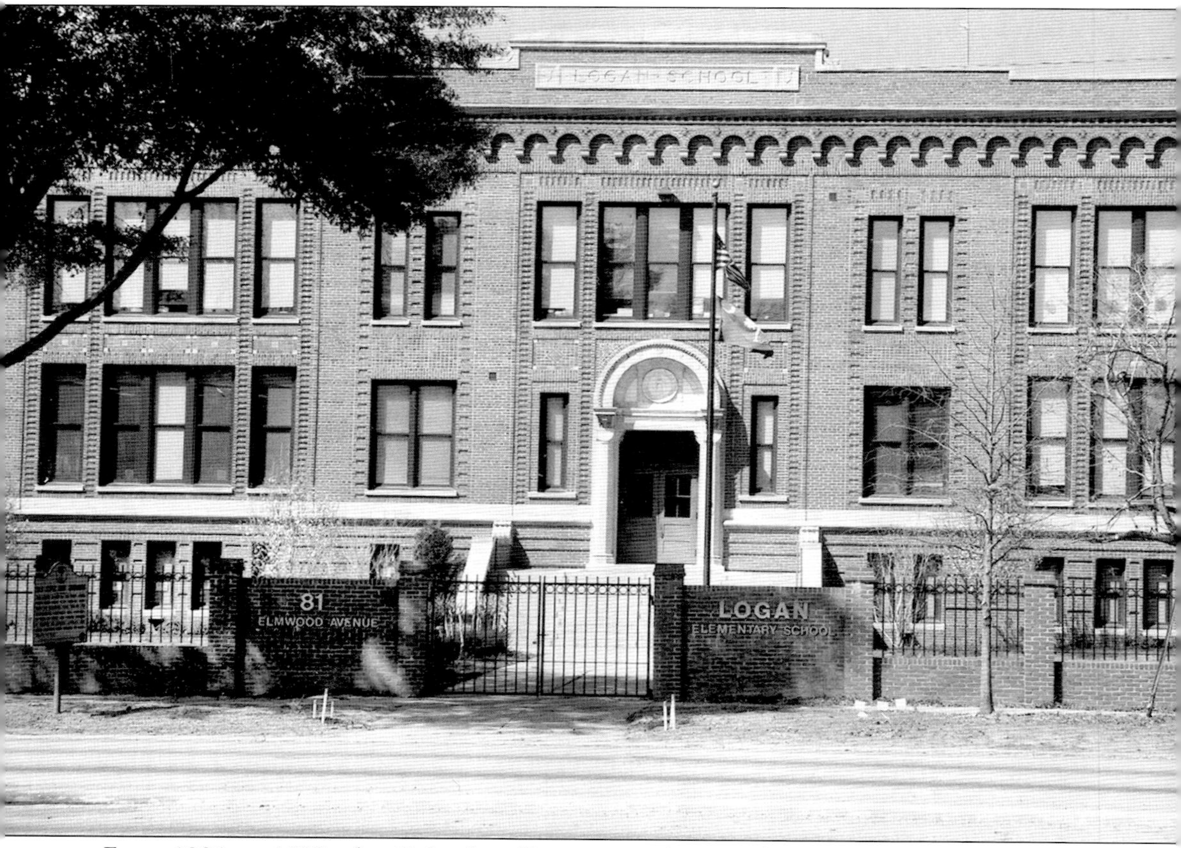

From 1904 to 1912, the Columbia Skyscrapers, Gamecocks, and Commies/Comers called Elmwood Field home, excluding 1908, when the Gamecocks gave the new state fairgrounds a try. The site has a long and varied history: it was a Confederate barracks and hospital during the Civil War, the location of the state fair before and after the war (up to 1903), a ballpark for nine years, and finally Logan Elementary School—which, as seen here, has remained for more than 90 years. Much like those at Chicago's yet-to-be-built Wrigley Field, fans often watched Elmwood Field games from neighboring rooftops. To give some perspective on this era, consider that the major league greats of the time were players like Honus Wagner, Cy Young, and Nap Lajoie. It would not be long before some of the players who hit the field here followed in their mighty footsteps. (Author's collection.)

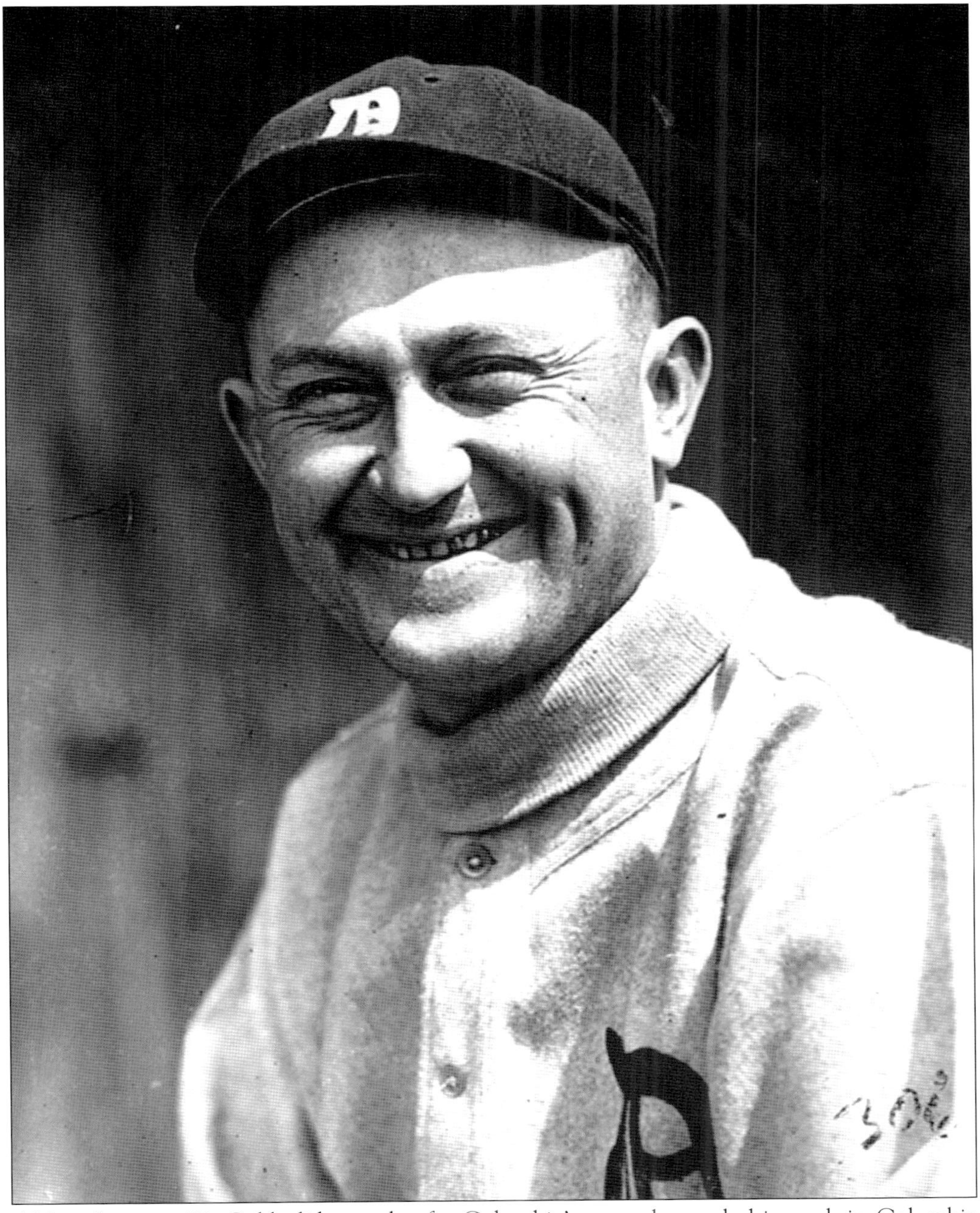

Although young Ty Cobb did not play for Columbia's team, he made his mark in Columbia baseball history right away. Columbia's first South Atlantic League season opened with a game against Augusta in April 1904. The Columbia Skyscrapers began the city's recognized professional baseball life with a victory, an 8-7 afternoon win, but it was the future legend of the game who stole the show: Augusta's star player crushed a home run and a double for the opposition. "The Georgia Peach" was the only player with two extra-base hits in the game. Columbia and Augusta ended that season as the bottom two teams in the six-team league. Cobb began his long Hall of Fame career the very next season in Detroit. (Detroit Tigers.)

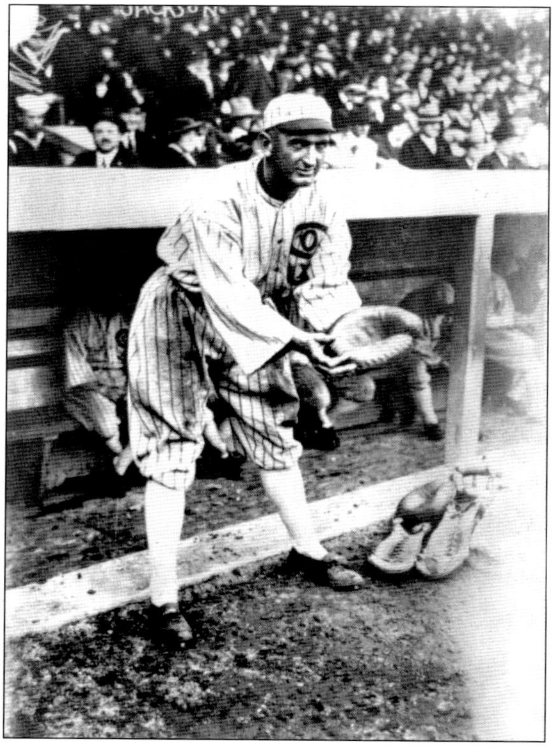

Another legend who passed through Columbia's Elmwood Field on the opposing side also happened to be one of South Carolina's finest: "Shoeless" Joe Jackson. Born in Pickens County in 1889, Jackson's tremendous hitting exploits made him a baseball immortal. The 1919 Chicago "Black Sox" scandal kept Jackson out of the Baseball Hall of Fame. (Bain Collection, Library of Congress.)

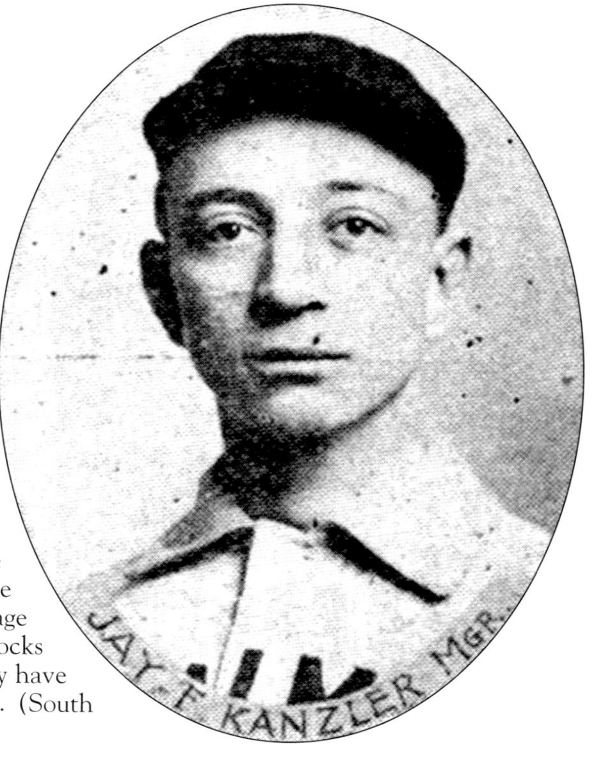

Manager Jay Kanzler led the Columbia Gamecocks at the start of the 1907 season. If you think that swapping out managers is a recent phenomenon, Kanzler's legacy may demonstrate otherwise. Although he began the season for Columbia, he did not manage to the end. The fact that the Gamecocks posted their lowest win total to date may have had something to do with the change. (South Caroliniana Library.)

Rather than feature a local player or coach of distinction on its cover, this scorecard for Columbia offered Charles Boyer, South Atlantic League president. Boyer arranged the original meetings in Savannah in late 1903 that formed the league. He served as Sally League president for the fledgling league's first five seasons. (South Caroliniana Library.)

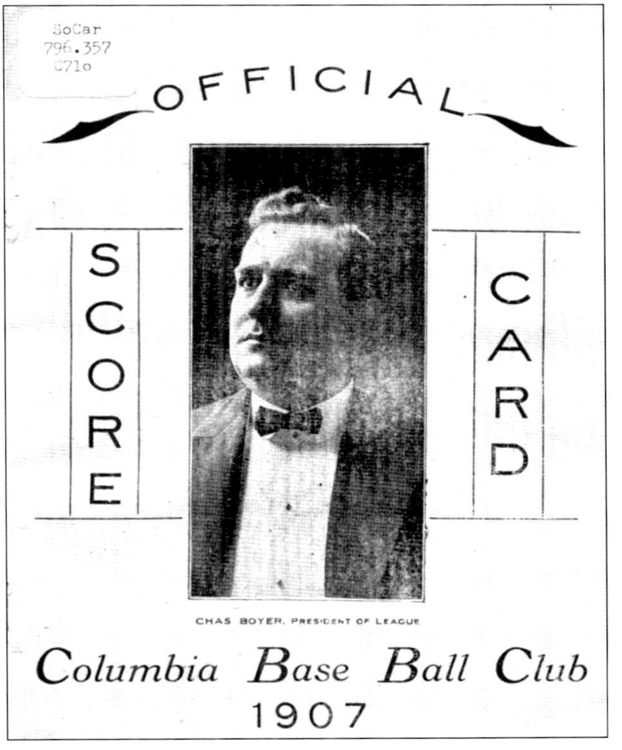

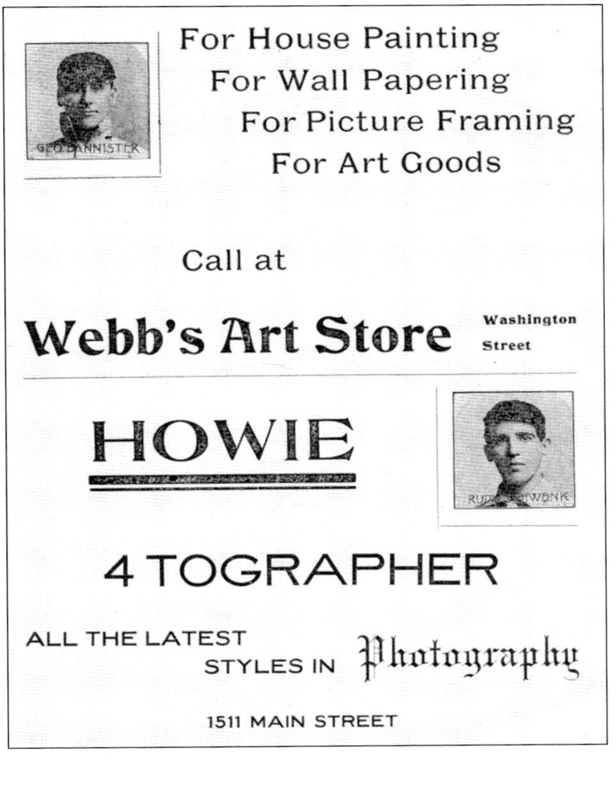

This image is a typical page from the 1907 scorecard: nearly all the ads in the book were for downtown businesses (many on Main Street), players were posted directly within advertiser spaces, and the players themselves were relatively unknown. The pictured duo had three games in the majors between them—George Bannister never made it, but Rudy Schwenk pitched three times for the Cubs in 1909. (South Carcliniana Library.)

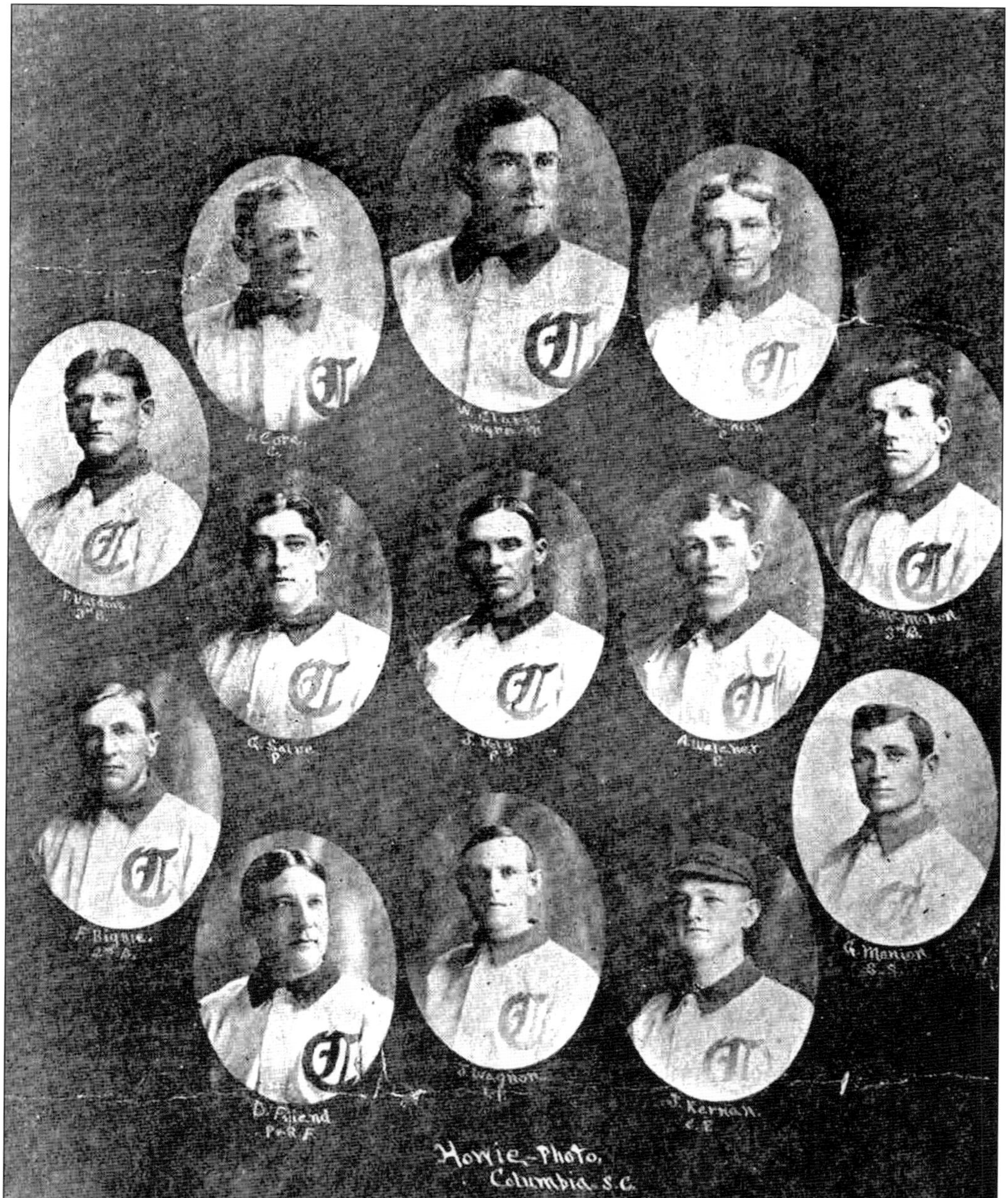

The Columbia team did not fare well for several years, finishing no better than fourth through 1910. The group in this team photo is most likely the 1908 squad, led by manager W.W. Clarke. The squad includes F. Bigbie and W. McMahon, who tied for the league lead in runs scored that year with 55, as well as J. Volz, leader in walks allowed with 91. (South Caroliniana Library.)

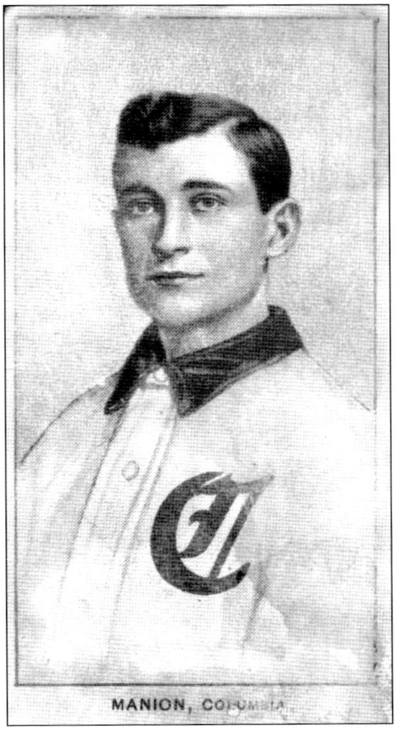

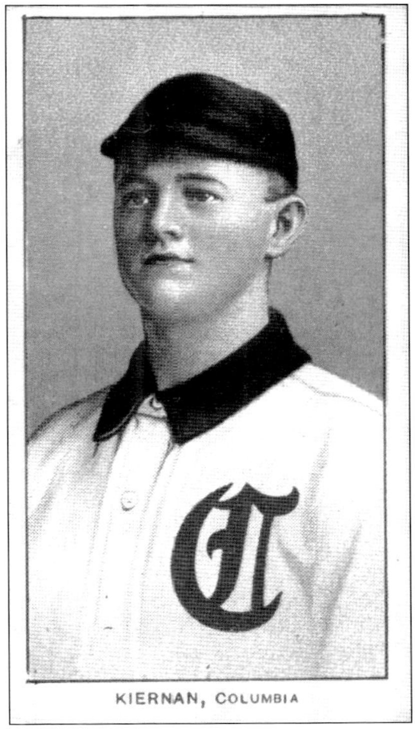

Baseball cards were significantly different in this era. Instead of bubble gum packagers or major card printers they were made by tobacco companies. The cards are not dated but come from c. 1908–1910. The George Manion and J.F. Kiernan cards above were printed in color by Piedmont. The Lewis/Martin/Redfern cards below, from Old Mill, are monochromatic full-length shots with red borders. The tobacco card makers generally issued sets by league rather than team, and each league was a separate series. (Bob and Fran Somogyi.)

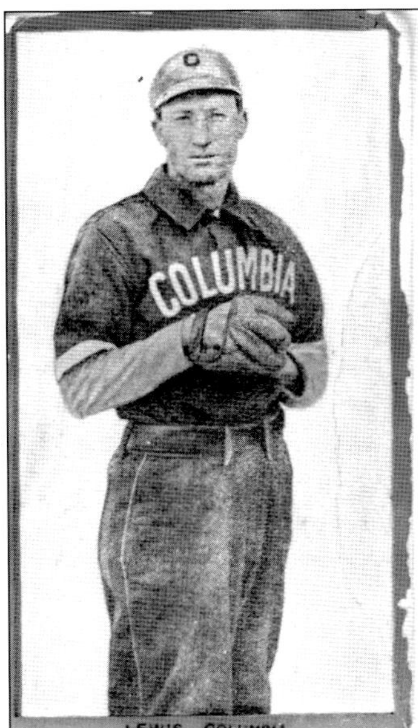

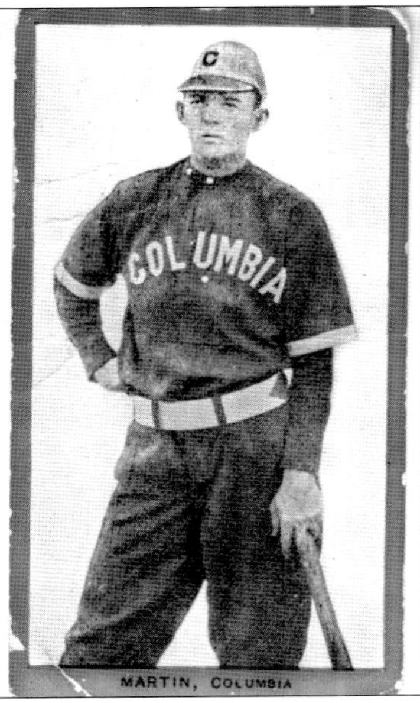

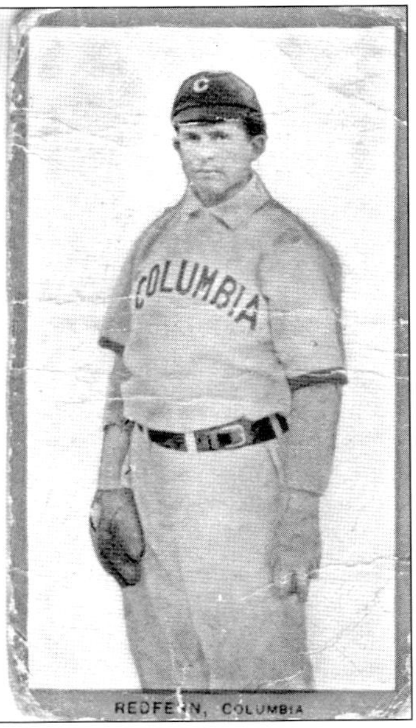

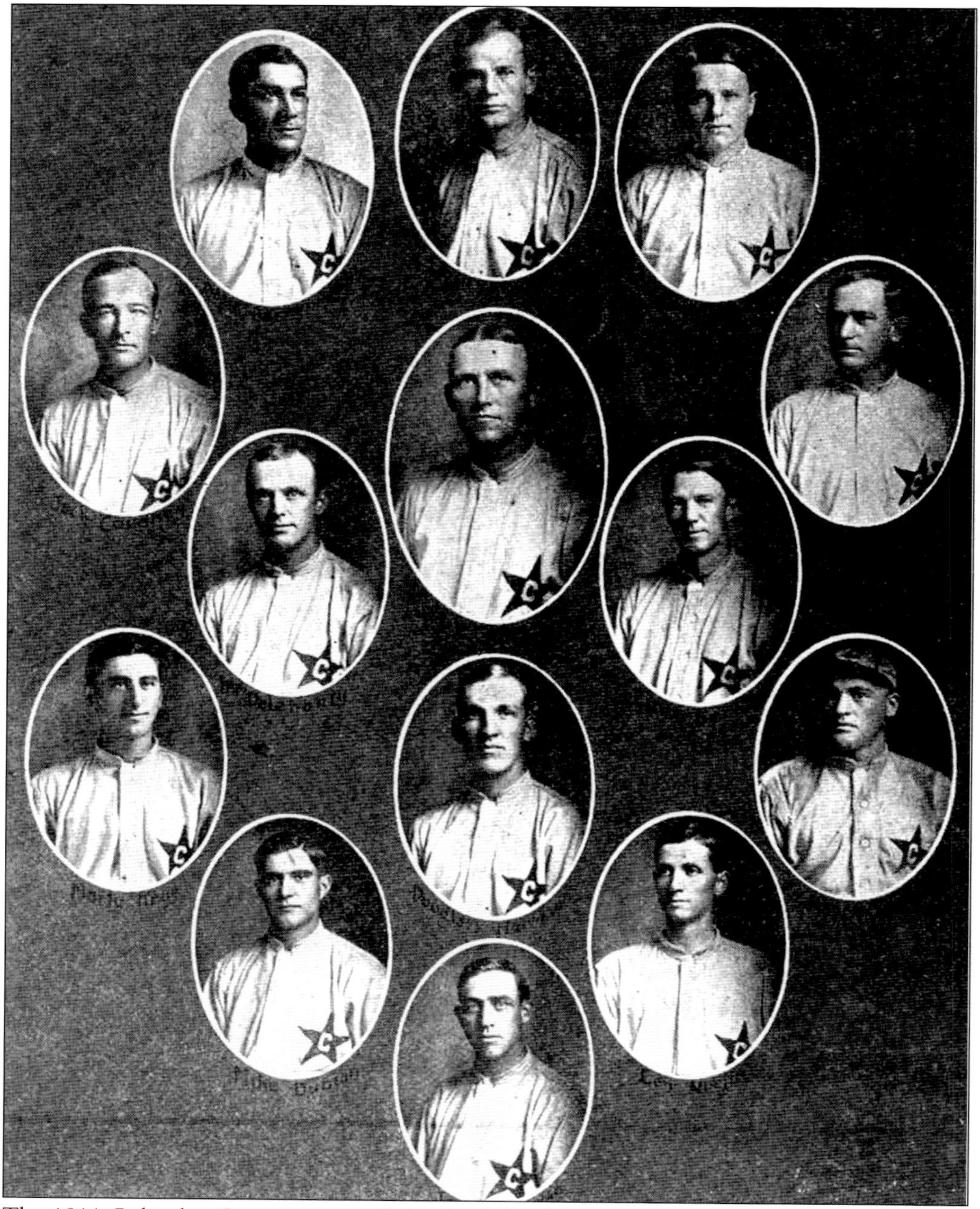

The 1911 Columbia Commies were Columbia's first legitimate on-field success story, winning the second half of a split-season format. Unfortunately, the squad lost the bid for the league title in a playoff, and the city's first championship remained years away. Looking over the early period of Columbia baseball, one notices the constant uniform alterations: the Old English C, the star with block C, "Columbia" arched across the chest, the diamond on the sleeve containing a C, a wide "Cincinnati-style" C, and still other variations. It would appear that the sartorial look of the squad had as many fits and starts as the teams themselves during these inconsistent years. (South Caroliniana Library.)

Two

Up and "Comers" in the National Pastime

When looking into Columbia's baseball past, people inevitably ask, "Why call them the Comers?" The new commissioner-based government of the time had a great deal of support, so the "Commissioners" seemed like a good idea for a name. Almost instantly it became "Commies," which would not have passed muster in later years, and settled down to the familiar "Comers."

The Columbia Comers established stability for baseball in the capital city and, just as importantly, established a high level of play as well. Championships would now belong to Columbia, and future legends of the game would begin their rise to greatness in the city. These years were a fascinating time for the Comers, as the country took a great stride forward into the 20th century, putting World War I behind and hitting the ground running for the Roaring Twenties. Baseball had tightened its hold as America's national pastime, and the Comers delivered all the thrills the game had to offer directly to the South Carolina Midlands.

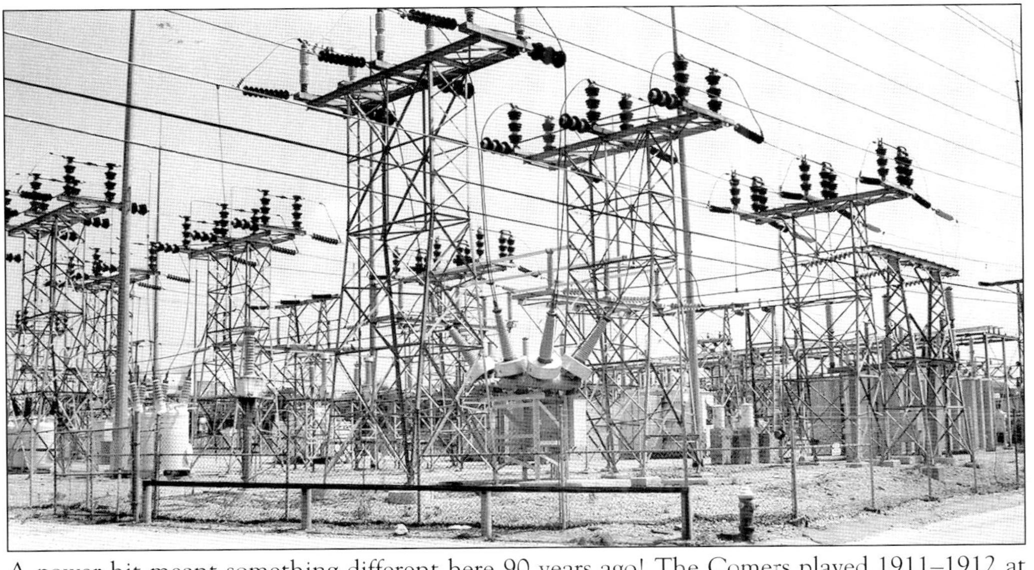

A power hit meant something different here 90 years ago! The Comers played 1911–1912 at the Elmwood site, but construction of the Logan School sent the team to a new location in the Congaree Vista. This spot, near the textile mill that now houses the South Carolina State Museum, only lasted as Columbia's home field for two seasons. After that, the team shared USC's Davis Field for several years. (Author's collection.)

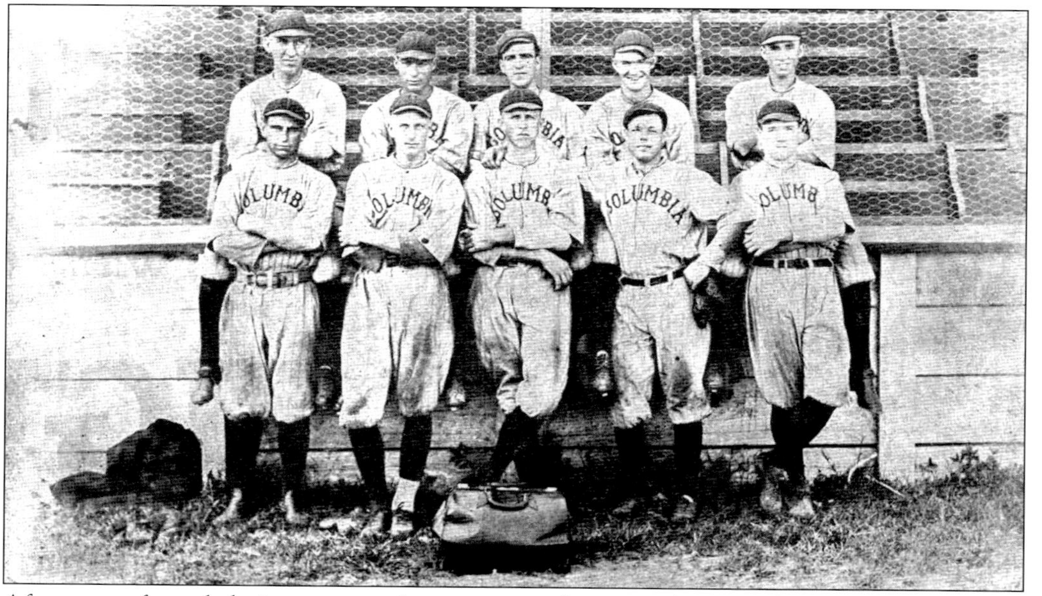

After years of mostly losing seasons, the momentum began to change in late 1915. The Comers, under manager Douglas Harbison, finished third in the second half and did well enough for a winning mark overall. The turn-around did not have immediate championship implications, but better days were soon to come. (South Caroliniana Library.)

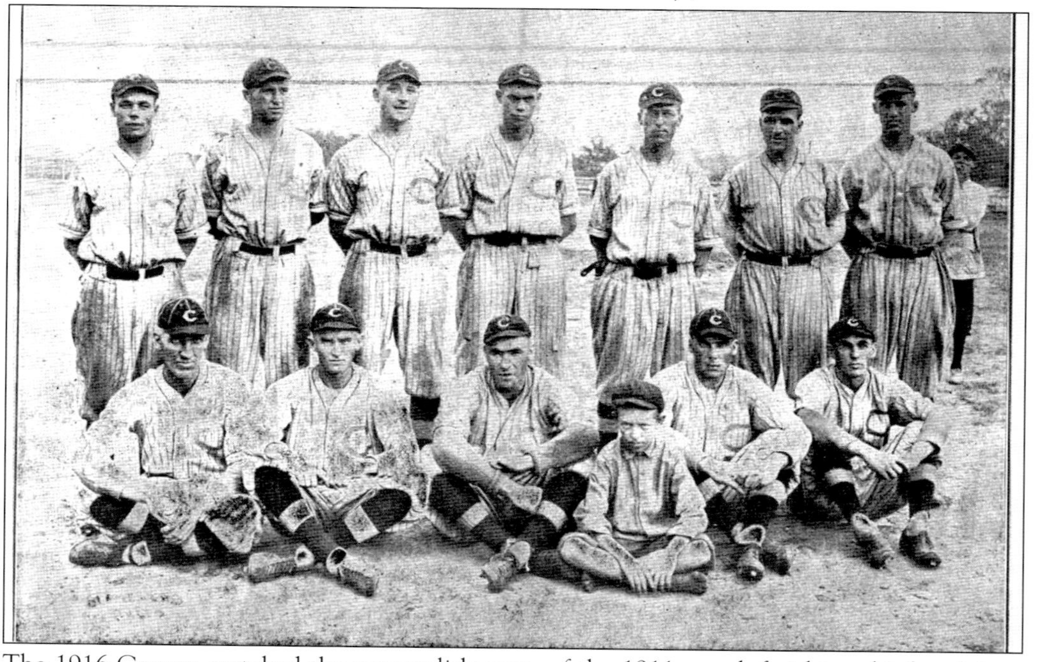

The 1916 Comers matched the accomplishments of the 1911 squad, finishing third and then first in the split season, only to lose the championship playoff. The next four Sally League pennants would all belong to Columbia. The first came in the war-shortened 1917 season. After the league suspended operations for all of 1918, the Comers got back to the business of winning championships the following year. (South Caroliniana Library.)

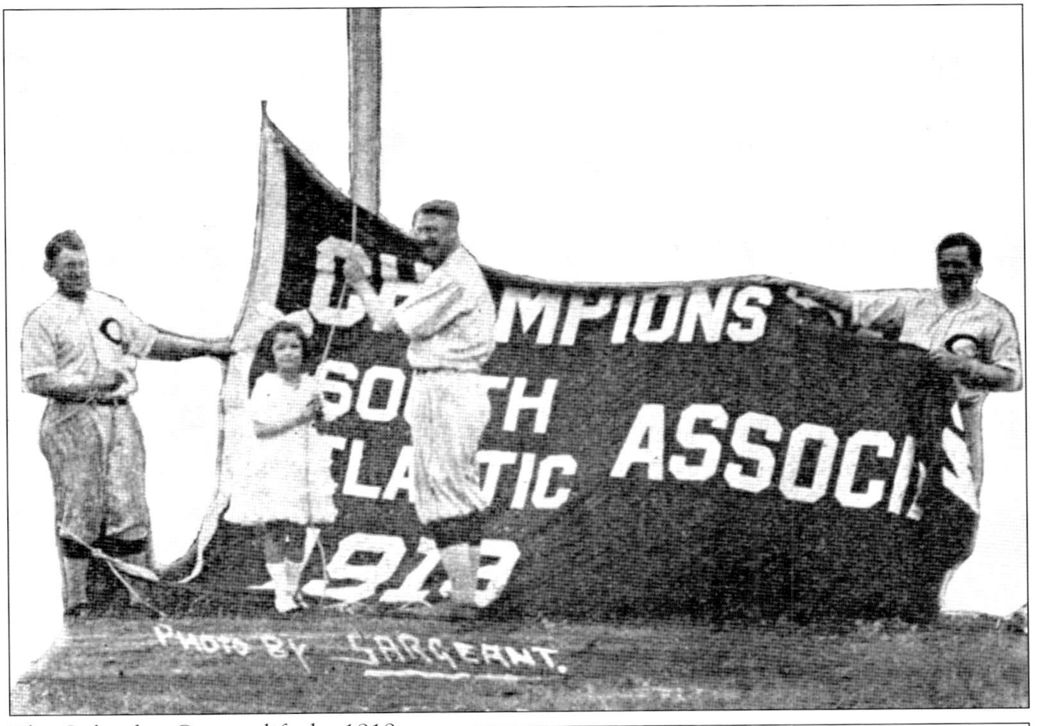

The Columbia Comers lift the 1919 pennant for the Champions of the South Atlantic Association, as it was then called. Although it is now just a remnant of baseball tradition, the pennant itself once represented the pinnacle of success for a team. The pennant, not trophies, rings, or other rewards, was the number-one goal for every team every season. (South Caroliniana Library.)

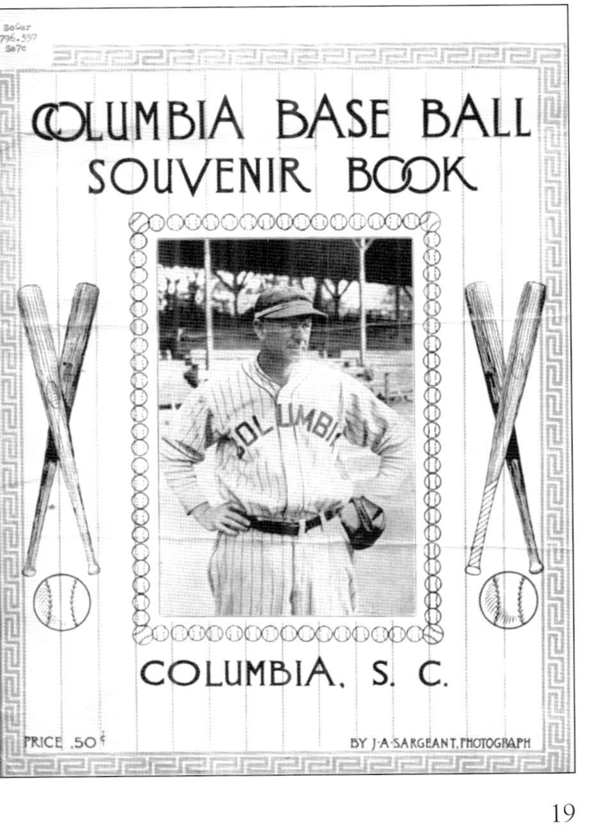

Manager Zinn Beck graced the cover of the 1920 team program. Notice that "base ball" had still not evolved into one word at this point. Beck was not far removed from his years in the majors as an infielder for the Cardinals and Yankees when he took over as player-manager for the Comers. He managed the team for three seasons and won two titles in that time. (South Caroliniana Library.)

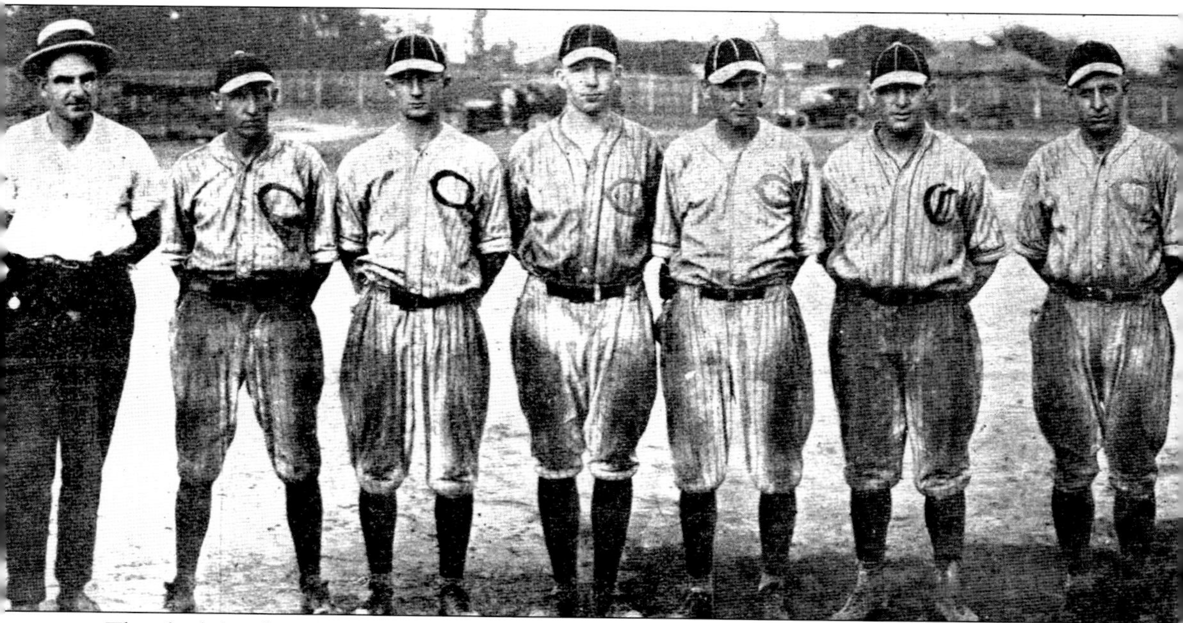

The duel for the 1919 pennant came down to an early September series in Charlotte. The Comers needed to split the six games to win the title. The games were hard-fought, including a 20-inning 5-5 draw. Pitcher Lynn "Lefty" Scoggins (seventh from right) tossed a complete-game shutout (six strikeouts, five hits) on Labor Day to clinch the pennant, earning a ride off

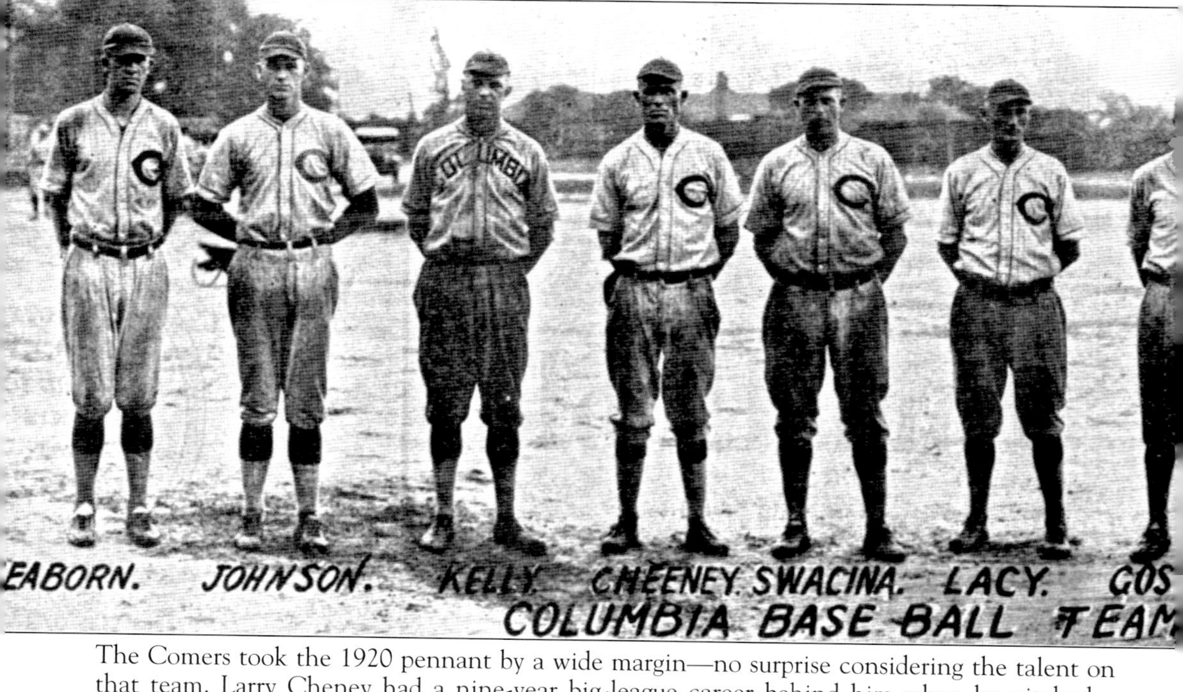

The Comers took the 1920 pennant by a wide margin—no surprise considering the talent on that team. Larry Cheney had a nine-year big-league career behind him when he pitched a league-leading 183 strikeouts and posted a 23-6 record. Teammate Earl Whitehill also won 20 games and had yet to start his 17 years in the majors. Crowd favorite Alva "Pick" Nally led

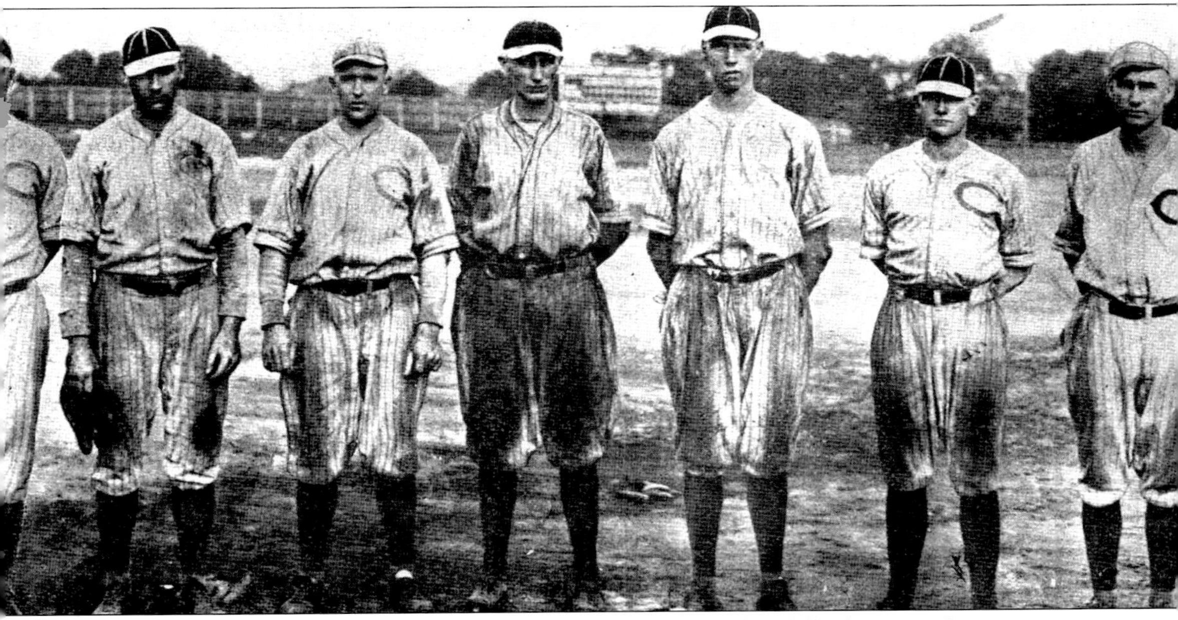

the field by visiting Columbia fans who presented him with a hat full of money. Scoggins, six years removed from his one-game career in the majors—a loss for the White Sox—died in Columbia four years later. (South Caroliniana Library.)

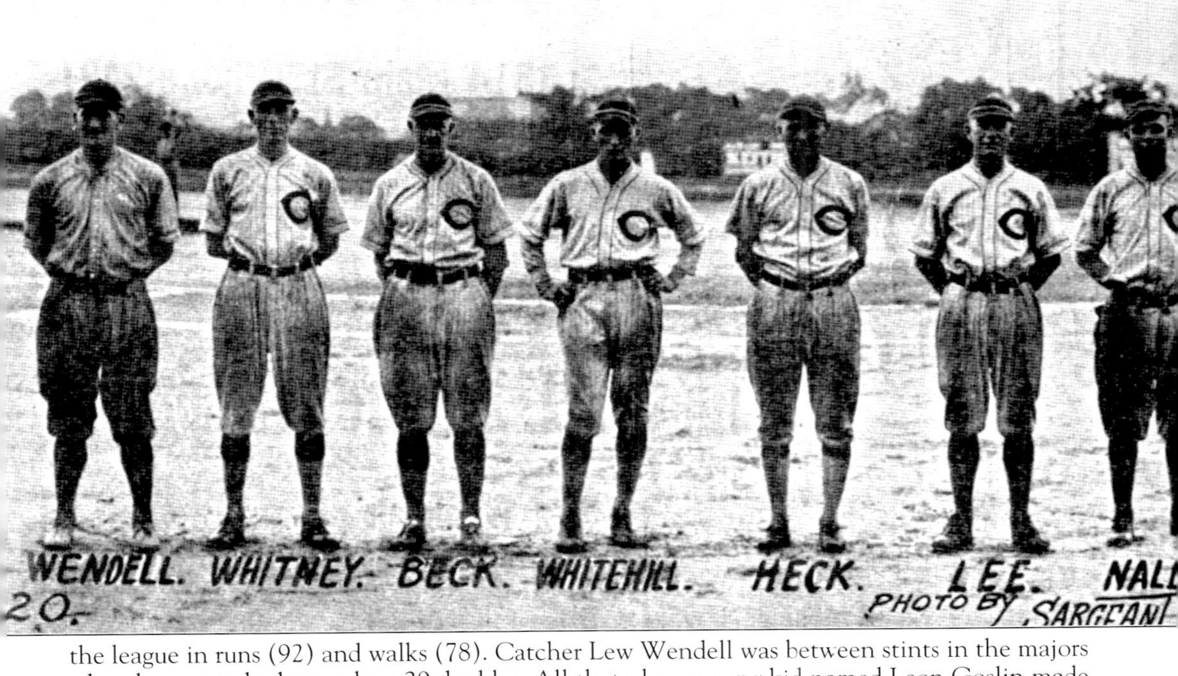

the league in runs (92) and walks (78). Catcher Lew Wendell was between stints in the majors when he swatted a league-best 29 doubles. All that plus a young kid named Leon Goslin made up the team. (South Caroliniana Library.)

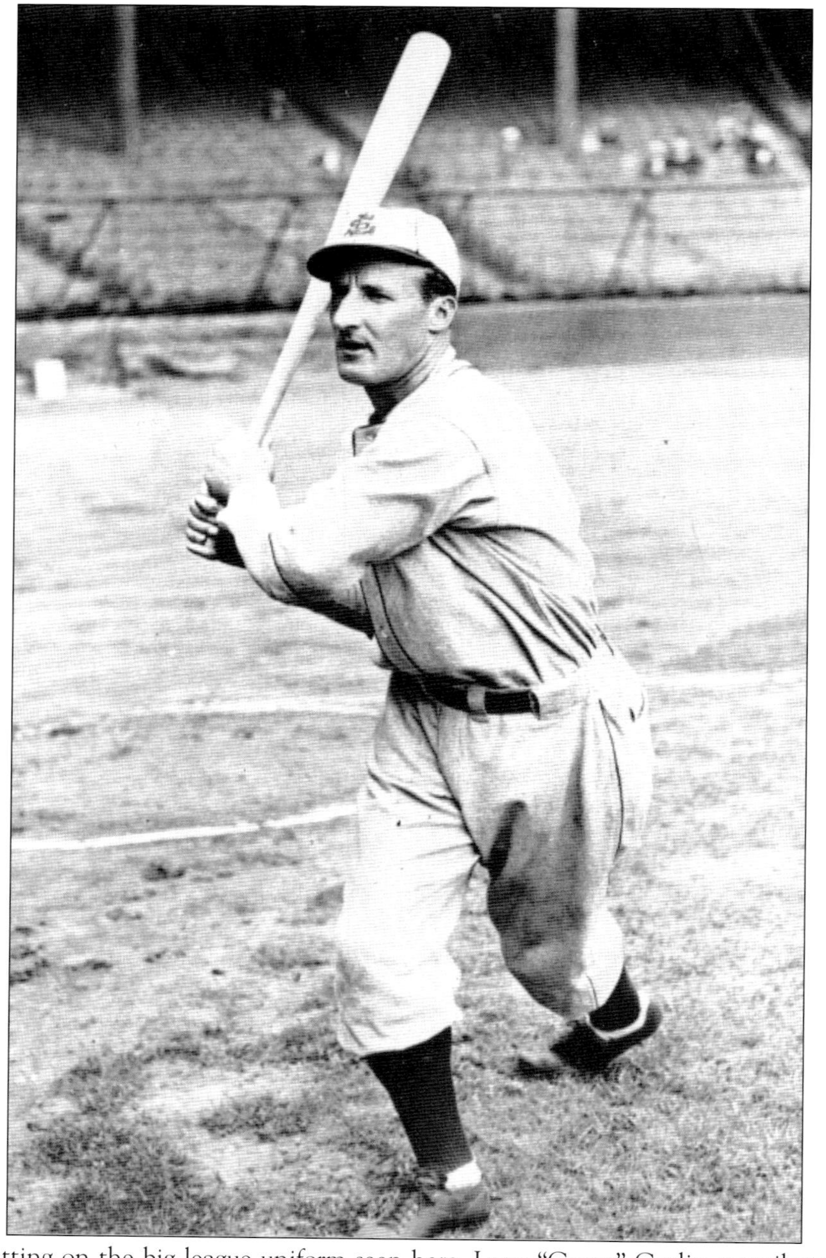

Before putting on the big league uniform seen here, Leon "Goose" Goslin contributed to the championship Comers teams in 1920 and 1921. Goslin truly came into his own in 1921, leading the league in batting average (.390) and runs (124). He also set team marks in hits (214), singles (147), total bases (325), and runs batted in (131). Goslin's stellar 18-year career in the majors, including five World Series with Washington and Detroit, earned him induction in the Baseball Hall of Fame in 1968. He once led the American League (AL) in runs batted in (129 in 1924) and twice led in triples (18 in 1923 and 20 in 1925). He also won the AL batting title with his .379 average in 1928, on the way to a career average of .316. Goslin entered the South Atlantic League Hall of Fame in 1995, its second year. (Bob and Fran Somogyi.)

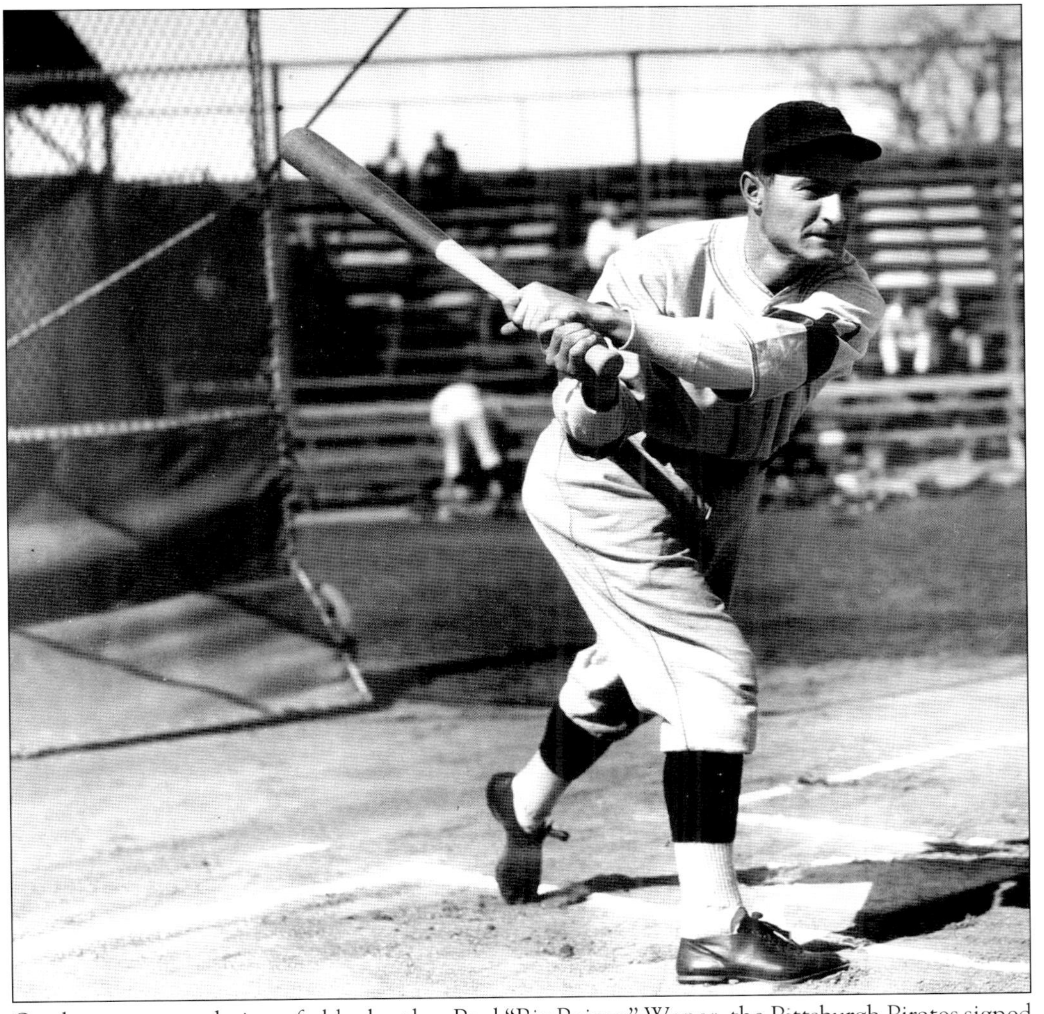

On the recommendation of older brother Paul "Big Poison" Waner, the Pittsburgh Pirates signed younger brother Lloyd "Little Poison" Waner to a contract in 1926 and sent him to Columbia. The Pirates had an affiliation with Columbia in the mid- to late 1920s and agreed to give Waner a chance in the Sally League. Waner responded by tearing up the league with an impressive .345 batting average. Despite playing for the worst team in the league that season—Columbia lost over 100 games and finished dead last—Waner earned league Most Valuable Player honors. The next year, Waner joined his brother in the Pittsburgh outfield in what would be the first year of an 18-season career meriting induction in the Baseball Hall of Fame in 1967. As for the nicknames, the legend has it that poison had little to do with it, but that pronunciation had more of a role. Reportedly when Pittsburgh paid a visit to Brooklyn, a fan pointed out the "big person" (poison) and the "little person" in the outfield, despite the fact that the brothers were virtually the same size. (Pittsburgh Pirates.)

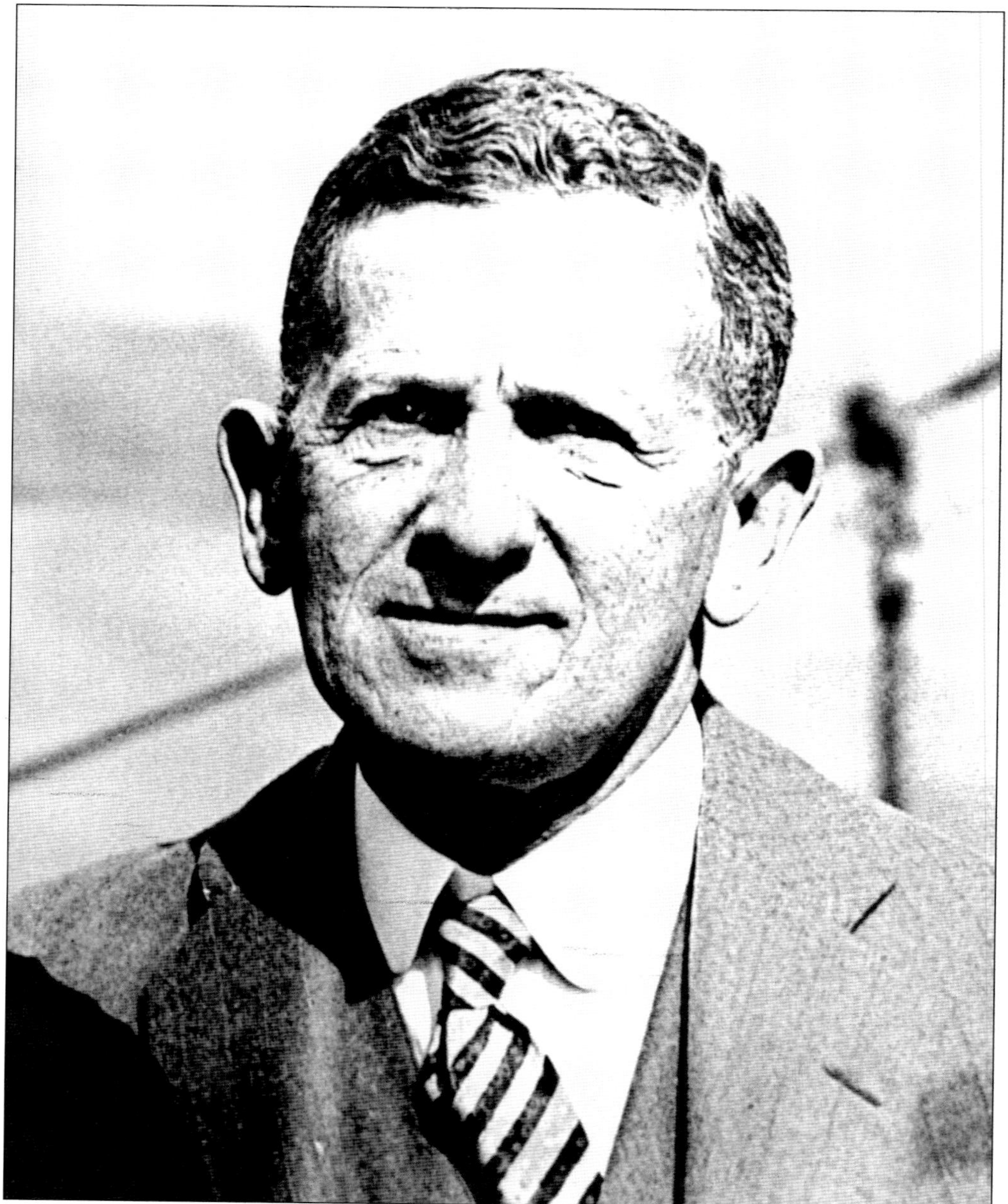

Barney Dreyfuss was a major figure in the affairs of professional baseball in the 1920s. The owner of the Pittsburgh Pirates, and later vice president of the National League, Dreyfuss gets due credit as one of the men who truly kept baseball alive in Columbia. When the field sharing at the University of South Carolina and the alternate field at the state fairgrounds were no longer options for home ballparks, Dreyfuss put up the capital necessary to build a new facility and keep his "Little Pirates" going in Columbia. Once the site was established and construction completed, the new ballpark was dedicated as Dreyfuss Field and would remain the home of Columbia baseball teams into the 21st century. Although the name Dreyfuss Field is no longer attached to the modern facility, the road that runs behind the ballpark off Assembly Street is still called Dreyfus [*sic*] Road. (Pittsburgh Pirates.)

THREE

A New Home for the Boys of Summer

In the mid-1920s, a group of Columbia businessmen rebuilt the Columbia Comers after a year with no baseball. Ten men contributed $1,000 each to purchase rights to the club and appointed L.L. "Louie" Propst from within the group as the operator of the team. With Propst and the backing of Barney Dreyfuss and the Pittsburgh Pirates, the Comers appeared ready for prosperity. A permanent new home was established for the team, lending further support. Finding the right spot took some time for city officials; although the chosen location was not the best, a new ballpark for Columbia had been agreed upon.

The Comers of these years did not live up to the promise of the pennant-winning days of Zinn Beck and Goose Goslin, but both Propst and the Pirates did all they could to ensure that the team would remain competitive in the Sally League every season. It seemed that the Comers would continue to make Columbia proud for many more years. Only something terrible and unforeseen could derail such an enterprise, right?

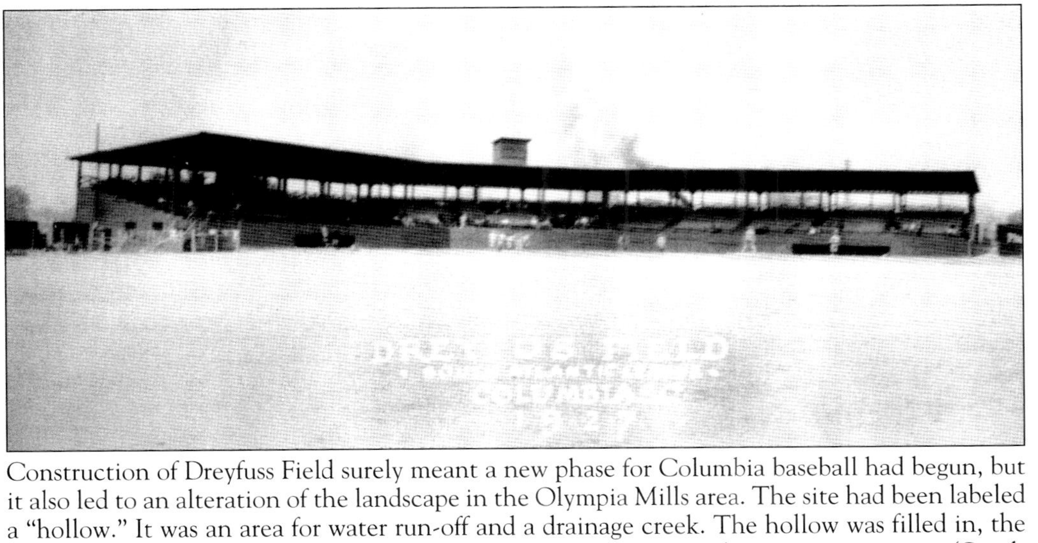

Construction of Dreyfuss Field surely meant a new phase for Columbia baseball had begun, but it also led to an alteration of the landscape in the Olympia Mills area. The site had been labeled a "hollow." It was an area for water run-off and a drainage creek. The hollow was filled in, the stadium was built, and drainage issues have often popped up over the many years since. (South Carolina State Museum.)

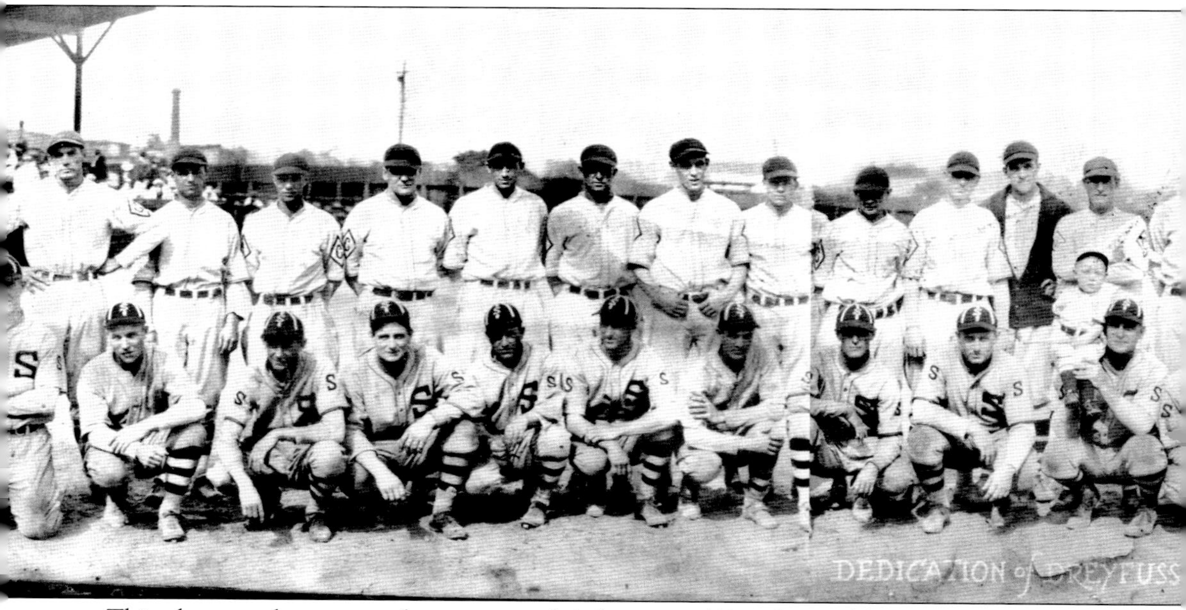

This photograph captures the ceremonial dedication of Dreyfuss Field in 1927. Although the various people in the photograph did not know it, this moment would begin the on-and-off relationship with baseball this location would have for nearly eight decades. Even without historical perspective, this event was still a momentous one for Columbia and for baseball in

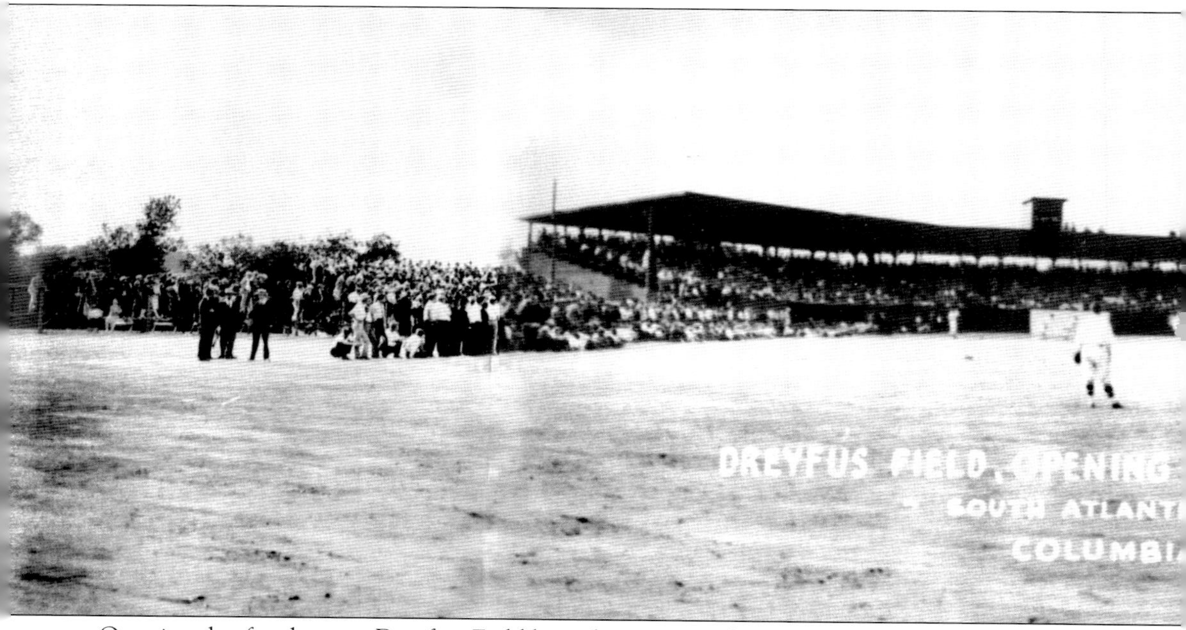

Opening day for the new Dreyfuss Field brought an excited, overflow crowd. The fans not only stuffed the grandstands, they also found any open space worthy of watching the Comers in action. That included lining up a few people deep down the foul lines on both sides, right on

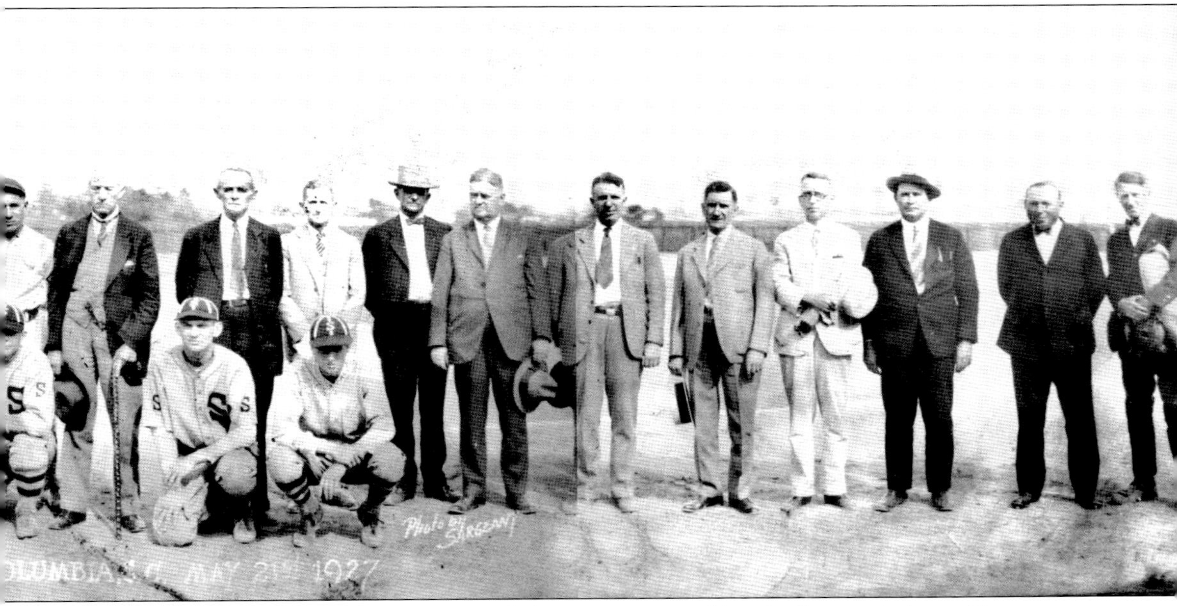

general. The dedication ceremony merited the appearance of baseball commissioner Kennesaw Mountain Landis (center, with cane). A former federal judge, Landis was baseball's first commissioner and presided over the game from 1920 to 1944. (CCB, from Mike Safran.)

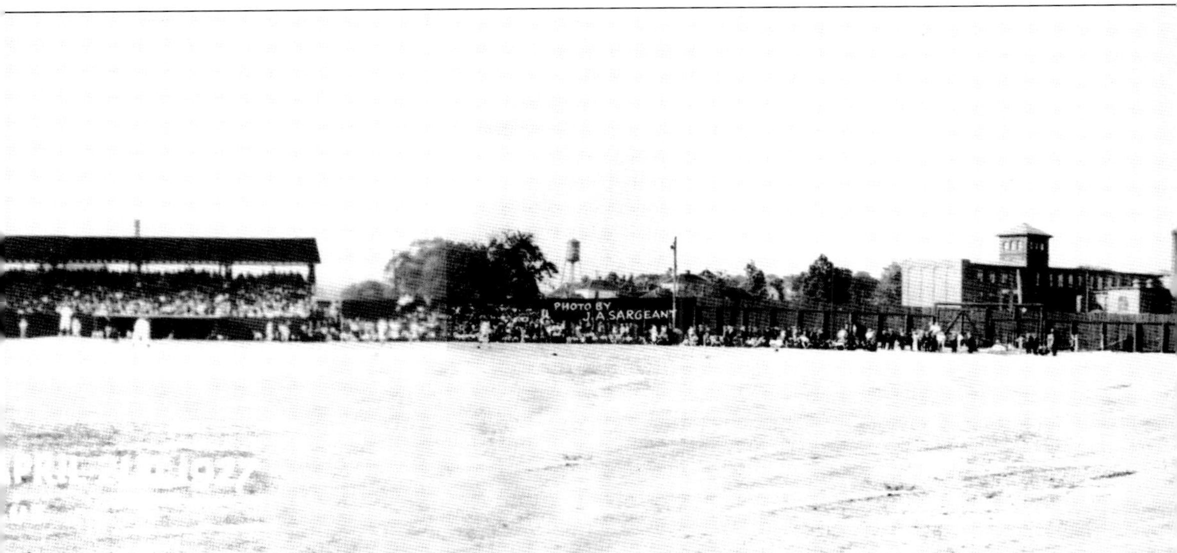

the field of play. This situation offers yet another reminder that the Comers played in a different day and age—can you picture fans being allowed in such numbers on the field at any ballpark today? (South Carolina State Museum.)

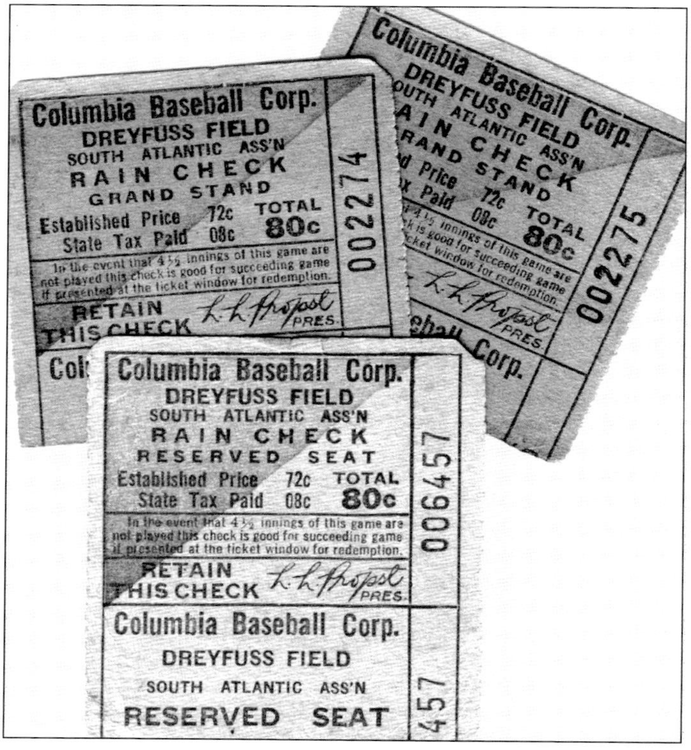

These ticket stubs are from the first season at Dreyfuss Field. Getting tickets like these meant a lot to people in town that year—but it meant even more to the proprietors of the team, anxious to make the most out of a permanent home after years of moving about or borrowing playing space. Note the signature of L.L. Propst on the tickets. (Bob and Fran Somogyi.)

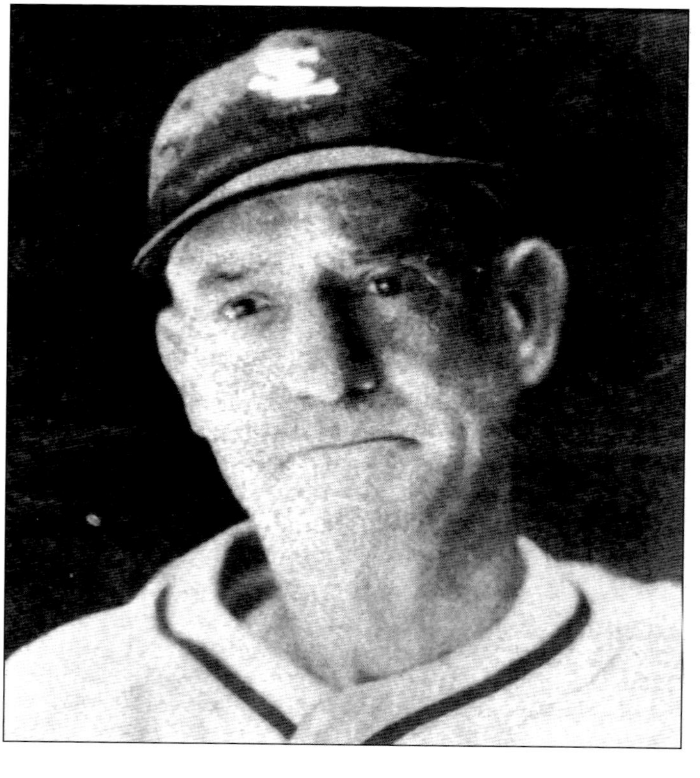

The manager for the Comers in 1927 was Charles "Gabby" Street. Known for his days as a catcher in the majors and for catching a ball dropped off the Washington Monument, Street still had his best days ahead of him. Just three years after managing Columbia, Street, seen here later in life, led the Cardinals to the National League pennant in 1930 and the World Series title in 1931. (Bob and Fran Somogyi.)

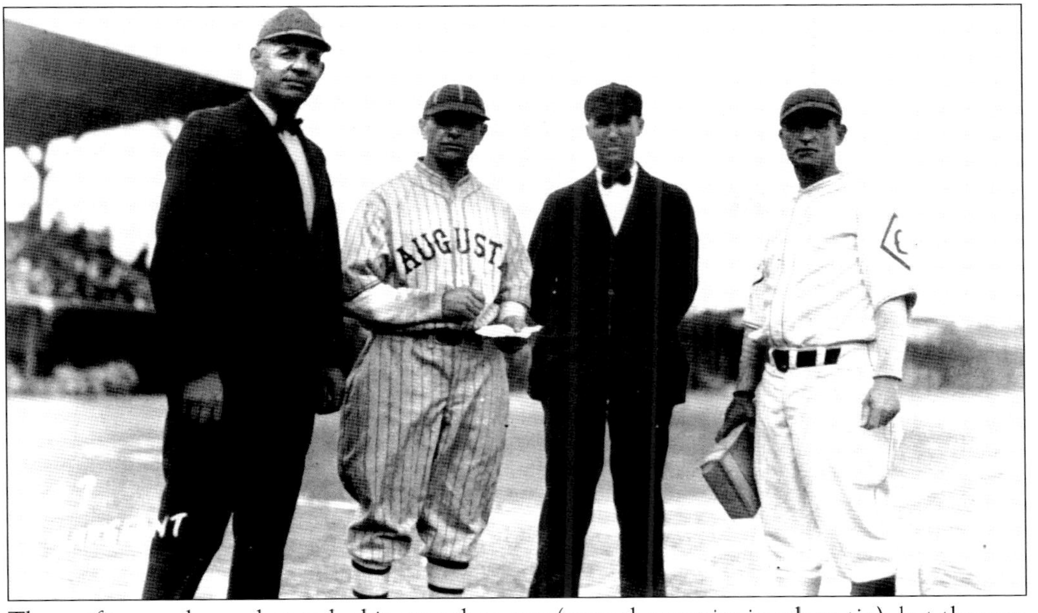

The outfits may have changed a bit over the years (note the umpire in a bow tie), but the pre-game exchange of lineups and discussion of ground rules has remained a tradition of the game. Notice the tome brought by the Columbia representative—it is a bit too big for a rulebook, so perhaps he thought a Bible was necessary. (South Carolina State Museum.)

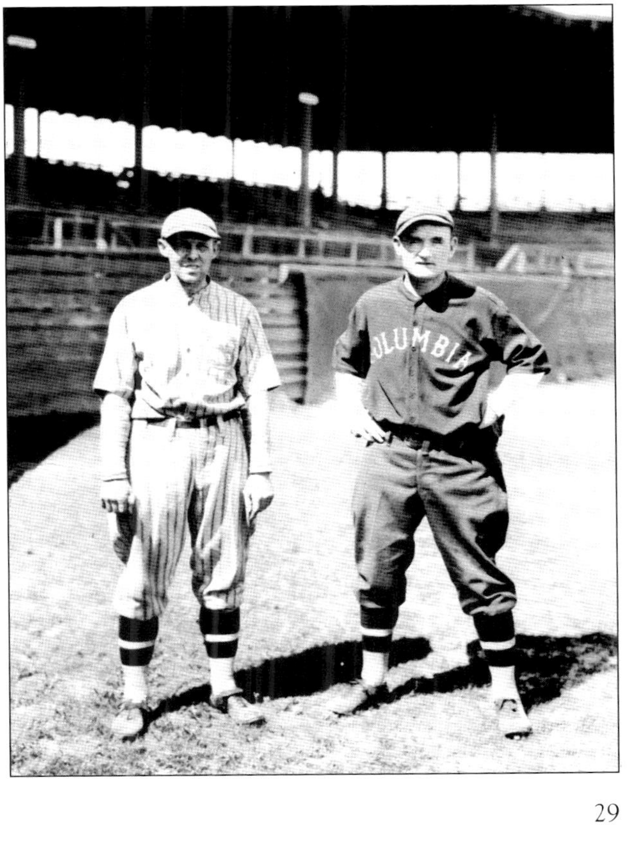

Salisbury manager George Whiteman and Columbia manager Joe Kelly posed together for this picture of L.L. Propst's two skippers. Propst not only ran the show for the Sally's Columbia Comers in 1928, he also headed the Salisbury Colonials of the Piedmont League. The teams trained together and sometimes even swapped players. A former big-league Pirate, Kelly led the Pittsburgh-affiliated Comers for two seasons. (South Carolina State Museum.)

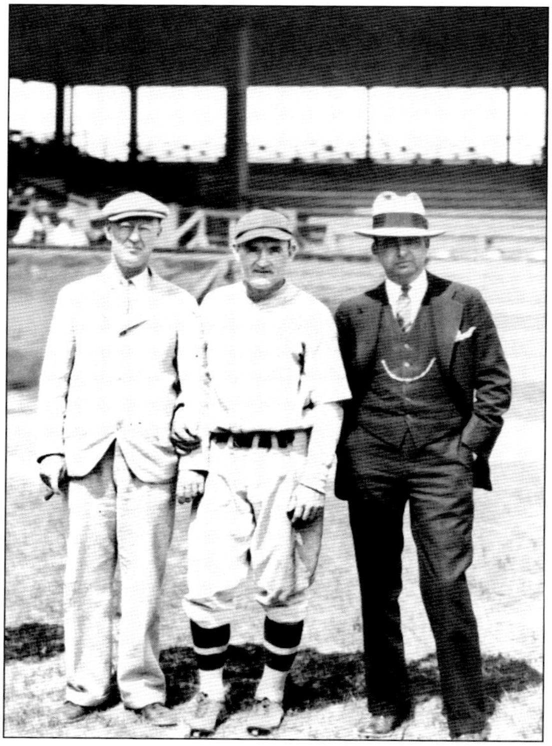

L.L. Propst, far right, deserves great credit for keeping baseball alive and well in Columbia in the 1920s. Propst was one of the youngest and most successful theater operators in the South when he helped bring the game back in 1925 after a year with no baseball. Away from the ballpark, Propst and his wife raised prize-winning Rhode Island Red Chickens. (South Carolina State Museum.)

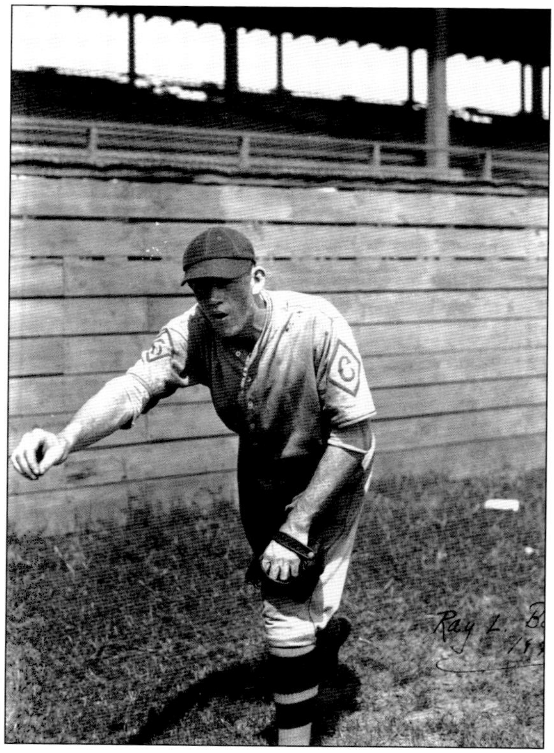

By the time Ray Benson and the 1928 Comers took the field, the championships of the early 1920s were already fading memories. From 1923 to 1930 (with no team in 1924), the Comers never finished better than sixth, except for one half-season in fourth place. Under manager Joe Kelly, Benson's team landed in sixth, about 30 games behind Asheville, the pennant winner. (South Carolina State Museum.)

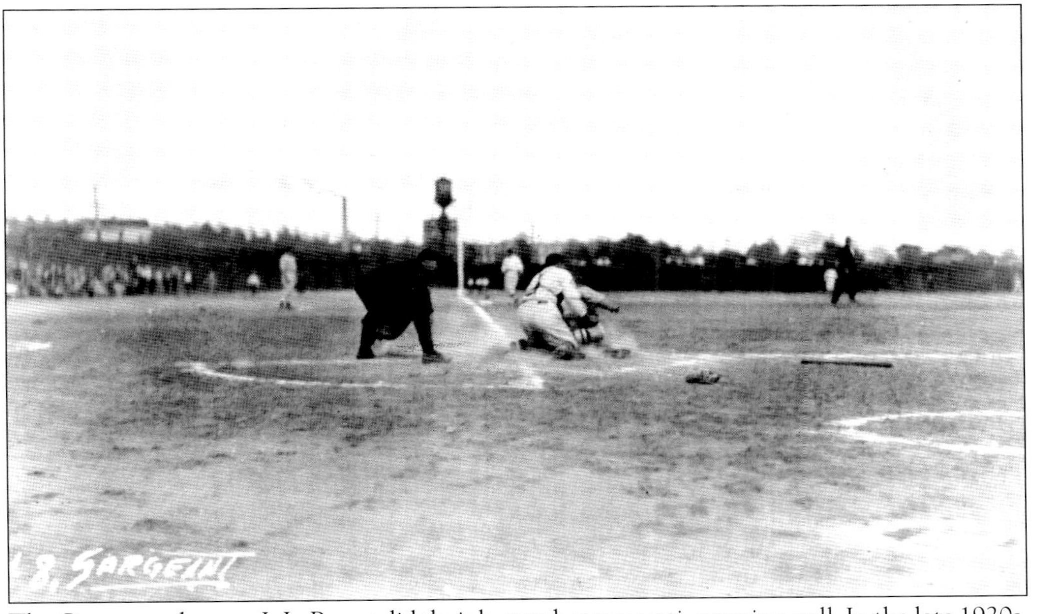

The Comers and owner L.L. Propst did their best to keep operations going well. In the late 1920s, they even made improvements where possible, like replanting the infield turf and renewing the grandstand roof in 1929. But like a play at the plate, a big impact lay ahead: between the 1929 and 1930 seasons, the stock market crash would change the face of America and its sports. (South Carolina State Museum.)

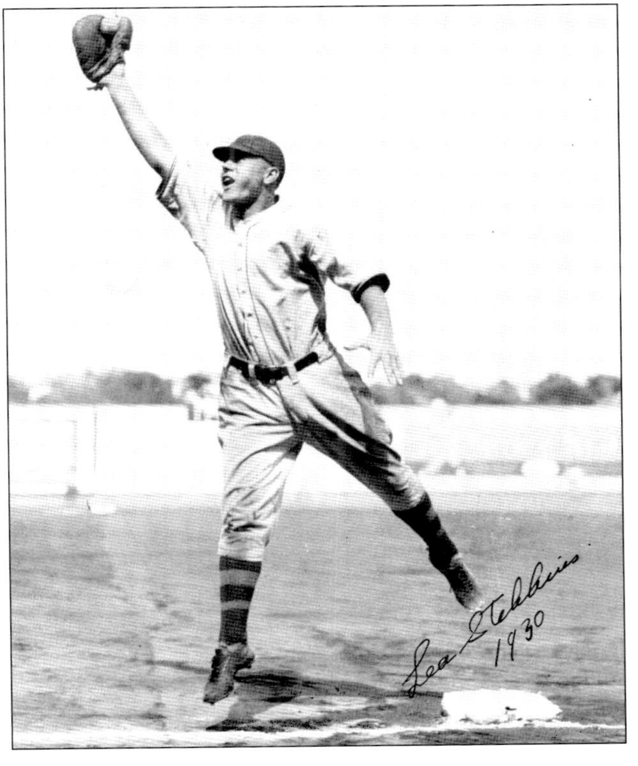

Player-manager Lem Stebbins set a team record in 1930 by only striking out 9 times in 117 games. Meanwhile, the Comers limped home to a losing finish, and that was not the worst of it. The Great Depression had begun, and Columbia was feeling its effects all the way to Dreyfuss Field. The team was losing money fast and was forced to suspend operations. The capital city had seen the last of the Columbia Comers. (South Carolina State Museum.)

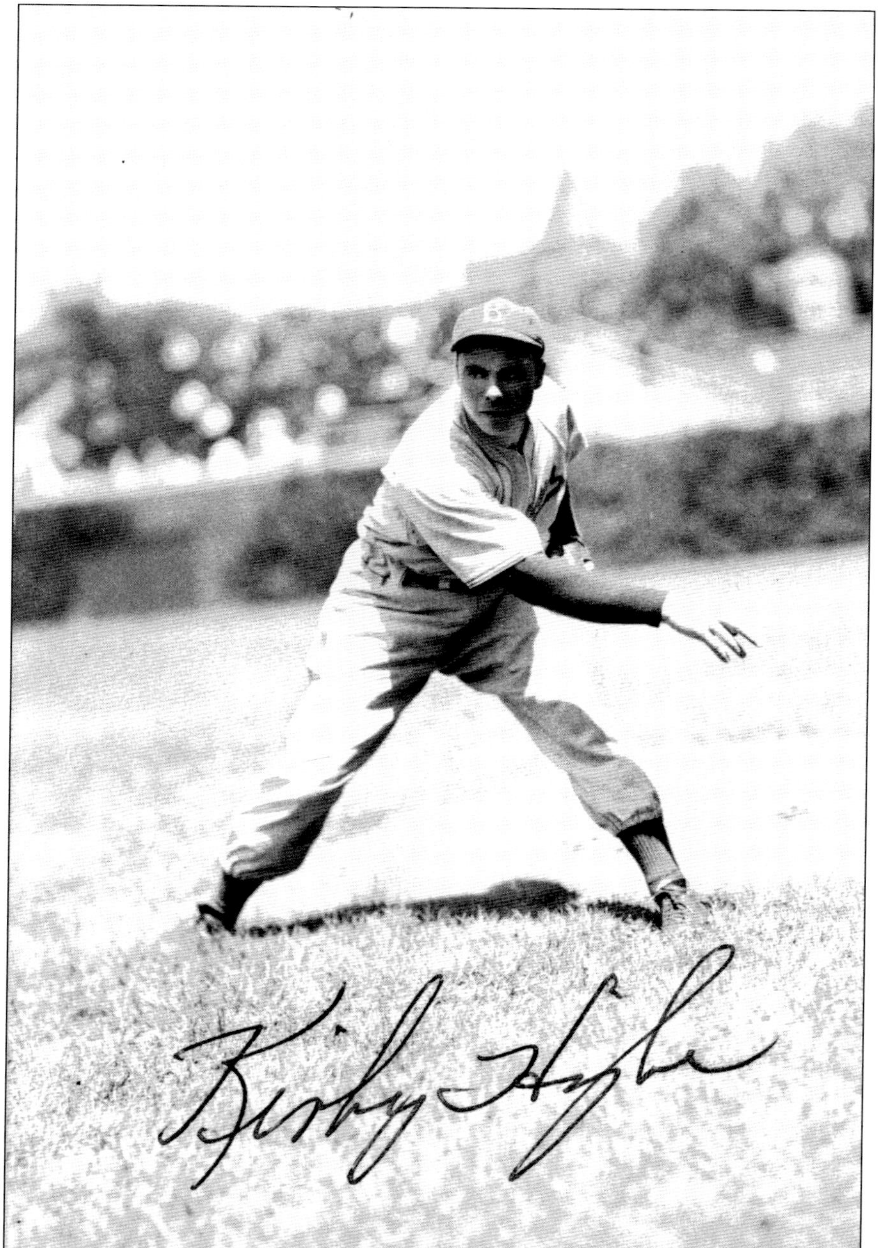

Columbia native Kirby Higbe, seen here in his Brooklyn Dodgers days, played for the Columbia Senators of 1936. After the Comers closed shop in 1930, no one played in town for three seasons. A Piedmont League team called the Sandlappers started the 1934 season in town but moved to Asheville before the year was over. Columbia was back in the South Atlantic League with the Senators in 1936 and 1937, but the Senators then gave way to the Columbia Reds, who found much more success for years to come. As for Higbe, he played 12 seasons in the majors and had his greatest success in the 1941 season for Brooklyn (22-9, 3.14 ERA). He also started a game in the World Series for the Dodgers that year. (Bob and Fran Somogyi.)

Four

The Columbia Reds Era

Columbia residents with long memories still remember going to the ballpark when they were young, seeing legends of the game in a golden era for baseball in the city. Those tales refer fondly to the days of the Columbia Reds. The Reds began playing in Columbia in 1938, and they would field a team every year through 1955—excluding, of course, the three-year hiatus for World War II (1943–1945). The Reds sent many promising players through South Carolina before bringing them to Cincinnati. Fans found plenty of great names to root for, like Ted Kluszewski, Johnny Temple, Pepper Martin, and Wally Post.

The team and the city formed a bond over the years, at its strongest in the early 1950s when the best squads of the Reds era took the field. Columbia got behind local heroes, like pitchers Barney Martin and Jim Kleckley, in those years. Ballpark attendees of the time also saw Columbia's baseball color barrier broken. Players like Frank Robinson demonstrated talent that eclipsed race and prejudice. Unfortunately, despite the pennant winners, playoff champions, and stellar players, waning attendance in Columbia and bright promises elsewhere eventually lured the Reds away.

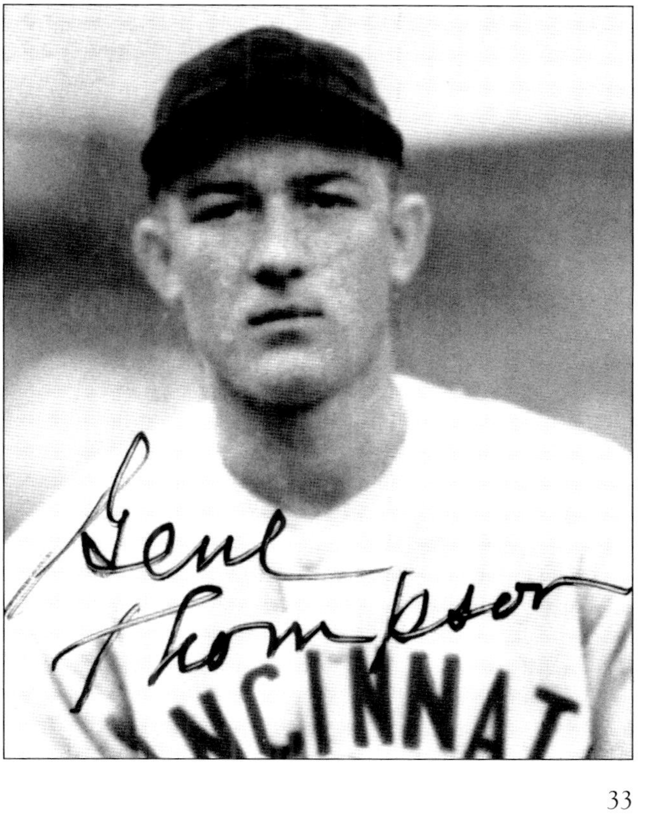

Gene Thompson played for the first Columbia Reds team in 1938. Thompson personified the typical player of those atypical times: he played for Columbia in 1938, played for Cincinnati from 1939 to 1942, served in the U.S. Navy from 1943 to 1945, and rejoined baseball with the Reds and Giants for 1946 and 1947. He stayed in the game years later as a scout. (Bob and Fran Somogyi.)

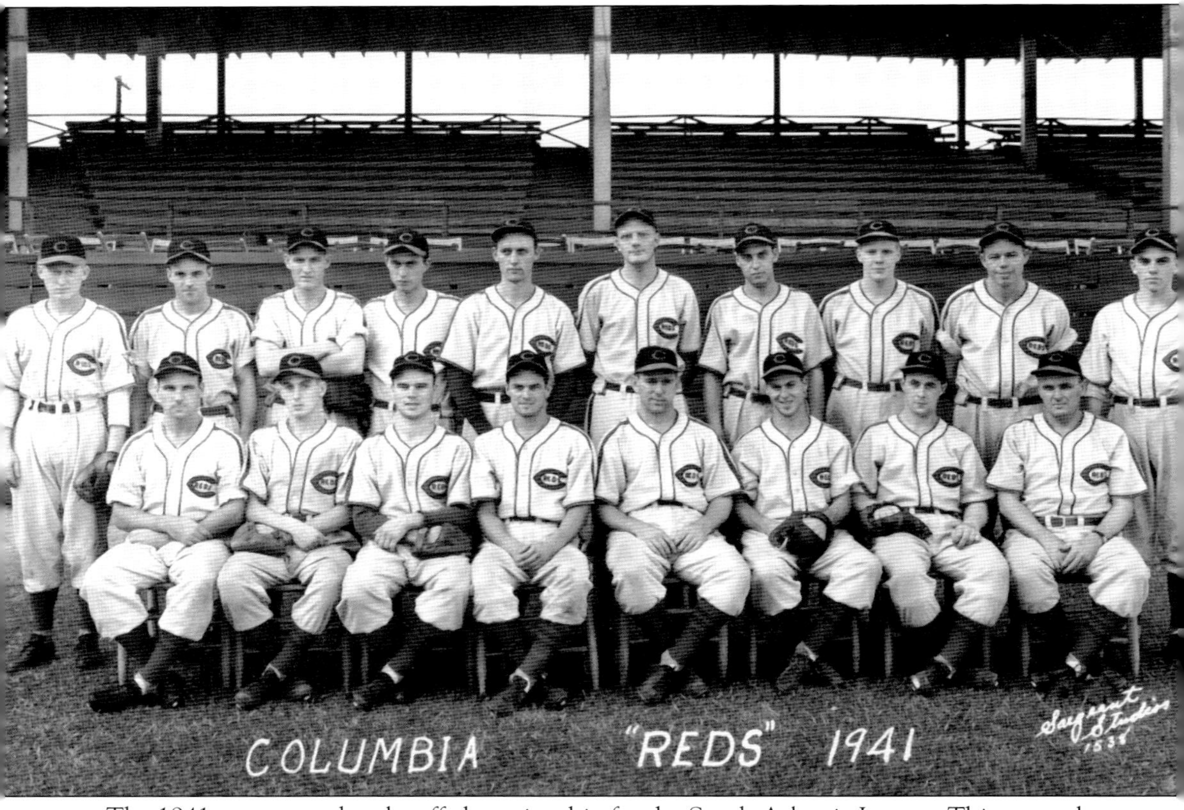

The 1941 team won the playoff championship for the South Atlantic League. This team photo captures the last squad to take the field in Columbia before America entered World War II. Shown, from left to right, are (seated) Nick Polly, Walter Flager, Len Bobeck, Buddy Day, Gordon Duff, Bobby Adams, Ted Maillet, and manager "Cap" Crosley; (standing) "Cotton" Ed Hill, Lenny Rice, Garland Lawing, Gene Hinrichs, Earl Pettit, Hal Erickson, Clyde Vollmer, Walter Loos, Lonnie Goldstein, and Ray Peeler. Out of this group, eight men would play in the majors: Rice, Lawing, Erickson, Goldstein, Polly, Flager, Vollmer, and Adams. Only the last two would be standouts in the big leagues. Vollmer made the majors the year after this photo, but the war intervened. He resumed his career afterward, playing in the outfield for the Reds, Senators, and Red Sox from 1946 to 1954. Adams spent most of his 14 big-league seasons in the Reds infield. (CCB, from Sue Heath.)

Pitcher George Burpo not only played for Columbia in 1946 but also in two games for Cincinnati that season. The 1946 campaign represented an odd return for many players, but the war had ended and the three-year hiatus for the South Atlantic League ended with it. Columbia finished second in the regular season that year. (Bob & Fran Somogyi.)

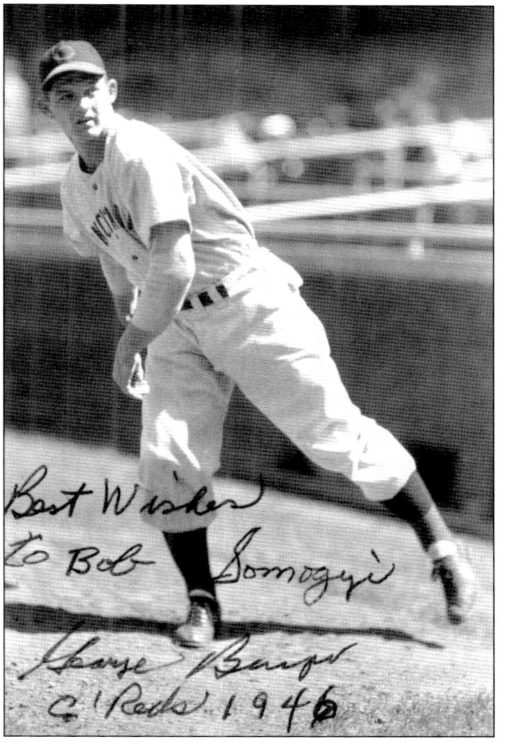

TIME OF GAMES

Sunday single games will start at 3:00 p. m.; Sunday double-headers at 2:00 p. m.; Night games at 8:15 p. m.; Night double-headers at 7:00 p. m.

PRICES

Box Seats	$1.15
General Admission	.90
Bleachers	.60
Ladies on Ladies' Night	.30
Child's General Admission	.25
Colored Bleachers	.50
Books of ten general admission tickets, good for any regularly scheduled Sally league games	$9.00

All Prices Include Taxes

TICKET SALE

Tickets may be purchased in advance at McGregor's Drug Store, 1308 Main Street. Tickets remain on sale at this location daily until 5:00 p. m. and until 12:00 noon on Sundays.

Ticket Offices at the ball park open 1 hour before game time.

For convenience, a Ticket Office is located opposite first base where you may purchase General Admission and Bleacher tickets. Box Seats are sold only at the Ticket Offices at the Main Entrance. Books of General Admission tickets may be purchased at McGregor's, or at any Ticket Office at the ball park.

This price list from the 1950 scorecard shows the racial reality of the times. Whites had their sections and prices, while African-American patrons were to sit in the "colored bleachers." The practice of separate grandstands was common for many years in Columbia and other cities. (Bob and Fran Somogyi.)

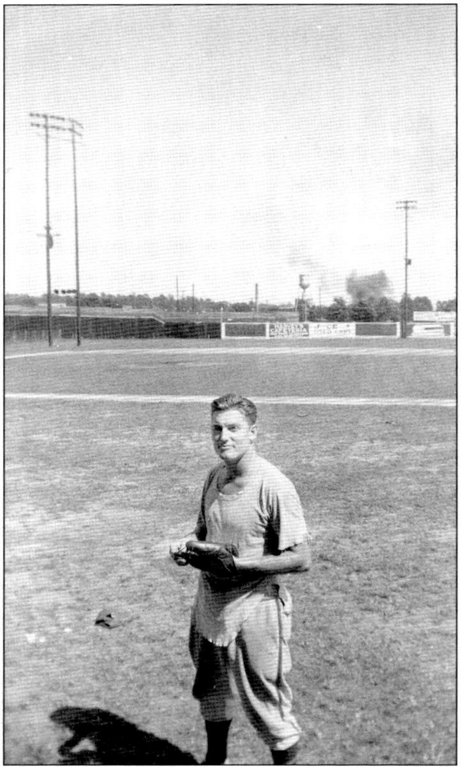

This unidentified member of the Columbia Reds took a break on the field for a candid photo at Capital City Park and offered his best Kirk Douglas look. Notice the water tower in the background, as seen in pictures of the ballpark from its dedication to the present day, but most intriguing is that this shot captured a fire burning beyond the left field wall! (CCB.)

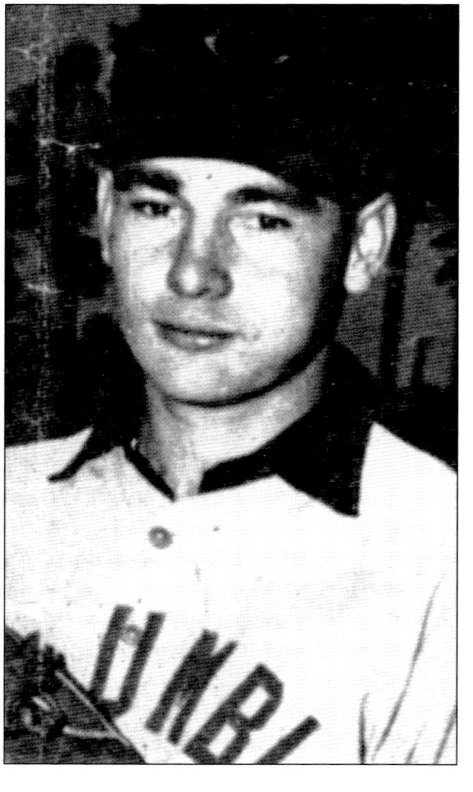

Johnny Temple became a mainstay at second base for the Cincinnati Reds in the 1950s, but first he was a star in Columbia. Temple finished third in the league with a .322 batting average in 1950, one spot ahead of teammate Bob Hazle (.313). In his 13 big-league seasons, Temple posted a career average of .284. (Bob and Fran Somogyi.)

A native South Carolinian, Bob Hazle naturally wound up with the nickname "Hurricane," a nod to the pounding Hurricane Hazel left on the Palmetto State. A popular player in Columbia, Hazle went on to play three years in the majors—including a World Series Championship with the 1957 Milwaukee Braves. Hazle hit .403 in 41 regular season games for the Braves that year. (Bob and Fran Somogyi.)

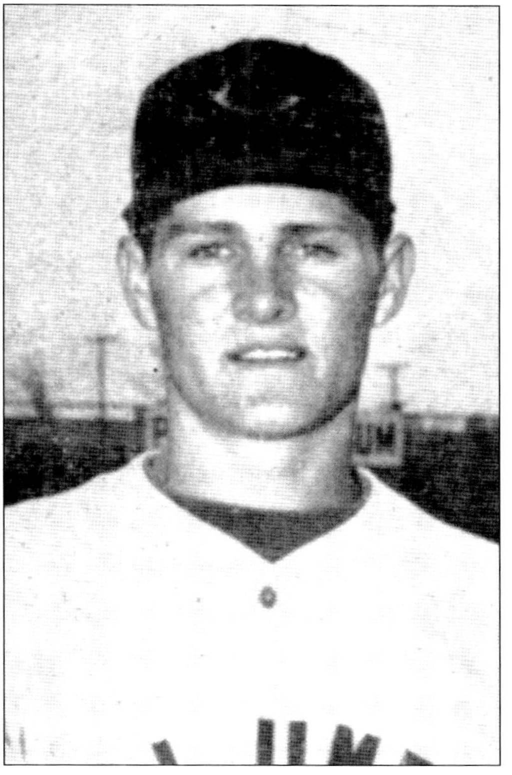

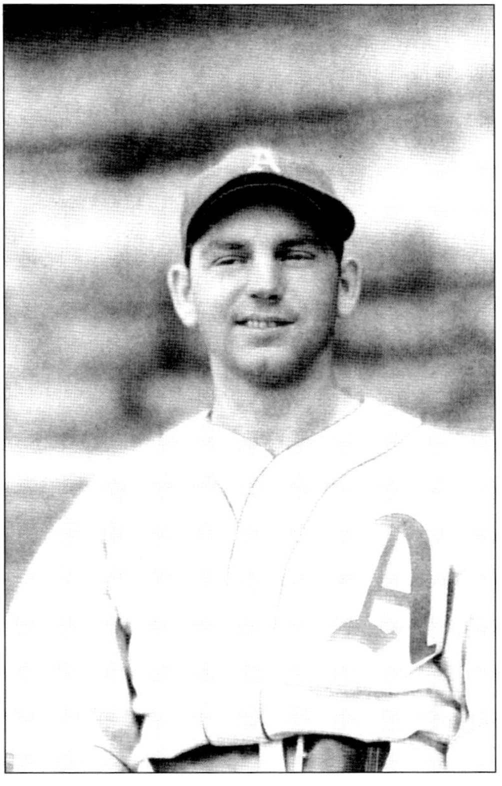

Buddy Hancken, manager of the 1951 Reds, suffered through a rough season in Columbia and an eighth-place finish. Seen here in his playing days, Hancken's career in the majors was an interesting one. He had one game with one putout for the Philadelphia Athletics but saw no pitches in his only trip to the plate. Instead, he watched a base runner picked off to end the inning. (Bob and Fran Somogyi.)

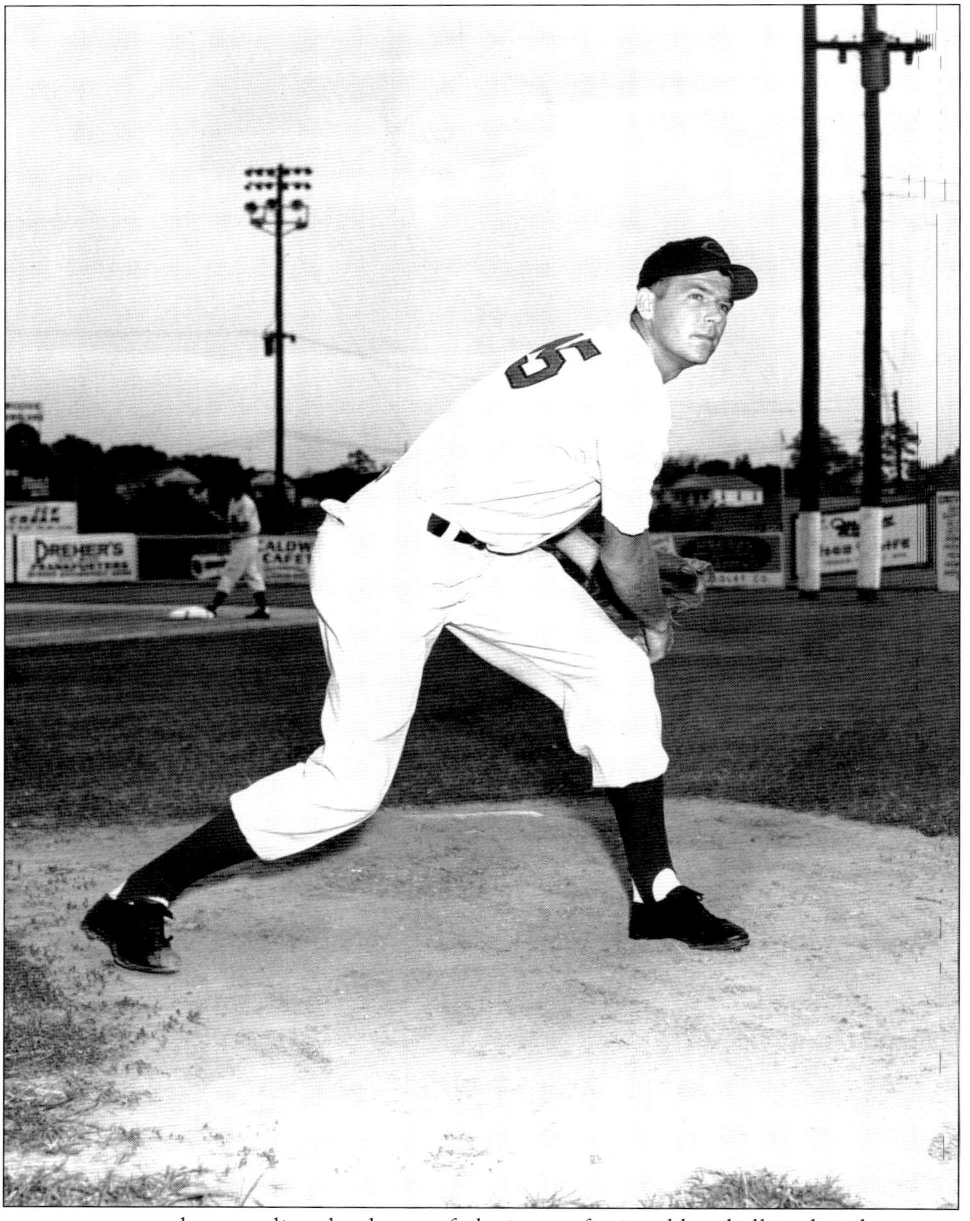

Not too many people get to live the dream of playing professional baseball in their hometowns, but fate worked out for West Columbia native and life-long resident Jim Kleckley, who played for the Columbia Reds in the early 1950s. Kleckley did not start his baseball career in the Reds organization, but it did not take long for him to find himself part of the Cincinnati system and the Columbia pitching staff. He lived through the rough last-place finish in 1951 only to see the team soar to unmatched heights the very next year. Kleckley also took the mound for part of the 1953 season in Columbia, but he soon moved on to other assignments in baseball. When the time came for him to make the life-altering choice of pursuing a potential career in the majors or answering his father's call to help with the family business, the decision came easy for Jim Kleckley: family first. (Jim Kleckley.)

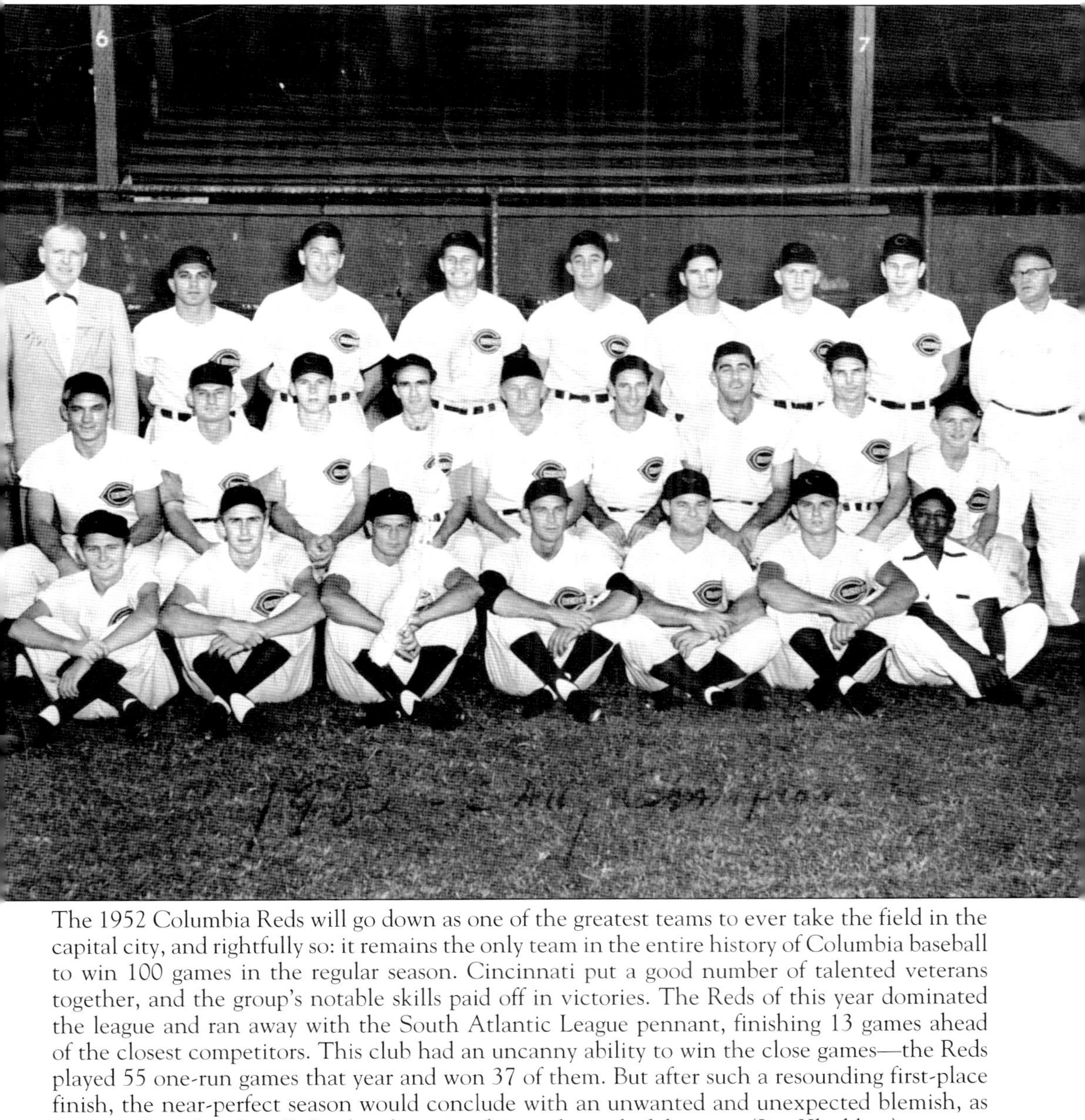

The 1952 Columbia Reds will go down as one of the greatest teams to ever take the field in the capital city, and rightfully so: it remains the only team in the entire history of Columbia baseball to win 100 games in the regular season. Cincinnati put a good number of talented veterans together, and the group's notable skills paid off in victories. The Reds of this year dominated the league and ran away with the South Atlantic League pennant, finishing 13 games ahead of the closest competitors. This club had an uncanny ability to win the close games—the Reds played 55 one-run games that year and won 37 of them. But after such a resounding first-place finish, the near-perfect season would conclude with an unwanted and unexpected blemish, as the team lost the playoffs for the championship at the end of the year. (Jim Kleckley.)

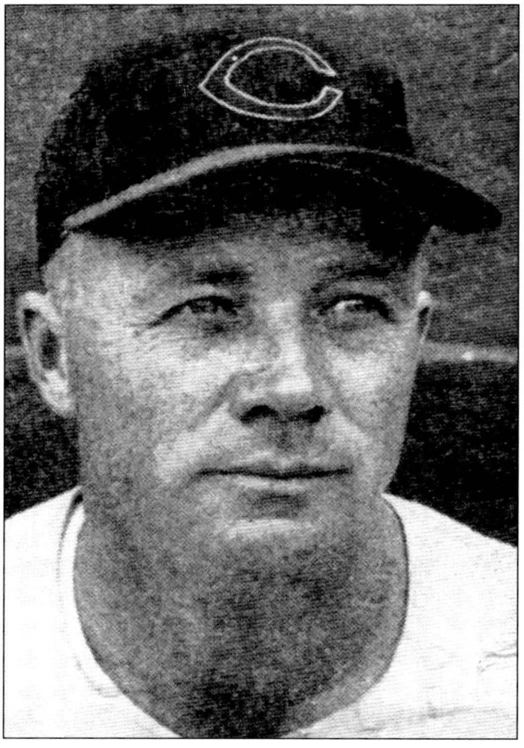

As a South Carolinian, Ernie White already had fans rooting for him—being a winning manager just made it easier. White led the Columbia Reds to four straight winning seasons, which included two regular season pennant winners (1952, 1955) and one playoff champion (1953). Before managing, White pitched seven seasons in the majors and won the only World Series game he played in with a complete-game shutout. (Bob and Fran Somogyi.)

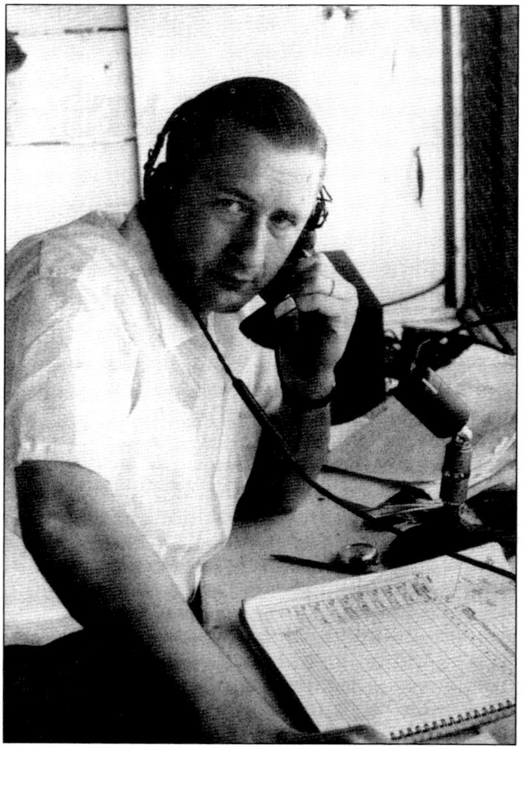

WNOK radio brought a young announcer named Bob Fulton to Columbia to broadcast Reds games starting in 1952. The hire would be historic not only for professional baseball in Columbia—he eventually called games for the Reds, Gems, and Mets—but also for how many people in South Carolina defined radio play-by-play: Fulton became the "Voice of the Gamecocks" for more than 40 years! (Bob Fulton.)

The starting centerfielder and leadoff batter for the 1952 Columbia Reds was Bob Wilson, whose clutch hitting came in handy time and time again. Wilson managed to keep his average consistently close to .300 all season long from the top of the order, while his team maintained its position at the top of the league standings. (Barbara Shealy.)

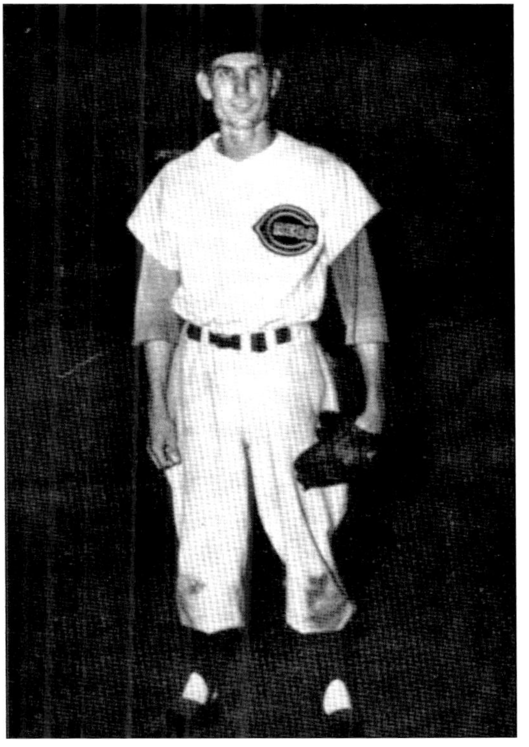

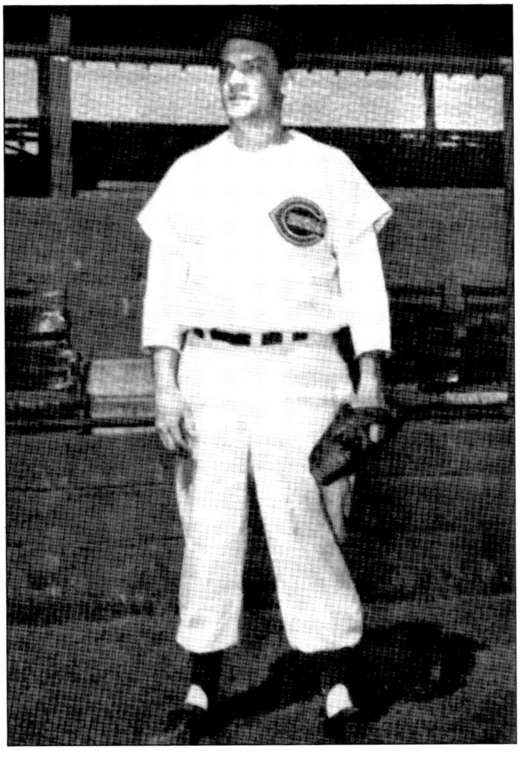

Bill Jankowski could succeed anywhere on the field. It is one thing to say a player can contribute at any position; it is another thing to see it. On a July night in 1952, Jankcwski played one inning at each position on the field. His performance included pitching a hitless first inning and hitting a 2 RBI double as part of a ninth-inning rally to beat Jacksonville. (Barbara Shealy.)

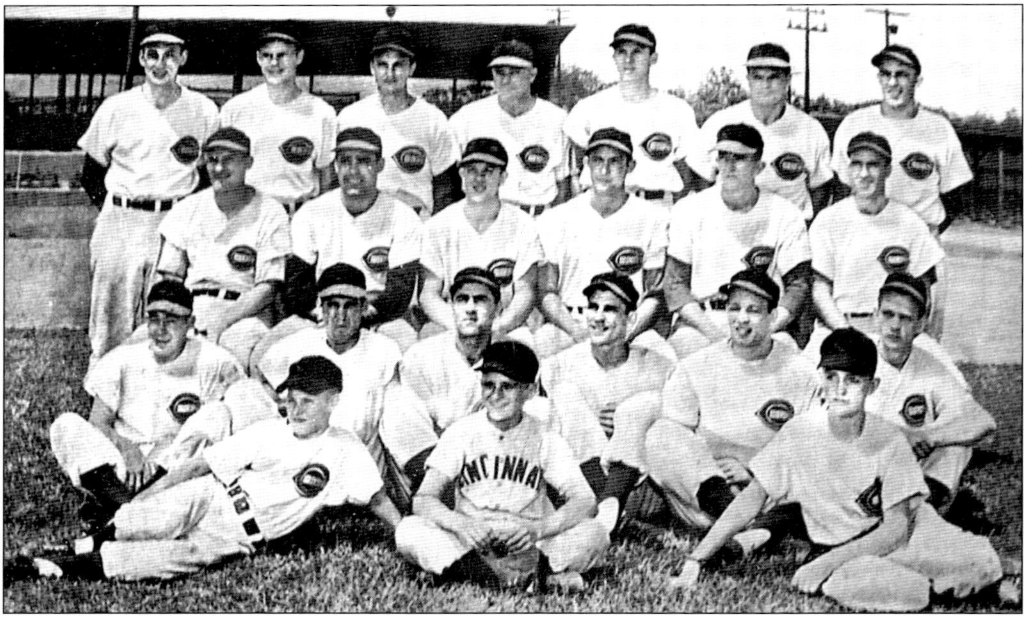

The 1953 team had quite an act to follow after the team's amazing 1952 season, and they were up to the task. The team won over 90 games for the second straight year and flipped the previous season's result: instead of a pennant and no championship, this team fell short of the pennant but found victory in the playoffs. (Bob Fulton.)

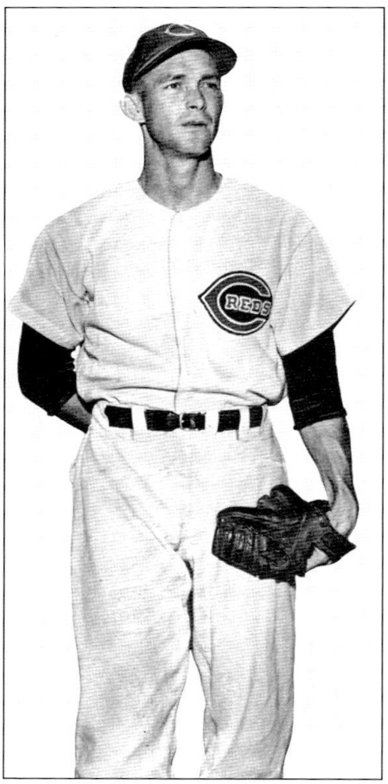

Barney Martin was not just a Columbia native, he was from the Olympia Mills neighborhood where the ballpark stood. The U.S. Navy veteran, who worked with the railroads in the off-season, became a standout for the great Columbia pitching staffs of the 1950s. Martin declined advancement opportunities that could have led to more big-league chances (he pitched one game in the majors), preferring to stay in his hometown instead. (Barbara Shealy.)

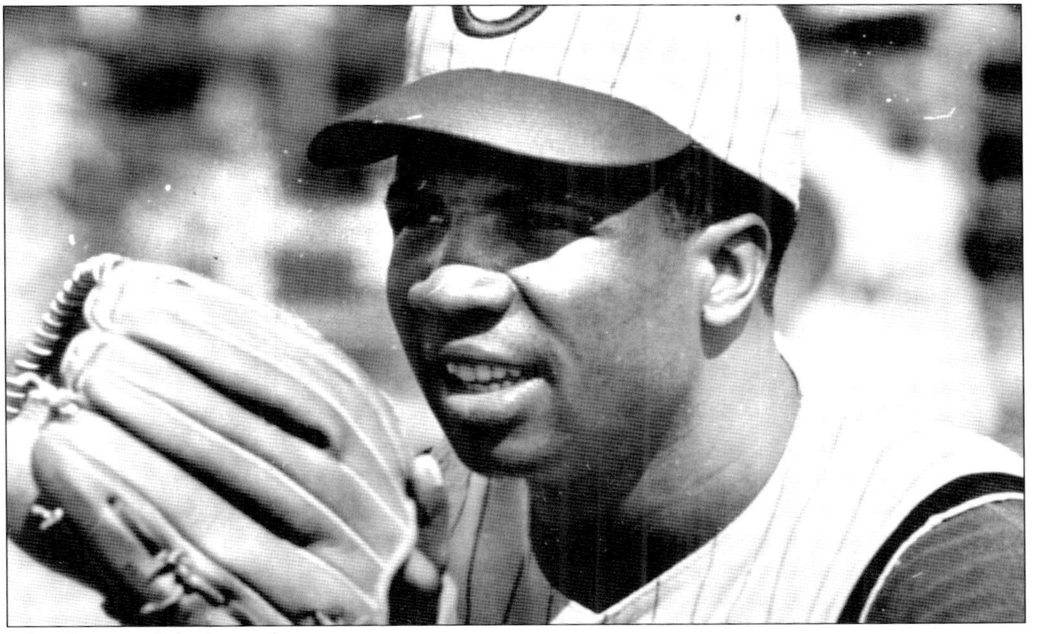

Clearly one of the best players to suit up for Columbia's teams from any era, Frank Robinson played for the Columbia Reds in 1954–1955. His numbers in the South Atlantic League were sensational, but his accomplishments after leaving became legendary: the only player to win the MVP award in both major leagues, the first black manager in the majors, and a member of the Baseball Hall of Fame, inducted in 1982. In his Columbia days, Robinson got pushed near the breaking point at times under the pressure of the era's racial climate, but his on-field performance never wavered. He was an inaugural inductee to the SAL Hall of Fame in 1994. (Bob and Fran Somogyi.)

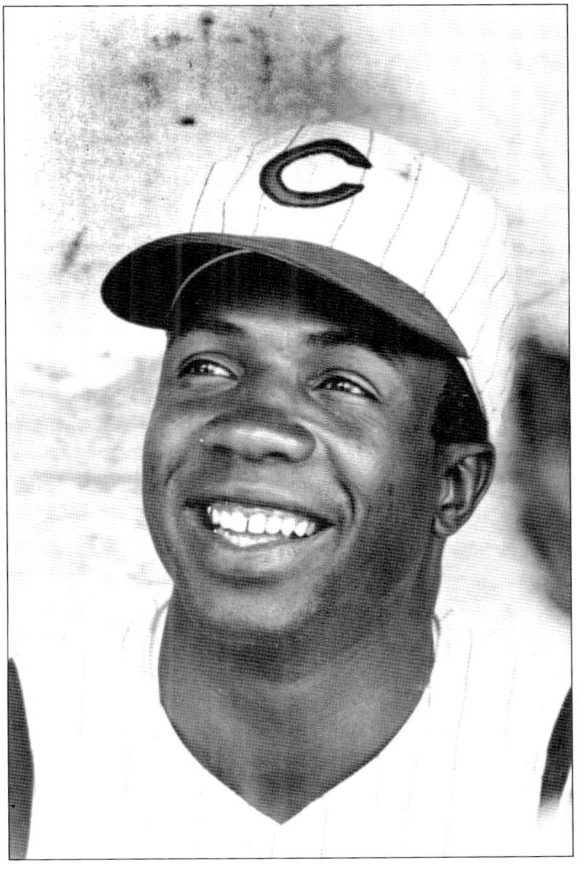

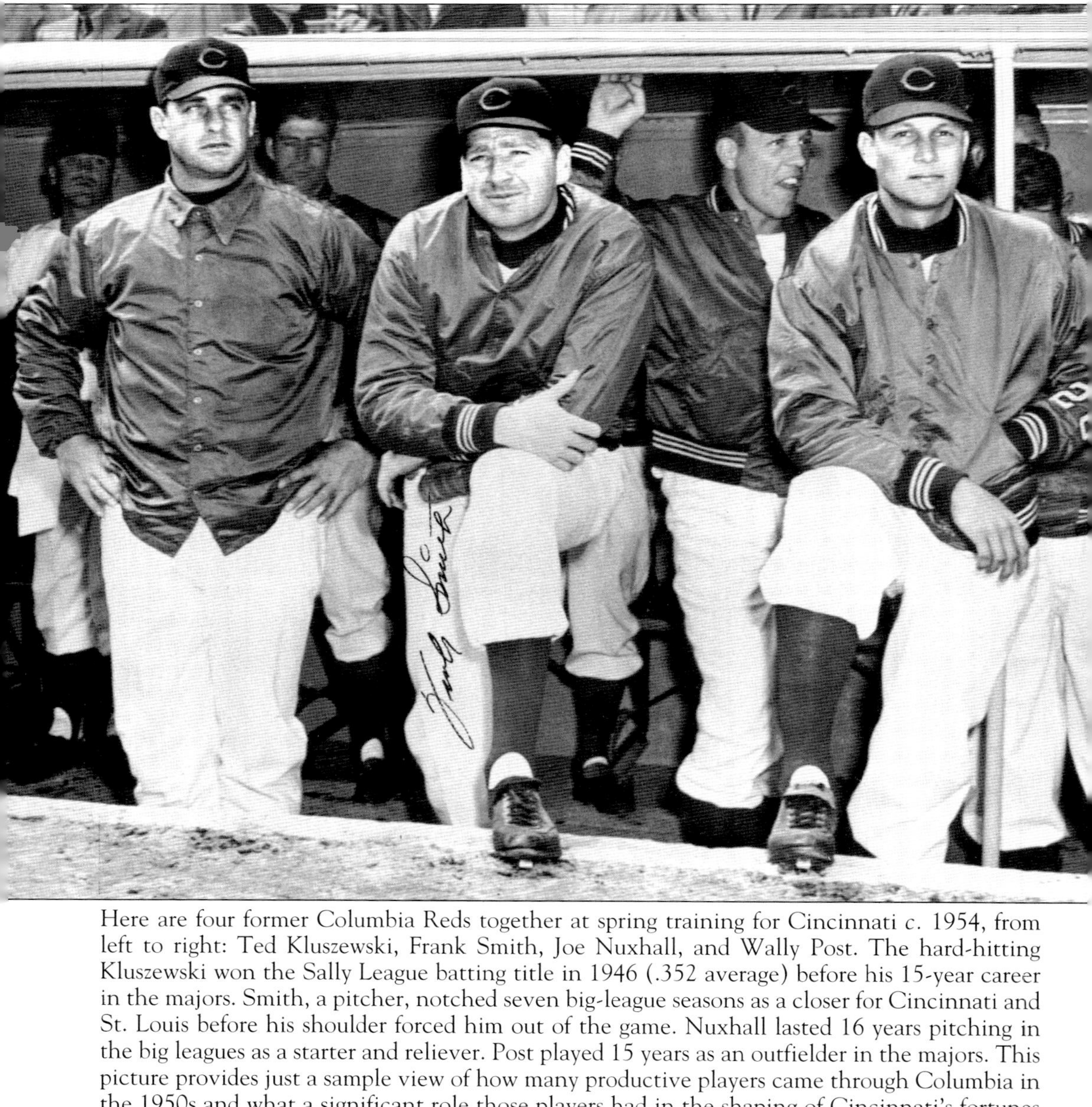

Here are four former Columbia Reds together at spring training for Cincinnati c. 1954, from left to right: Ted Kluszewski, Frank Smith, Joe Nuxhall, and Wally Post. The hard-hitting Kluszewski won the Sally League batting title in 1946 (.352 average) before his 15-year career in the majors. Smith, a pitcher, notched seven big-league seasons as a closer for Cincinnati and St. Louis before his shoulder forced him out of the game. Nuxhall lasted 16 years pitching in the big leagues as a starter and reliever. Post played 15 years as an outfielder in the majors. This picture provides just a sample view of how many productive players came through Columbia in the 1950s and what a significant role those players had in the shaping of Cincinnati's fortunes for those years. (Pat Reddick.)

Five

Trying to Save Baseball

The clamor over the Columbia Reds in the early 1950s had quieted a bit by the middle of the decade. Despite another pennant-winning year in 1955, the season was a financial loser. Dwindling crowds took their toll on the team's operation, and Cincinnati officials wanted their team elsewhere. The Reds turned to Savannah for the next few seasons, a city near the estate of Cincinnati owner Powell Crosley. Distraught baseball lovers and concerned city representatives went to bat for Columbia and succeeded in getting Kansas City to place a squad in town. That team, the Gems, lasted two seasons. They fell short of the talent of previous seasons, and efforts at rejuvenating attendance did not seem to work.

After two vacant years, the ballpark saw the return of the Reds, who had done no better in Savannah. The reunion of Columbia and the Reds fared the same as the Gems—two seasons and they were done. What no one knew was that the wait for another pitch would far exceed any of the delays or stoppages that had come before.

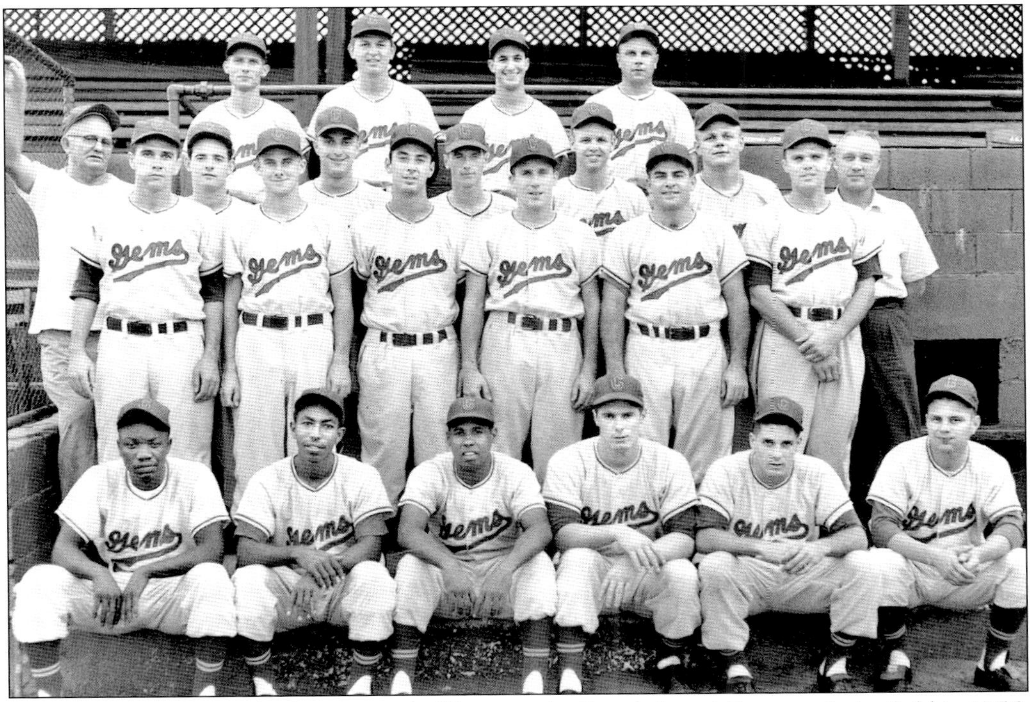

With the Reds gone in both name and affiliation, the Royals-based Gems took the field in 1956. Something else also came to an end: a run of four straight winning seasons and title contenders. The first Gems team posted a 64-76 mark, only good enough for fifth place. The 1957 team would flirt with triple-digit losses (59-95) on the way to a seventh-place finish. (CCB.)

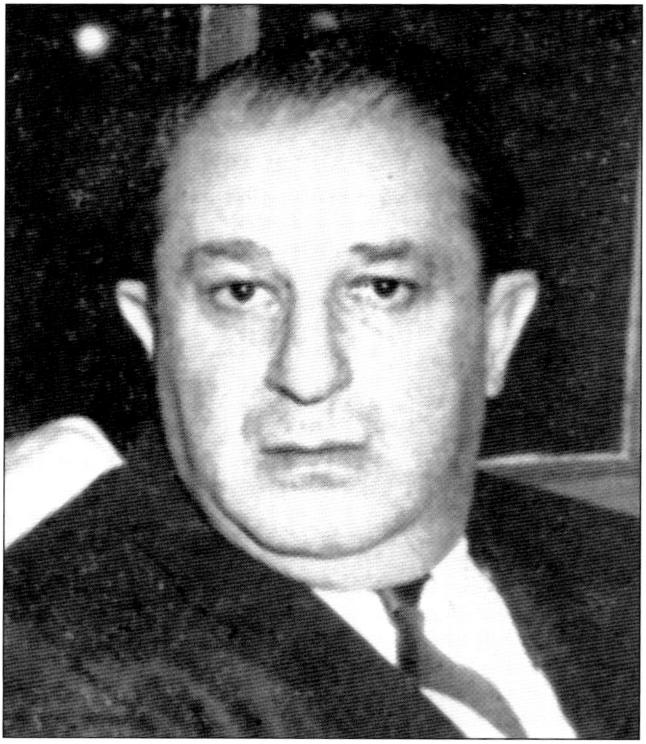

Julius Love never shied from a leadership role. The textile/garment businessman stayed active in the community on many fronts. Sport was a great area of contribution for Love, and keeping professional baseball going in Columbia became his calling. He convinced Kansas City to send players, and he operated the club himself. (Bob and Fran Somogyi.)

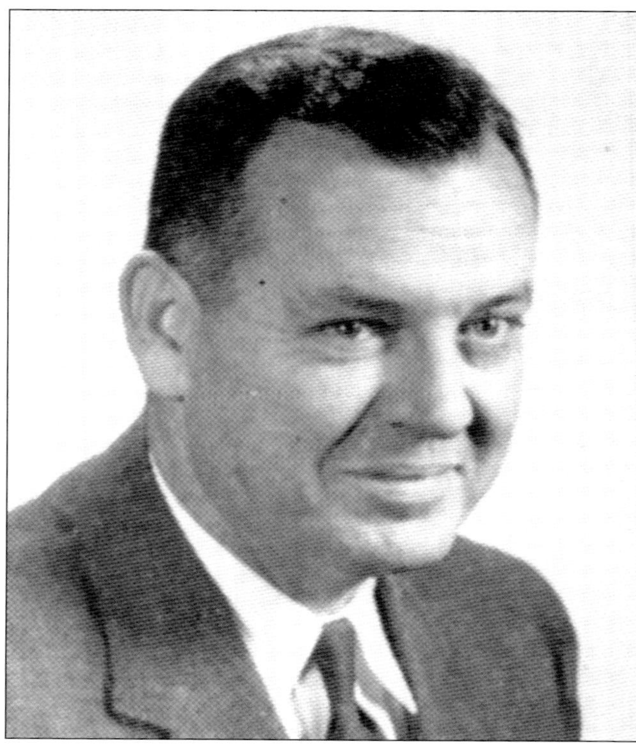

Bill Ouzts has been one of the strongest proponents of baseball in Columbia. Like Julius Love, he took a direct hand in keeping baseball alive in the 1950s. Ouzts also worked hard to get a team going again in the 1980s. His tireless efforts in the private sector and as a Columbia city councilman were eventually recognized in the naming of Ouzts Field at Capital City Stadium. (Bob and Fran Somogyi.)

With attendance woes mounting, the Gems and announcer Bob Fulton (left) staged a promotional stunt to spur ticket sales. Fulton bet the Savannah announcer that the Gems could outdraw Savannah over two weeks. Fulton lost the wager and spent 12 days and nights on the ballpark roof! Partner Lou Essex (right) joined Fulton for one night. Youth groups sold enough tickets to get Fulton back down. (Bob Fulton.)

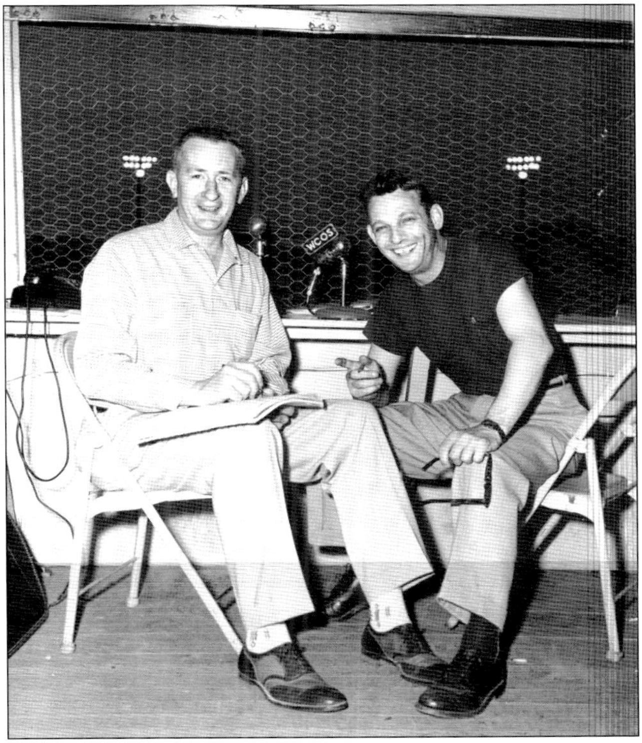

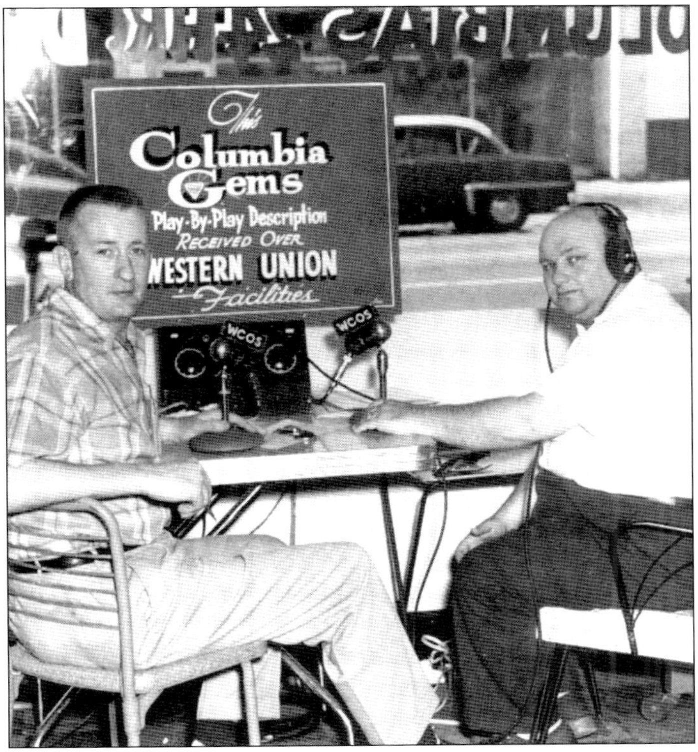

Bob Fulton (left, with color announcer Bob Truere) called road games from the window of the Taylor Street Pharmacy. He took in game descriptions by wire and recreated the game for the radio audience. Since the play-by-play lagged behind, Fulton gave coded clues on the air so that owner Julius Love could get the game result and go to bed early. (Bob Fulton.)

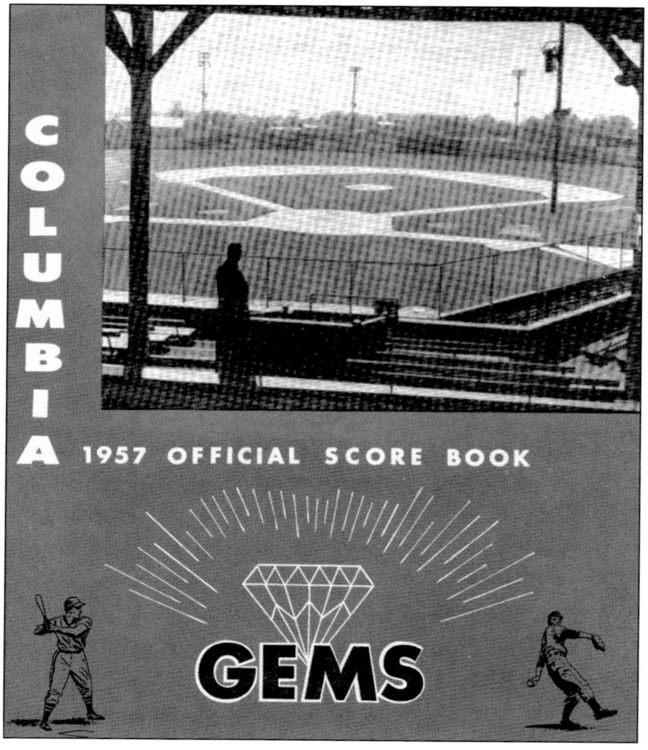

Popular Columbia Reds manager and South Carolinian Ernie White returned to town in 1957 to lead the Gems, but he could not do much with what the Royals provided. Shrinking crowds and mounting losses made the season increasingly difficult. The Gems came in seventh in the league and lost nearly 100 games. (Bob and Fran Somogyi.)

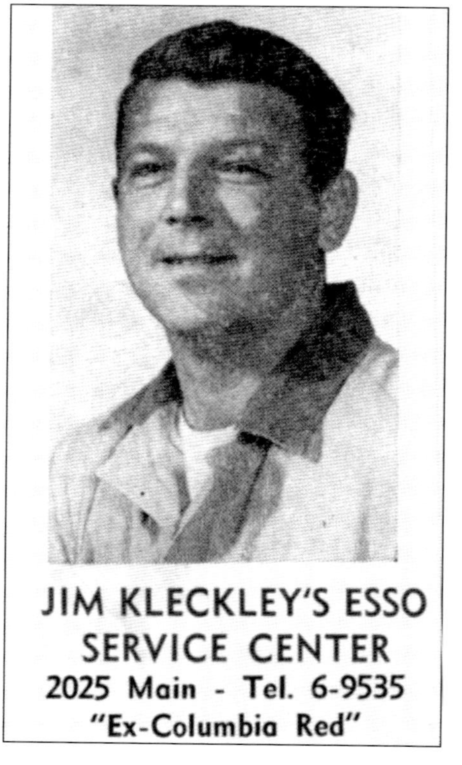

This advertisement came from the 1957 Gems scorebook. In a good show of sportsmanship and business sense across the years, former Columbia Red Jim Kleckley advertised with the Gems. Like the arrival of Ernie White, the ad for Kleckley's Esso tried to connect the Gems to the beloved teams of Columbia's not-so-distant past. (Bob and Fran Somogyi.)

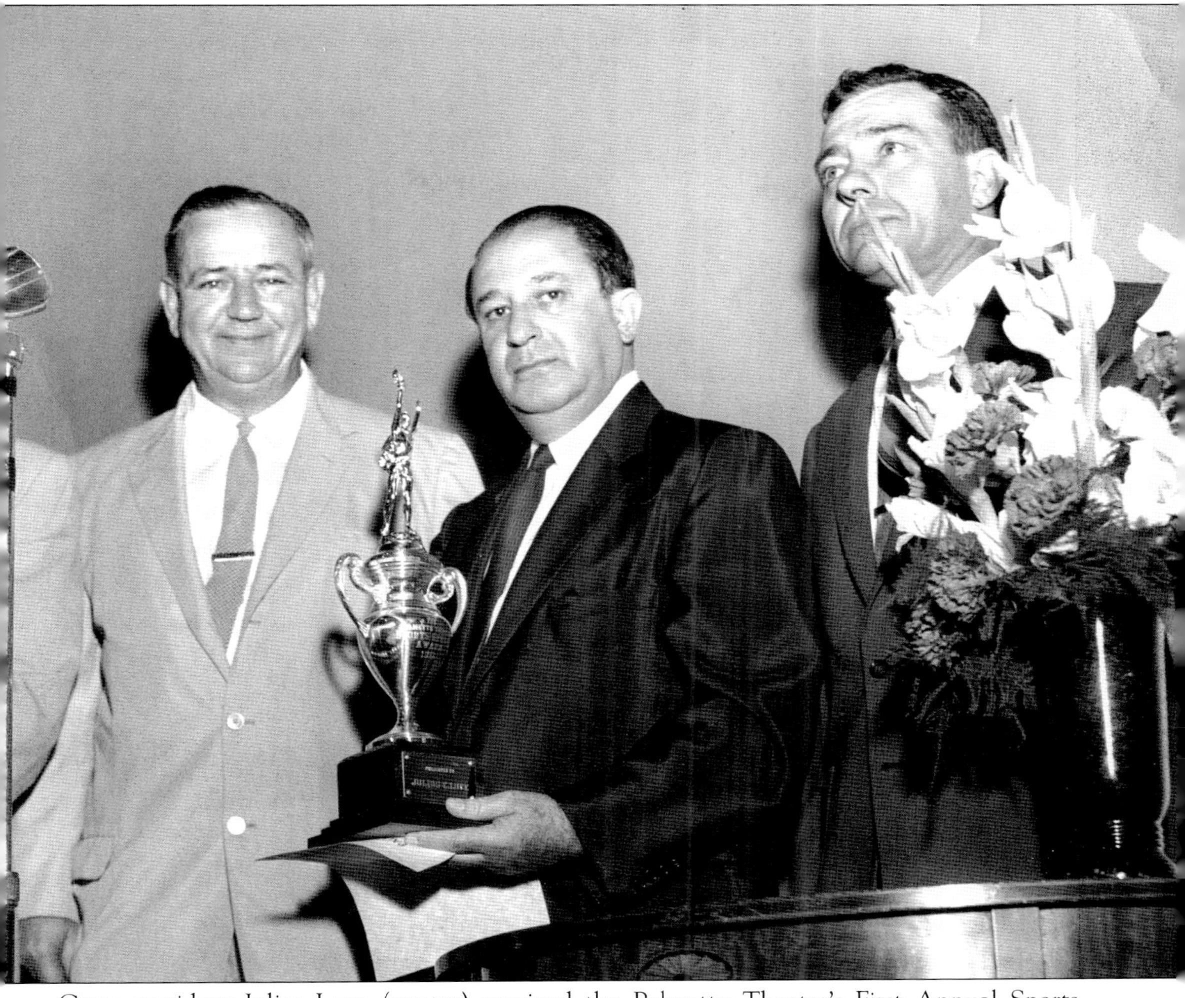

Gems president Julius Love (center) received the Palmetto Theater's First Annual Sports Service Award in July 1957. The award was created to honor local figures making valuable contributions in the Columbia sports environment and was designed to stimulate sports leadership in the community. It was given to Love primarily for his dedicated efforts to keep baseball going in Columbia, despite the departure of the Reds after the 1955 season. From left to right are University of South Carolina athletic director Rex Enright, Julius Love, and Columbia mayor Lester Bates. It is an unfortunate irony—and no fault of Julius Love—that just months after this ceremony, Columbia would be without professional baseball in a non-war year for the first time since 1935. (Michael Love.)

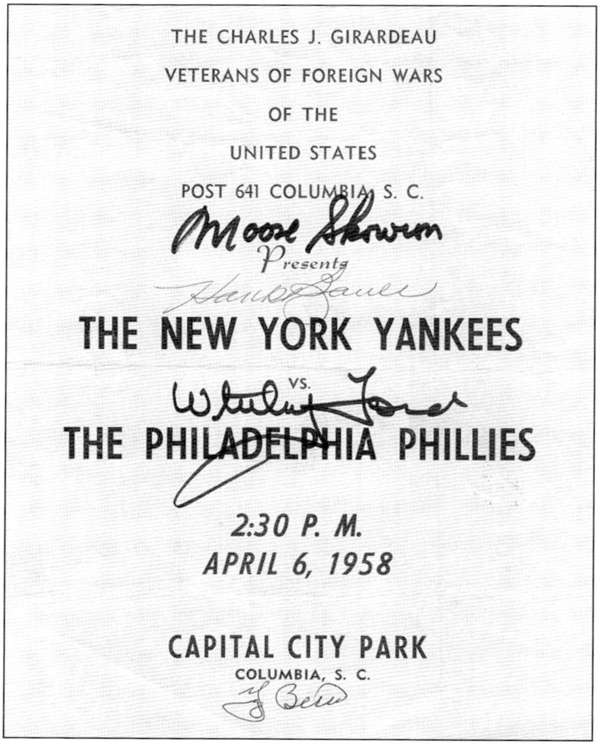
THE CHARLES J. GIRARDEAU
VETERANS OF FOREIGN WARS
OF THE
UNITED STATES
POST 641 COLUMBIA, S. C.
Presents
THE NEW YORK YANKEES
VS.
THE PHILADELPHIA PHILLIES
2:30 P. M.
APRIL 6, 1958
CAPITAL CITY PARK
COLUMBIA, S. C.

Even without a regular team, baseball lived on in Columbia, as Capital City Park hosted an exhibition game between the Yankees and Phillies in 1958. It was more common for big-league clubs to make such barnstorming stops in this era, even with big names like the ones on this autographed program: Moose Skowron, Hank Bauer, Whitey Ford, and Yogi Berra. (Bob and Fran Somogyi.)

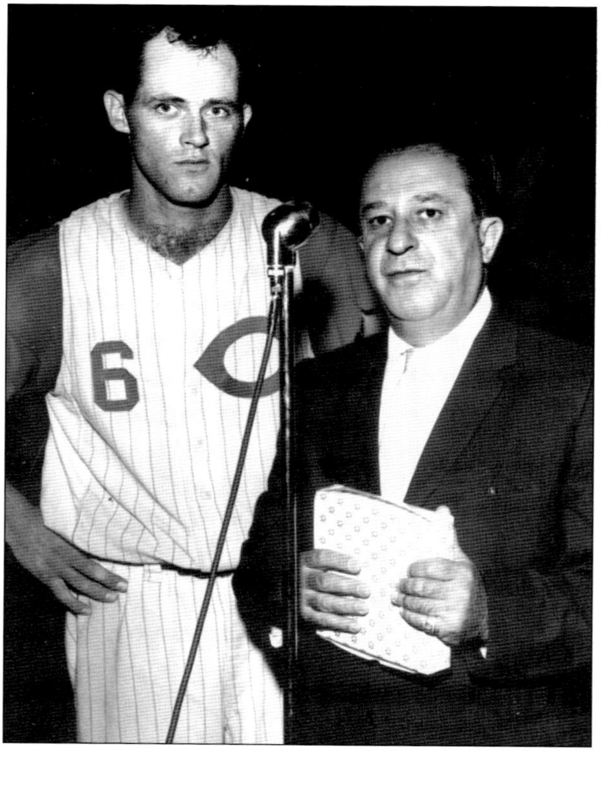

Turning the tables a bit on the typical player award presentation, catcher Dutch Dotterer gave Julius Love a thank-you gift from the Reds after a first place finish in 1960. Yes, the Reds were back in Columbia: Love and other city dignitaries had successfully persuaded Cincinnati to return after four years in Savannah. (Michael Love.)

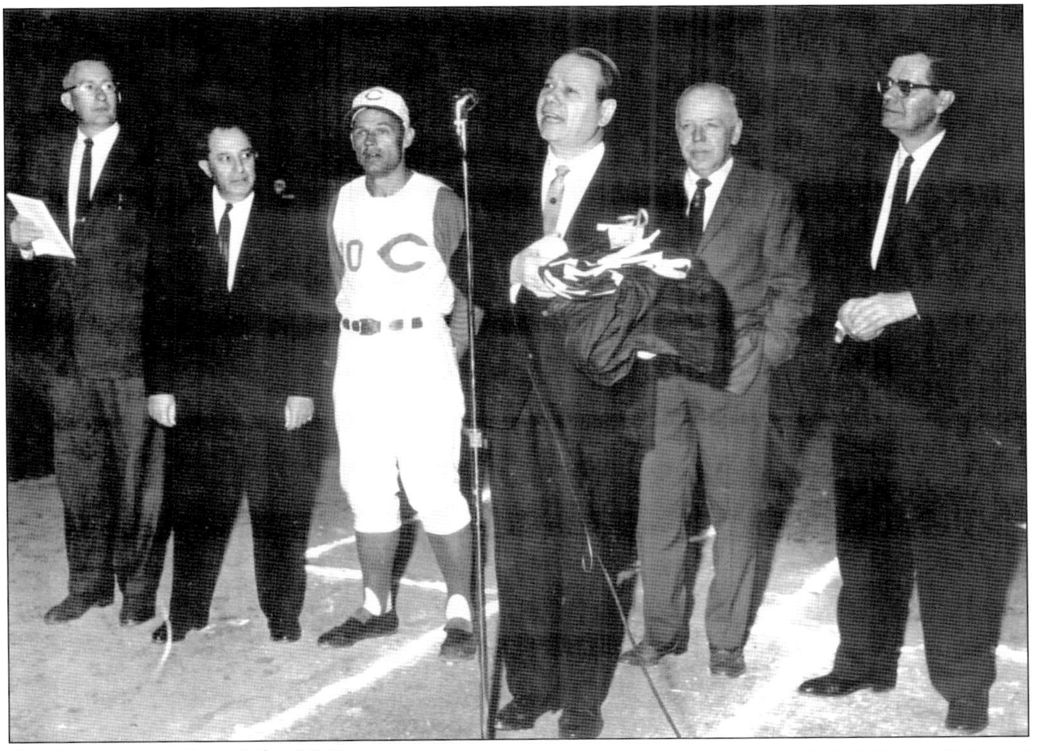

At the opening day of the 1961 season, Columbia mayor Lester Bates addressed the crowd before presenting the 1960 pennant to the Columbia Reds. From left to right are Reds announcer Bob Fulton, president Julius Love, field manager Ted Beard, Mayor Bates, business manager Art Kowalski, and Greenville mayor Kenneth Cass (Columbia played Greenville that night). (Bob Fulton.)

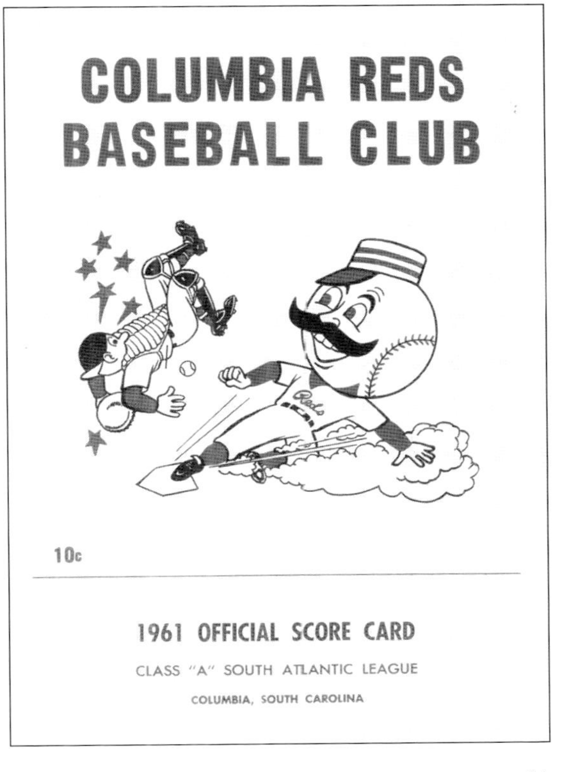

The Reds mascot may have smiled at the time, but this scorecard would later symbolize an end to baseball in Columbia. Manager Ted Beard's 1961 club finished with a winning record but out of contention. The Reds pulled out of Columbia following the season, and the town went without a team for 22 years. (Bob and Fran Somogyi.)

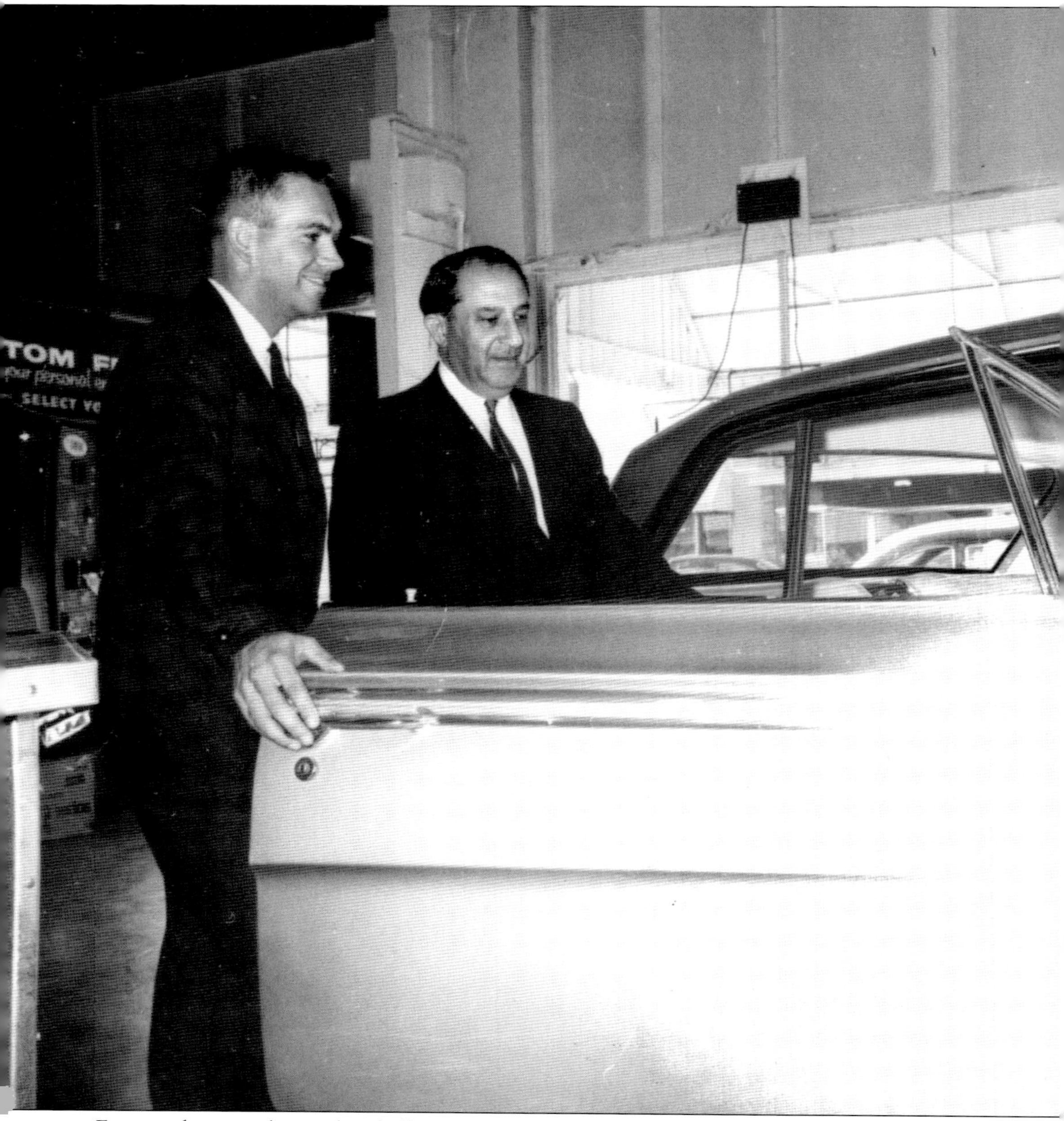

Even with minor league baseball out of Columbia, Julius Love kept in touch with the baseball community. Here we see Love offering New York Yankees great Bobby Richardson a role with Love Chevrolet. Richardson, a native of Sumter, spent 12 seasons with the Yankees. He played in seven World Series and earned MVP honors for the 1960 Fall Classic—he is the only player to do so while playing for the losing team. Richardson went on to coach the University of South Carolina baseball team from 1970 to 1976, including a trip to the College World Series for the Gamecocks in 1975. Meanwhile, Love had obviously changed his business direction since his days with Columbia Garment Mills. The automobile dealerships that Love established are still thriving in the Midlands today. (Michael Love.)

SIX

Back to the Ballpark with the Mets

When the 1961 Reds packed up and moved out, it was nothing new for Columbia. Departures and gaps between teams had been part of the city's baseball scene since before the days of the Comers, so fans may have expected to see a new squad suit up after a year or two. This time things turned out differently, and the gap lasted 22 years, removing a generation from the town's baseball timeline.

The push for baseball's return gathered life in the 1980s. A professional sports presence had been absent too long, and several community leaders stepped up to the plate to try to change that. The solution came in two parts: a businessman willing to invest in a team and a team needing to move. Those roles were filled by Herb Wishengrad and the Shelby Mets. The Shelby Mets became the Columbia Mets in 1983, and the third great period of baseball for the city had begun. That team changed hands and switched names over the years, but the same franchise still operated in 2004.

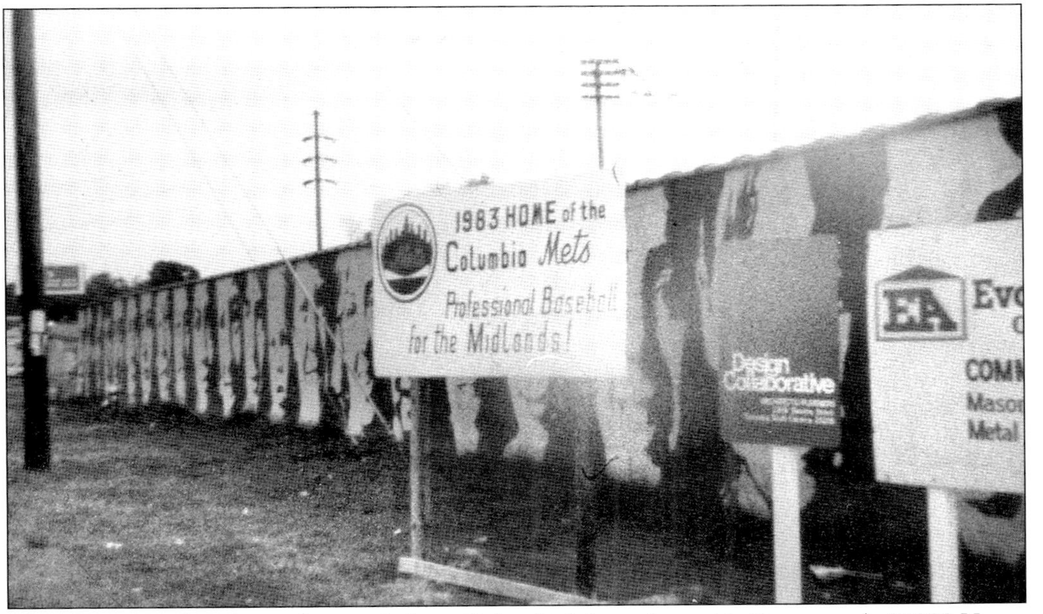

This sign erected in front of a mural along Columbia's busy Assembly Street reads, "1983 Home of the Columbia Mets—Professional Baseball for the Midlands." Old Capital City Park was about to wake up after two decades without a team. Getting the place in baseball shape was not easy, but a strong community effort ensured the facility's readiness. (CCB.)

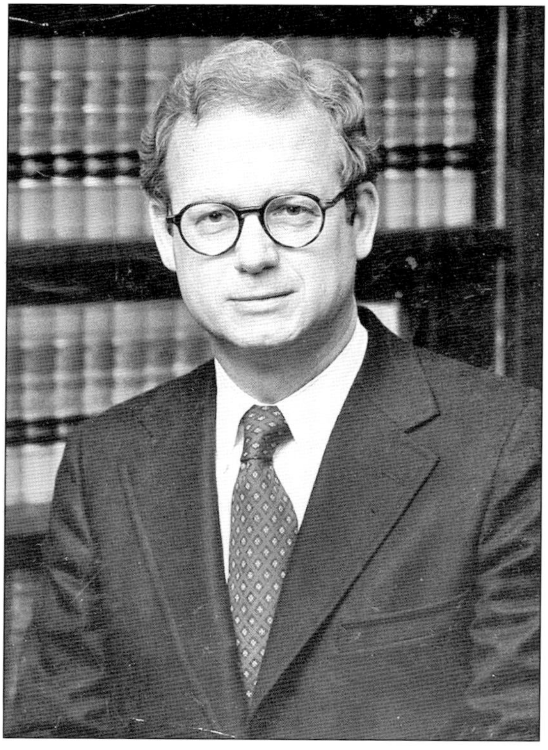

Columbia mayor Kirkman Finlay Jr. spearheaded years of effort to get pro baseball back in the capital city. That hard work finally paid off in 1982 with the impending move of the Shelby, North Carolina franchise. Some of Finlay's dreams for the city's future still have an impact in the 21st century, such as his goal of revitalizing the Congaree River Vista, an area in which some have envisioned a possible new ballpark. (CCB.)

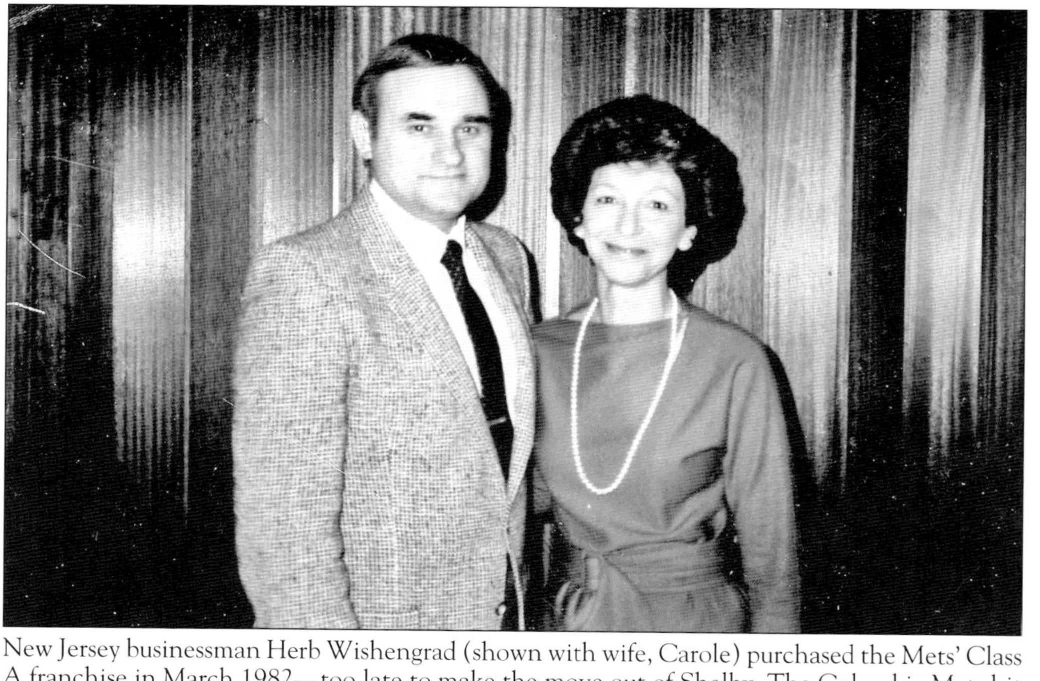

New Jersey businessman Herb Wishengrad (shown with wife, Carole) purchased the Mets' Class A franchise in March 1982—too late to make the move out of Shelby. The Columbia Mets hit town in 1983, the second year for the new owners. Wishengrad was chairman and CEO of a company making packaging and other paper, plastic, and aluminum products. (CCB.)

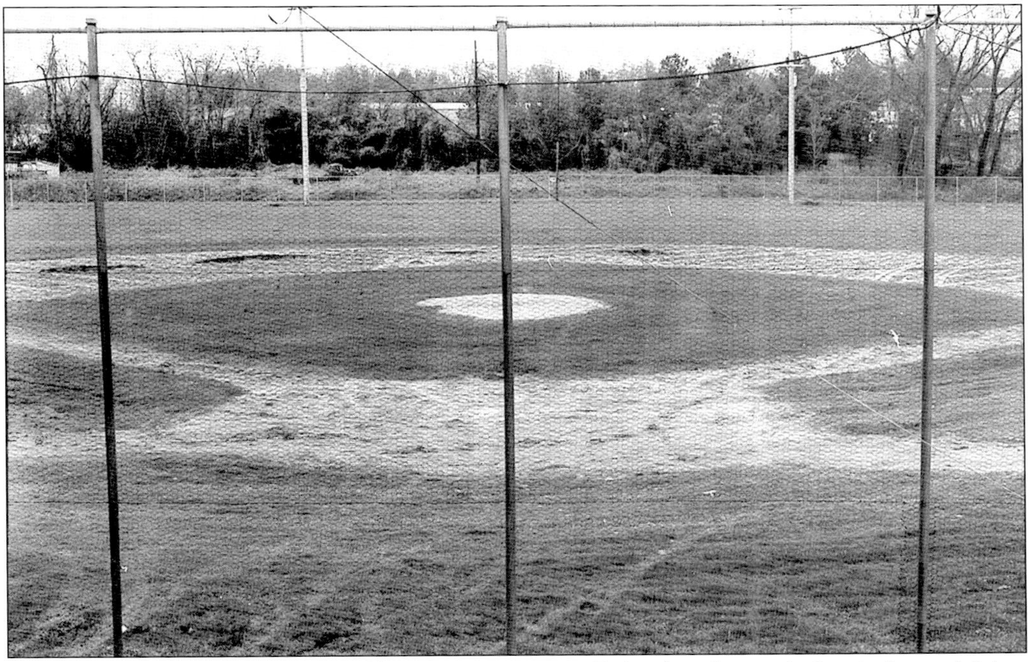

Years of political and business efforts got a team to Columbia, but only hard physical labor cleared the way, and this image shows that task in progress. Overgrown weeds and significant amounts of litter had already been removed by the time this picture was taken. Workers had to correct a playing surface pocked with holes and gullies and build a new outfield wall. (CCB.)

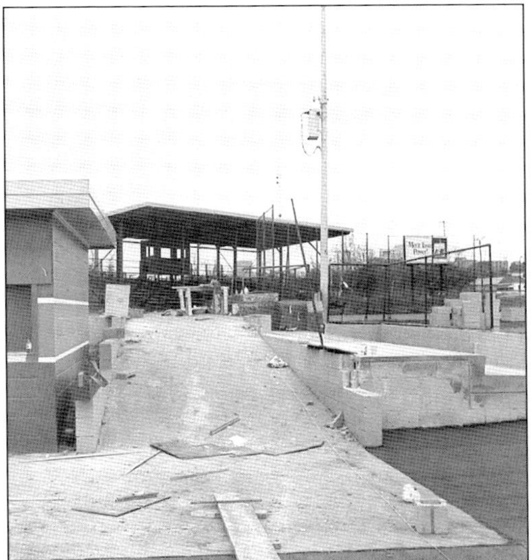

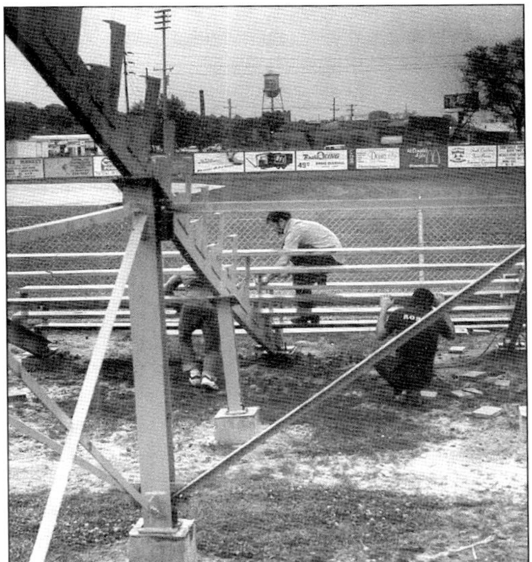

Construction debris littered the landscape as concession stands and walkways took shape around the old wooden stands. Completing additional new grandstands for the ballpark required plenty of teamwork. Many seats were hand-me-down bleachers donated from Richland School District One. Volunteers installed the seats after Fort Jackson crews moved them to the site. The team added aluminum box seats purchased from a racetrack. A Richland District Two shop class built the stadium's new press box. (CCB.)

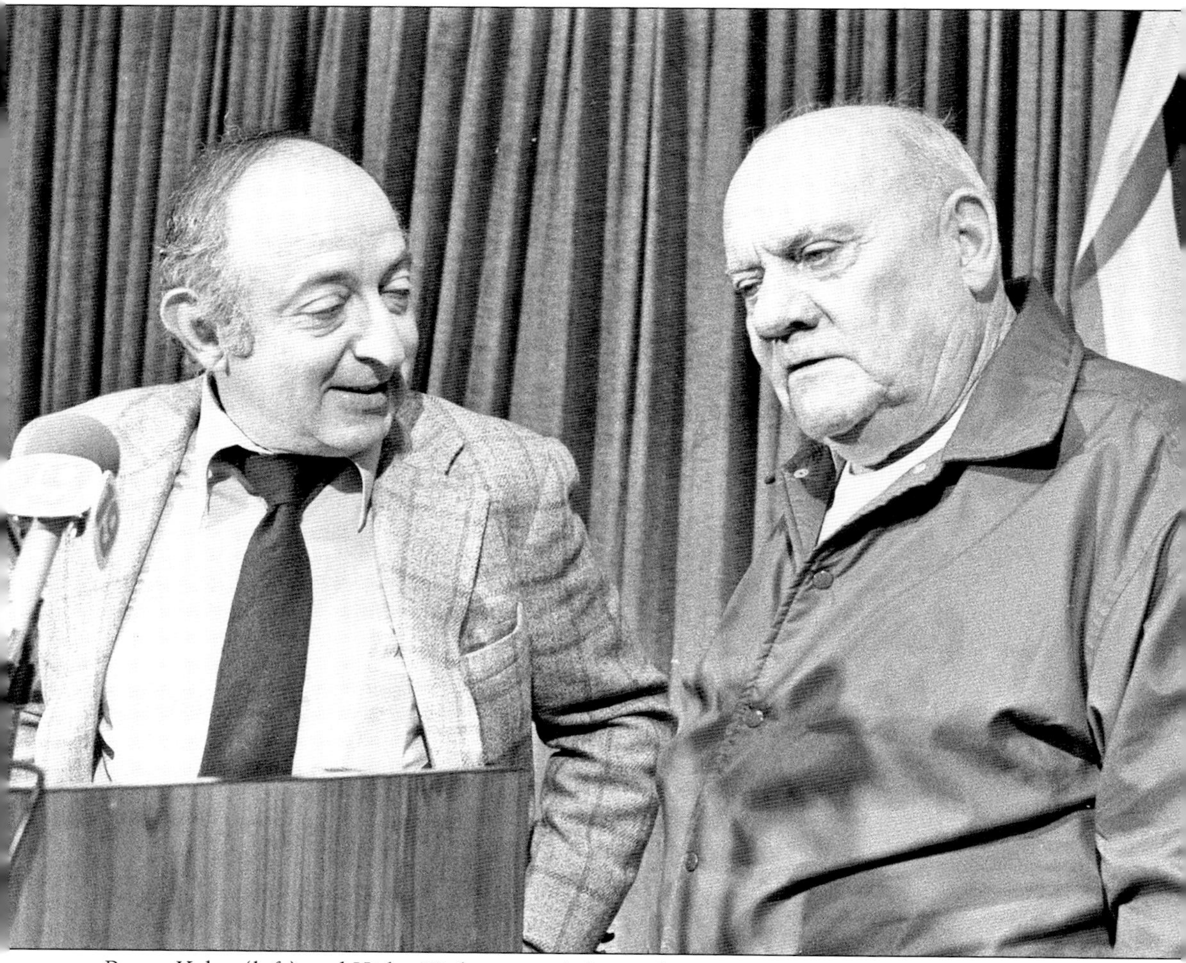

Roger Kahn (left) and Kirby Higbe greeted the media at a preseason press conference in 1983. Kahn, bestselling author of *Boys of Summer* and other baseball books, bought an interest in the team and assumed the role of president. He acknowledged his hopes to tell the story of the Columbia Mets in a book to be called *Diamond in the Rough*. Before midseason, Kahn stepped down following health problems, and the book never materialized. Later that same year, he bought into the Utica Blue Sox, and the experience became his book entitled *Good Enough to Dream*. Higbe was a Columbia native who played minor-league ball in town in the 1930s before his successful career in the majors with the Brooklyn Dodgers and other teams. He threw out the first pitch for the 1983 home opener. (CCB, from *Columbia Record*.)

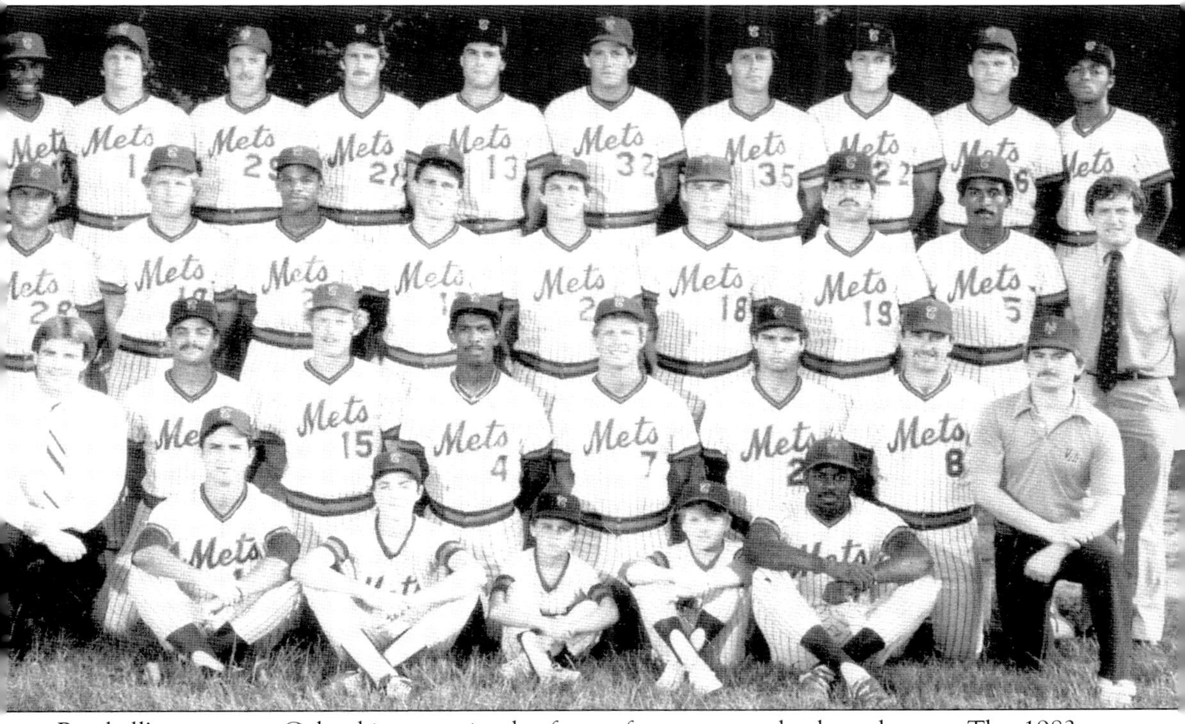

Baseball's return to Columbia came in the form of a strong and talented team. The 1983 Columbia Mets finished 88-54, losing the championship series to Gastonia. The team, from left to right, is (first row) Ed Pruitt, batboys Byron Roberts, John Tamargo Jr. and Paul Prince, and John Wilson; (second row) assistant general manager Neil White, Ken Harris, Dennis Glynn, Julio Paula, Steve Phillips, Joe Klink, Billy Welch, and trainer Sam McCrary; (third row) manager John Tamargo, Steve Springer, Herman Lewis, Kevin Brown, Mickey Weston, Randy Myers, Paul Hollins, Frank Moscat, and general manager Bill Blackwell; (fourth row) Lou Thornton, Wade Schexnayder, Barry Lyons, Scott Murray, Stu Foulks, Craig Weissman, pitching coach Greg Pavilick, Dave Magadan, David Jensen, and Floyd Youmans. From this exceptional group, eight played in the majors: Klink, Springer, Weston, Myers, Thornton, Lyons, Magadan, and Youmans. In addition, Phillips went on to become the general manager of the New York Mets and Tamargo Jr. eventually played pro ball in Columbia. (CCB.)

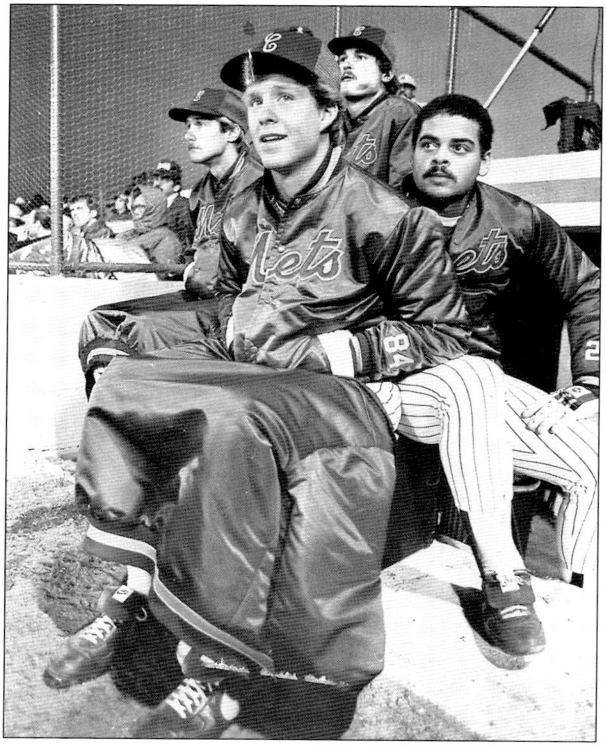

Early in the Mets' inaugural season, Columbia got a cold snap that forced fans and players alike to bundle up. From left to right in this shot are Scott Murray, Steve Phillips, Marlin McPhail, and Ken Harris. None of them played in the majors, but two had lasting effects on the organization. Phillips spent several years as the Mets general manager. After trying his hand at coaching, McPhail became New York's area scout based out of Irmo. (CCB, from *Columbia Record.*)

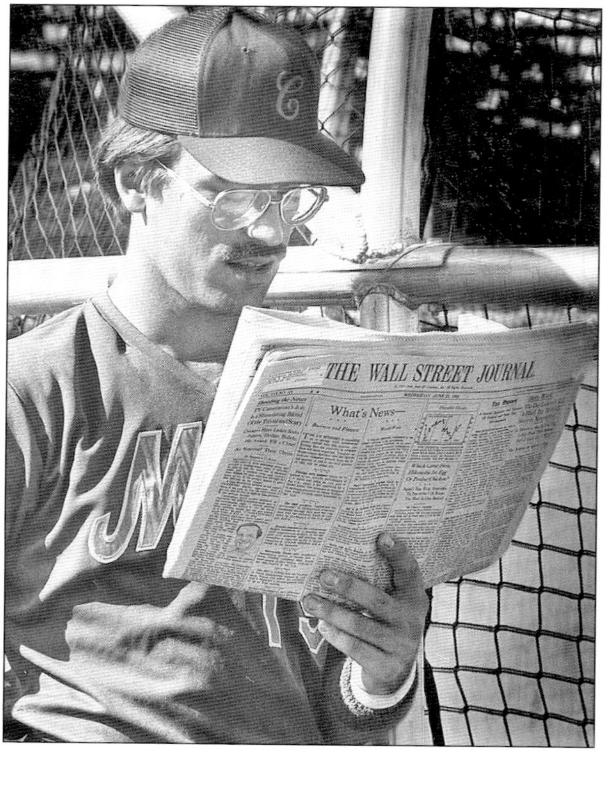

In this classic staged photograph, of the type you might have seen three decades prior, Paul Hollins demonstrated his business acumen by checking stocks. Hollins was a rare player in recent Columbia history—a former USC Gamecock who played pro ball in town as well. Hollins's 97 RBIs in 1983 had only been matched or surpassed by three players through the end of 2003. (CCB, from *Columbia Record.*)

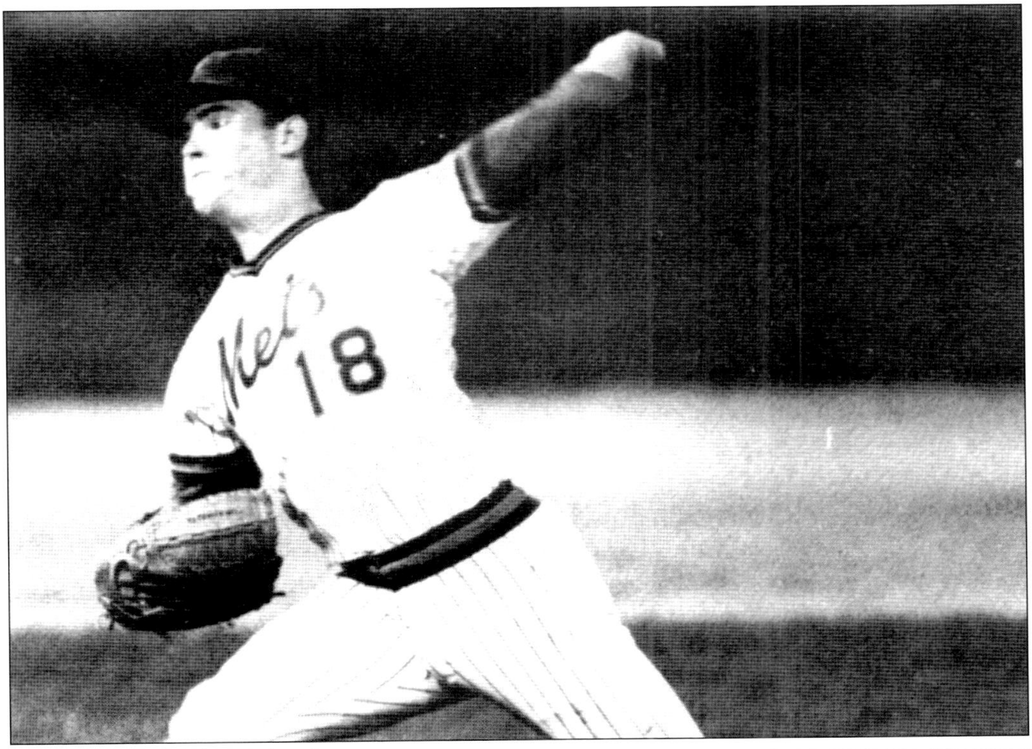

A workhorse for the Columbia Mets in 1983, Randy Myers started 28 games, earning 24 decisions (14-10), and pitched 173 innings. Myers made the final SAL All-Star list for the year and found continued success after leaving the team. He made his debut for the New York Mets in 1985 and began a long career in the majors. Myers found his calling as a big-league reliever, racking up 347 career saves. (CCB.)

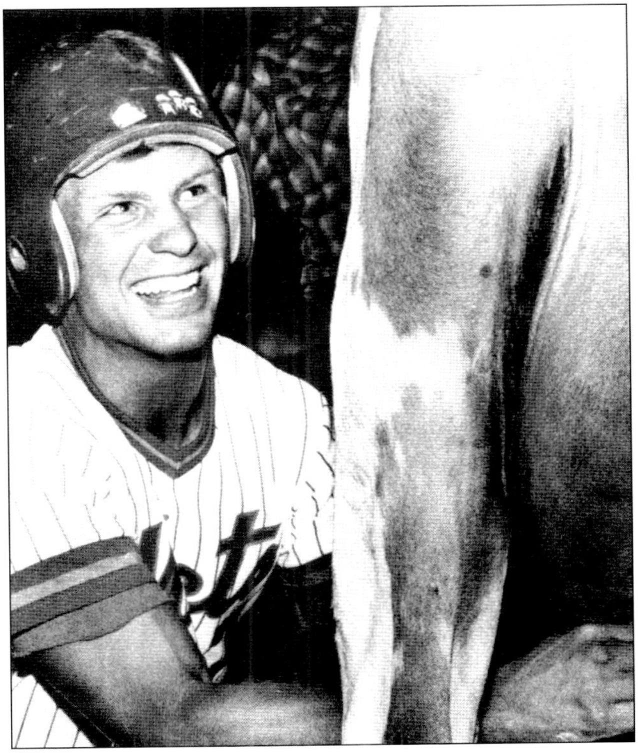

Columbia Mets infielder Steve Phillips was all smiles during this classic minor league promotion: the cow-milking contest. For years, stunts like this one have kept fans amused and maintained a high community profile for the team, while also making sponsors happy. With that kind of arrangement, everyone wins—even the cow! (CCB.)

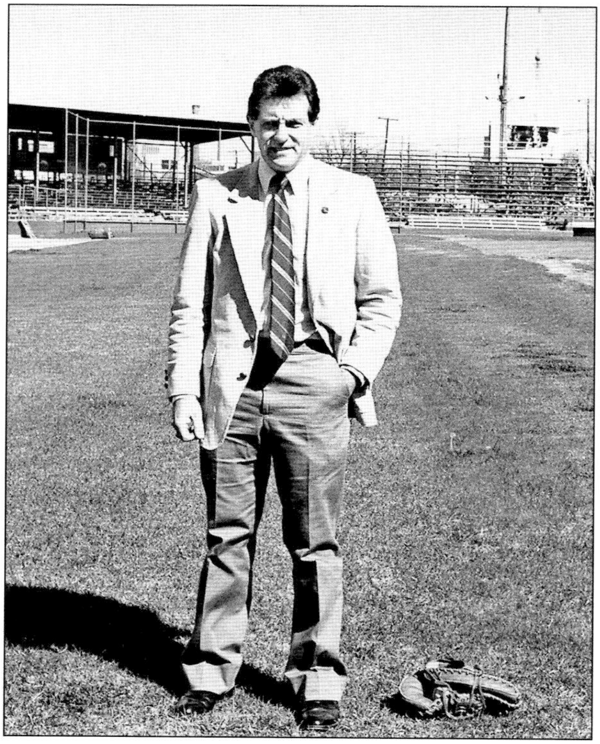

Bill Blackwell, the Columbia Mets' first general manager, had a broadcasting background when team owners brought him aboard in 1982. Blackwell ran team operations for the holdover year in Shelby and then got things started in Columbia. He stayed with the Columbia Mets through 1987 and has since remained in baseball. He began his third season as GM of the Charlotte Knights in 2004. (CCB.)

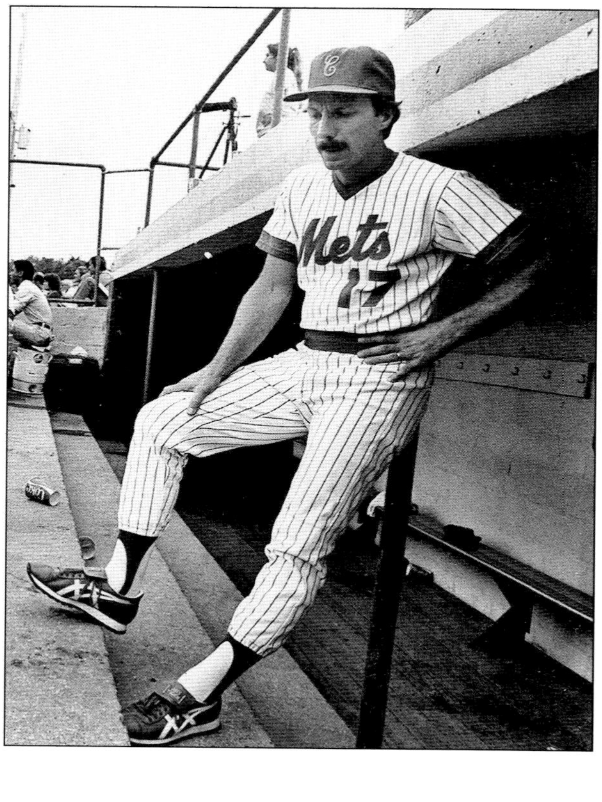

The Mets turned the reins over to Rich Miller for 1984. Miller led Columbia to the league's best overall record but not to a playoff berth, an unfortunate side effect sometimes when leagues play a split-season format. Miller returned to manage most of the season in 1985 and was seen again many times over the ensuing years as a roving instructor for the Mets organization. (CCB, from *Columbia Record*.)

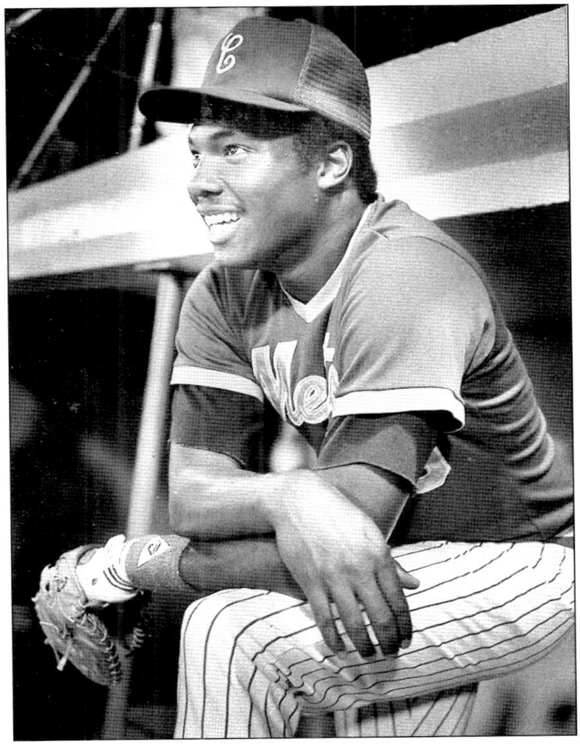

After swatting a home run against Anderson early in 1984, Andy Lawrence had to smile in the dugout. Lawrence played in the first two seasons for the Columbia Mets, but he made his greatest contribution in 1984, playing in 138 out of 139 games that year! (CCB, from *Columbia Record.*)

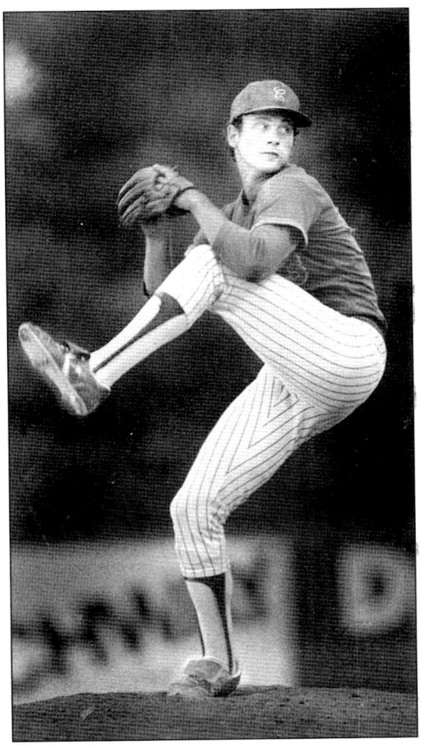

Columbia Mets pitcher Tom Edens gets ready to let loose in this shot from 1984. On the night this was taken, Edens surrendered a hit in the sixth to lose a no-hit bid. Edens moved on to a successful career in the majors. (CCB, from *Columbia Record.*)

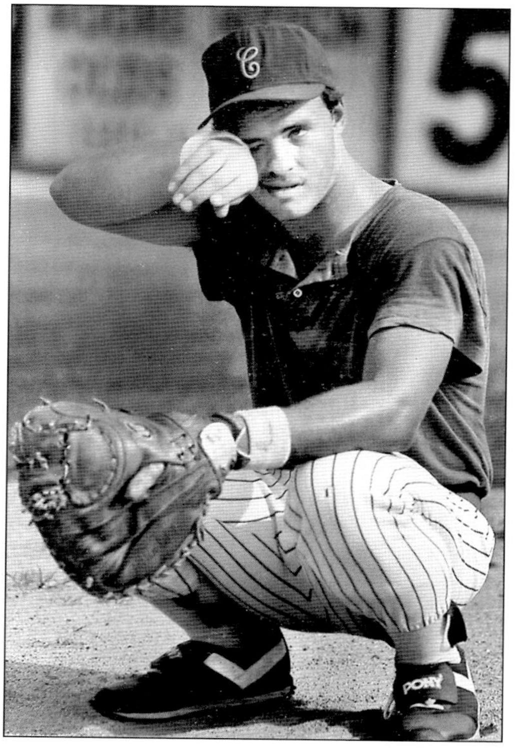

Catcher Allen Wilson tries to wipe the sweat from his eyes during practice at the ballpark in 1985. All of Columbia's players have learned that the city can be oppressively hot during baseball season. Imagine how tough it got in the days of wool uniforms. (CCB, from *Columbia Record*.)

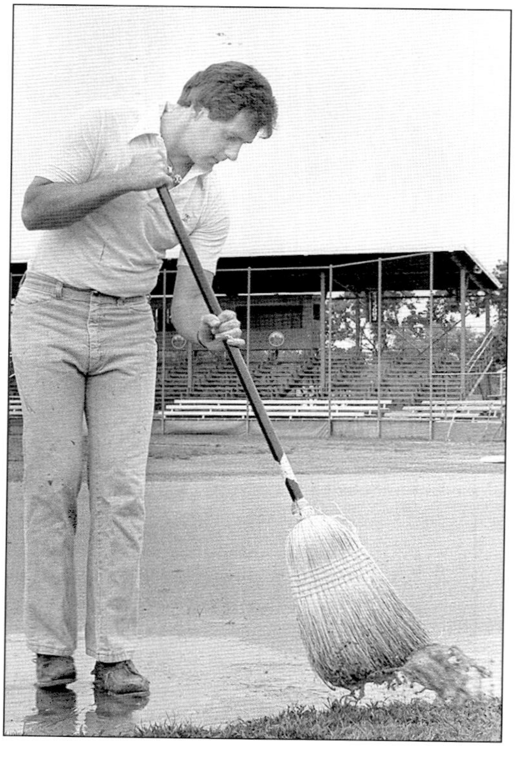

This is not what is meant by a series sweep, but it does show that getting a waterlogged field ready for play means trying anything that might work. That list can include brooms, rakes, squeegees, fans, and even towels—plus, of course, the absorbent materials spread to try and create a new surface for playing baseball. (CCB.)

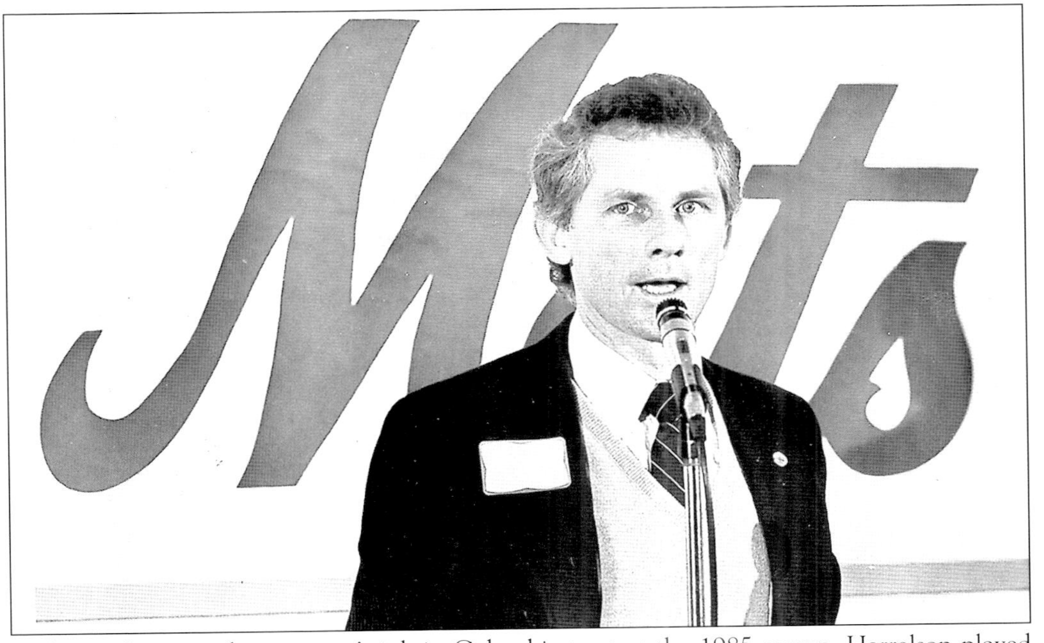

Bud Harrelson got the manager's job in Columbia to start the 1985 season. Harrelson played 16 years in the majors, mostly as a shortstop for the Mets. Early in the year, Harrelson got a big reassignment: coaching third base for the parent club. He replaced Bobby Valentine, who had just taken the job as manager in Texas. Rich Miller returned to lead the club the rest of the way. (CCB, from *Columbia Record.*)

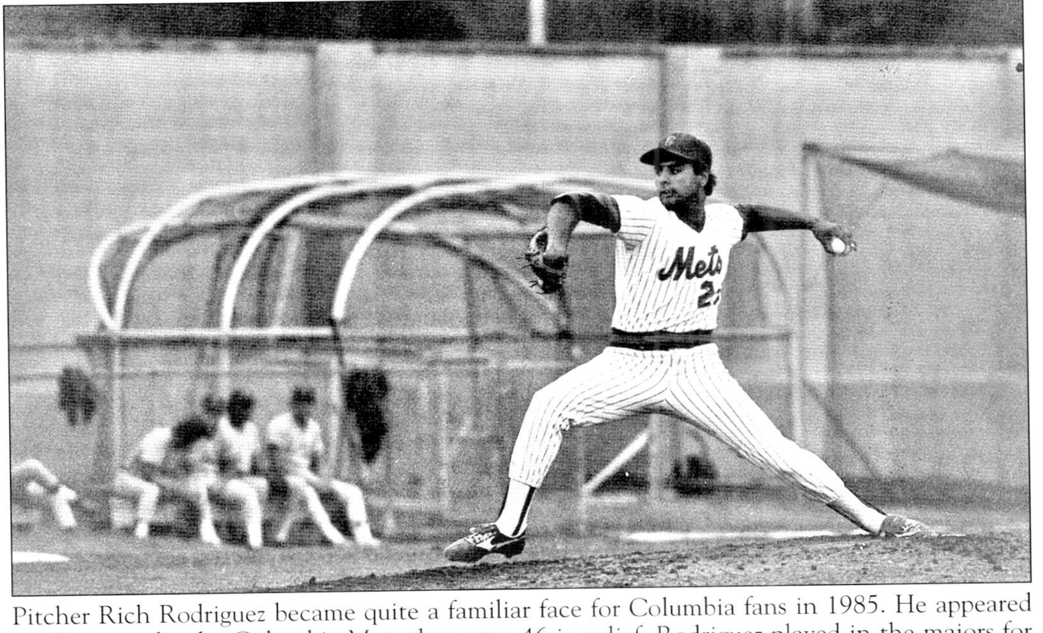

Pitcher Rich Rodriguez became quite a familiar face for Columbia fans in 1985. He appeared in 49 games for the Columbia Mets that year, 46 in relief. Rodriguez played in the majors for several years after making his big-league debut in 1990 for the San Diego Padres. (CCB, from *Columbia Record.*)

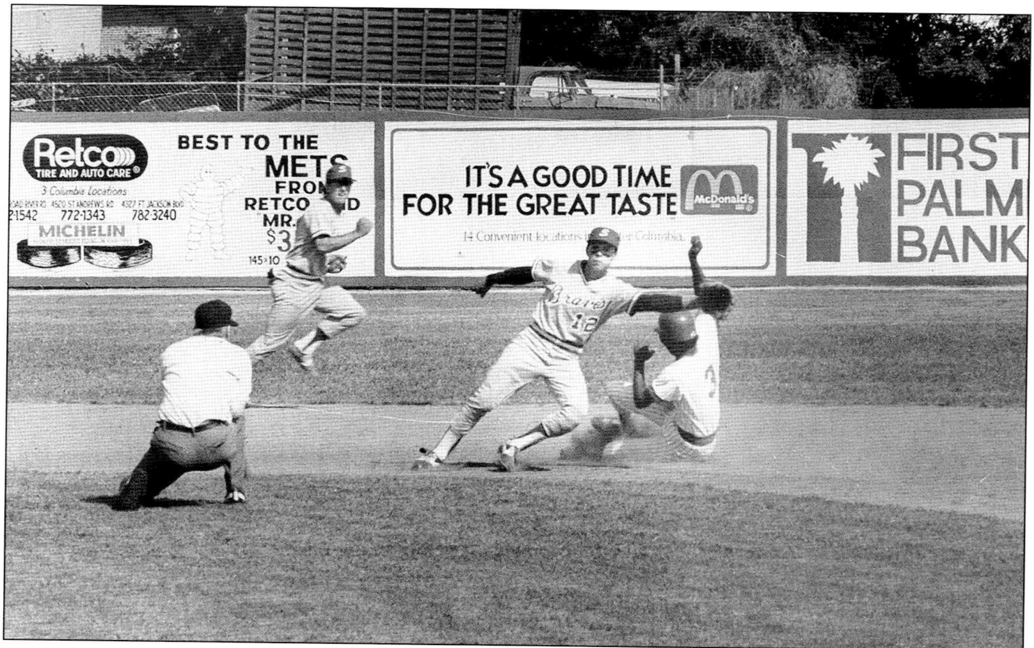

Here we see Marcus Lawton in the act, stealing one of the many bases he snared in 1985. The victims on this day were the Sumter Braves, and you can see second baseman—and future Atlanta Brave—Mark Lemke does not yet have the ball (it is passing in front of his collar) when Lawton is at the bag. (CCB, from *Columbia Record.*)

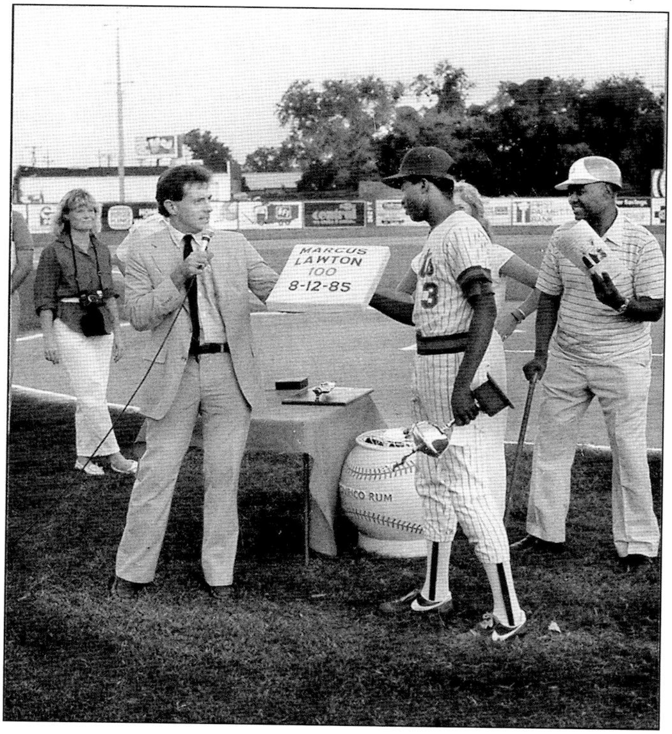

In this pre-game ceremony, Columbia Mets general manager Bill Blackwell saluted speedy outfielder Marcus Lawton for reaching 100 stolen bases. In 2004, Lawton remains the only player in franchise history to hit the century mark in steals. Going along with his 111 stolen bases that season, Lawton also scored 113 runs—another record that still stood in 2004. He made it to the majors but only played 10 games for the Yankees. (CCB.)

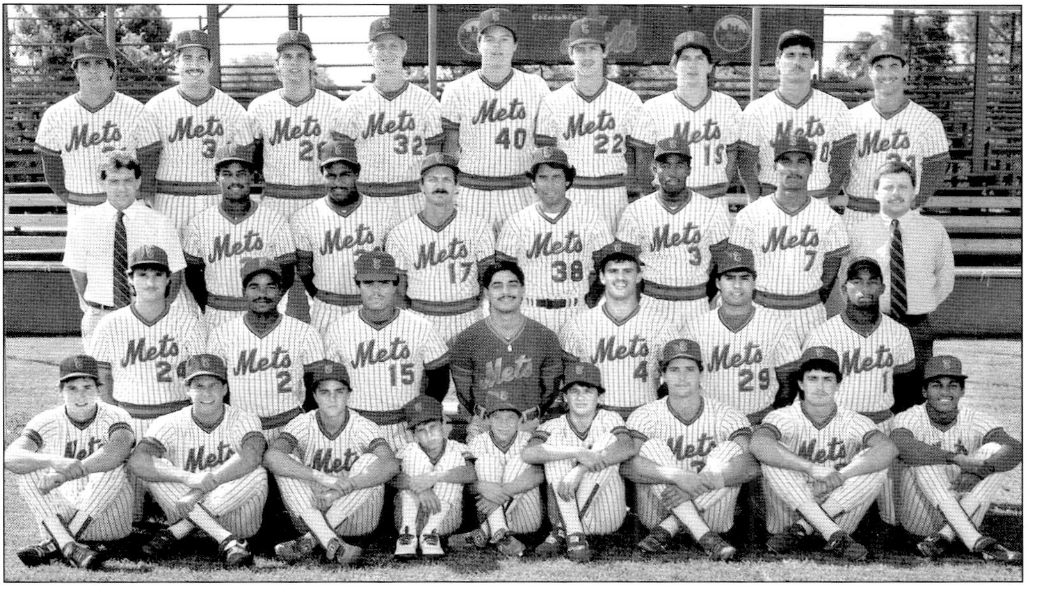

The 1985 team photo included four Columbia Mets who made the majors: Rich Rodriguez (#29, second row), Marcus Lawton (#3, third row), Dave West (#32, fourth row), and Mauro Gozzo (fourth row, far right). While Lawton was busy stealing bases, another player on this team was very busy setting a lasting record: Angelo Cuevas (#15, second row), whose 101 RBIs remained a franchise-best through 2003. (CCB.)

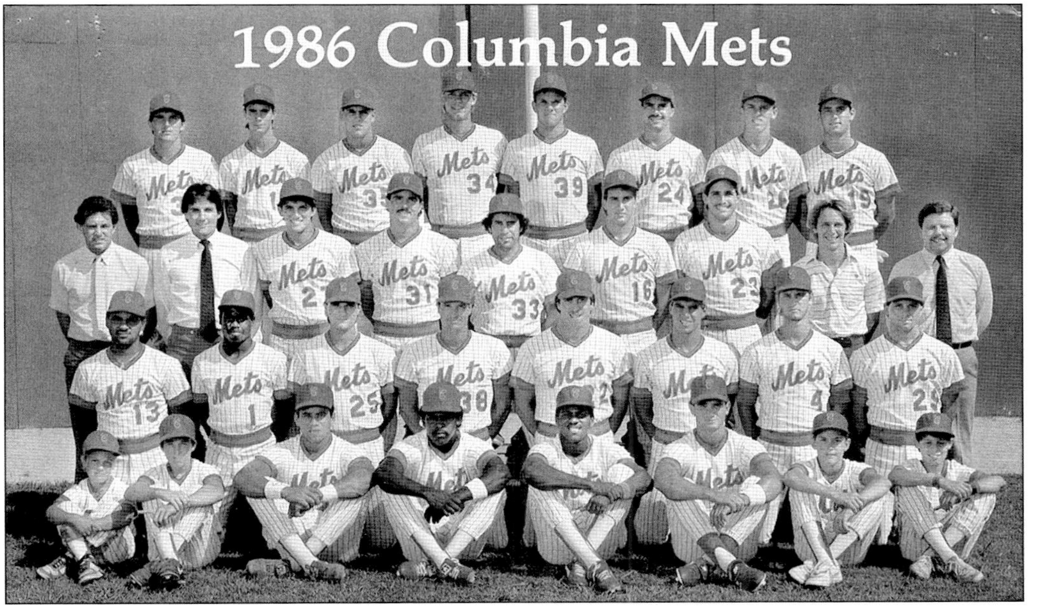

The 1986 Columbia Mets made quite an impression on the South Atlantic League. Four players and manager Tucker Ashford made the final All-Star list as the team marched to the league title. That success did not translate to future greatness, as only one player in this team photo went on to play in the majors: Brian Givens (#39, fourth row), who did not make his debut until 1995. (CCB.)

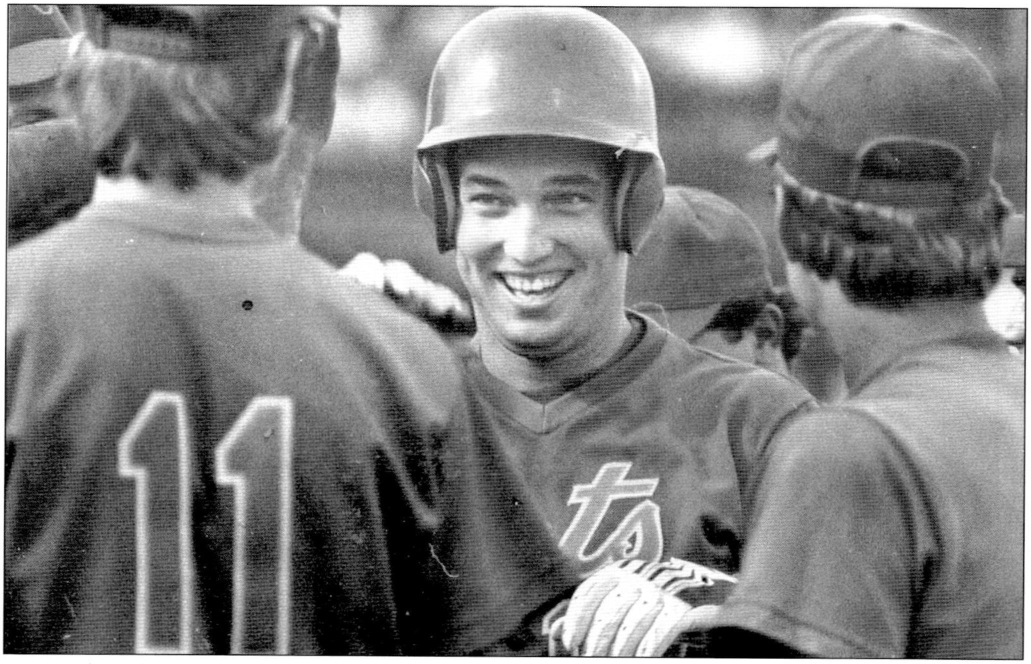

A grand smile on Brandon Bailey's face followed a grand slam during the 1986 season. Bailey finished with 14 home runs that year and returned in 1987 to set the franchise single-season home run record (at 24). Although three players have topped that record since then, Bailey's two-year total of 38 home runs still stood going into 2004. (CCB, from *Columbia Record.*)

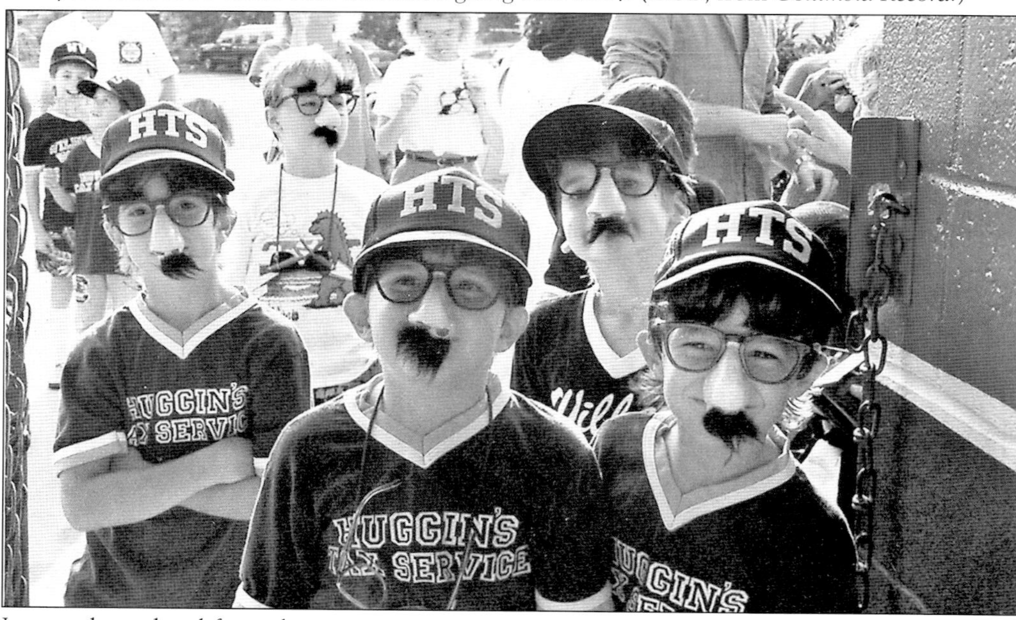

Just to show that life in the minors requires a sense of humor, the Columbia Mets enjoyed a "funny nose and glasses" giveaway promotion in 1986. During the game, plenty of fans were found wearing the novelty gifts, plus staff members and even batboys sported the comic look. Just about anything can be a promotional event at the ballpark if it is packaged right. (CCB.)

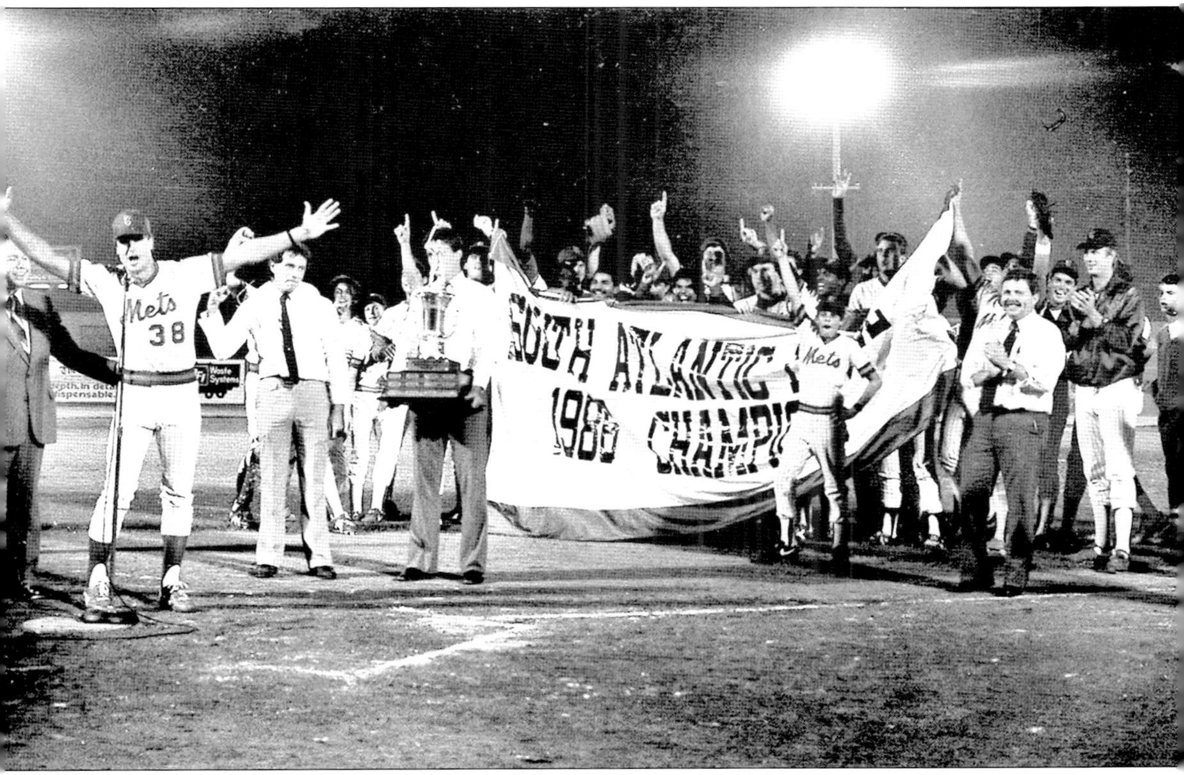

Manager Tucker Ashford takes the microphone at home plate while his team celebrates behind the championship pennant they just earned. The 1986 team steamrolled to first-place finishes in both halves of the divided season with a total record of 90-42; they also set a franchise record for runs scored with 836, more than 6 runs per game. Through 2003, no other team had gotten within 50 runs of that mark except for the very first Columbia Mets in 1983 (819 runs). The pennant was the first for the Columbia Mets and Columbia's first since the days of the Columbia Reds, ending a long drought for the city. (CCB.)

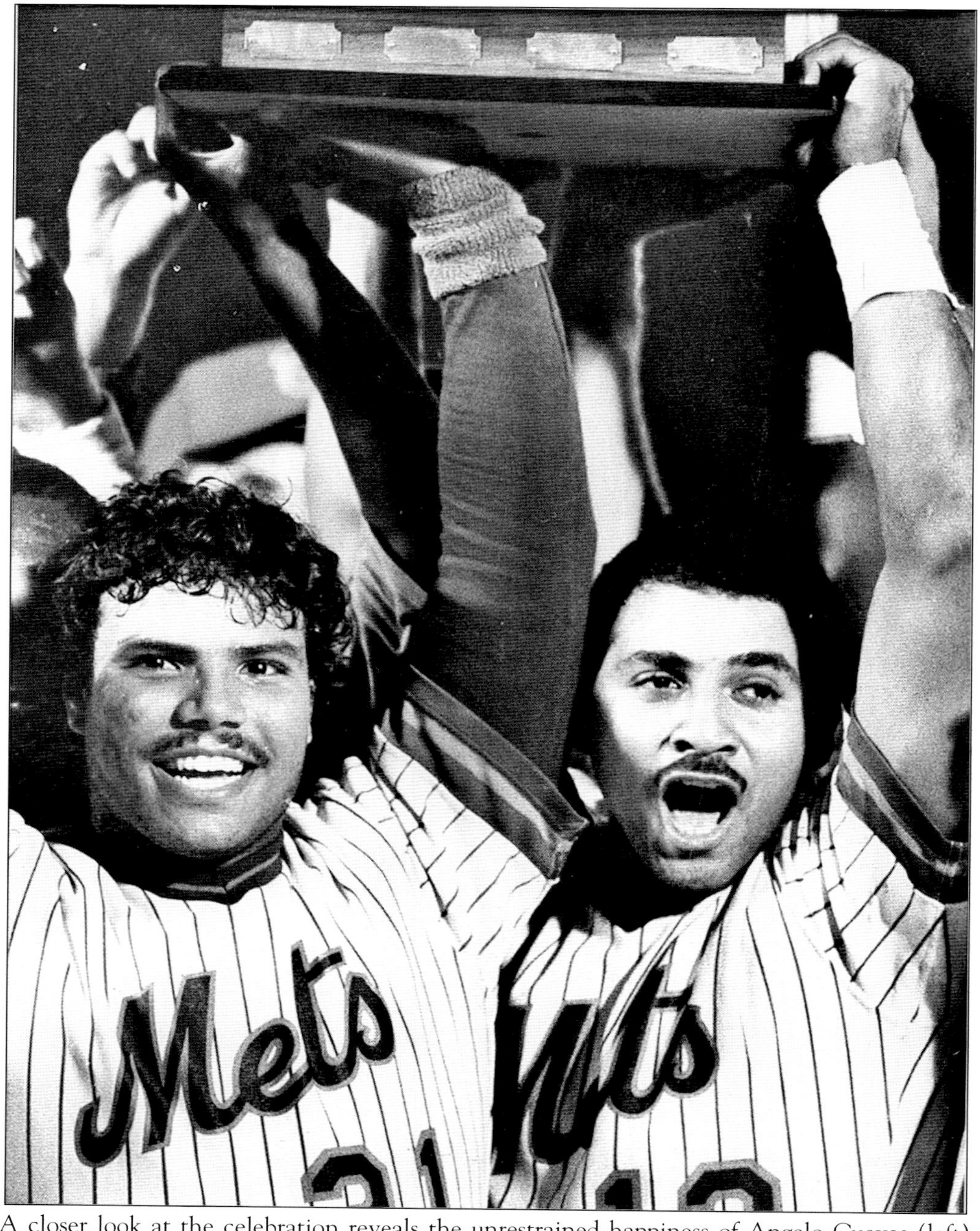

A closer look at the celebration reveals the unrestrained happiness of Angelo Cuevas (left) and Johnny Monell as they hold up the 1986 SAL Championship trophy. Although players in the minors do have the seemingly selfish goals of advancing their own careers, they also take pride in playing and winning as a team. Earning a championship ring at any level is a significant accomplishment. The managers actually have the toughest task in this light: they must simultaneously improve players as individual talents and prospects while also proving that they can coach the team as a whole to victories and maintain good team chemistry. Nothing establishes all these desired goals more than winning it all. (CCB, from *Columbia Record.*)

Manager Butch Hobson (left) and pitching coach Bob Apodaca watch from the dugout. Hobson, formerly a big-league infielder, led the team in 1987–1988. Neither of his Columbia Mets teams made the playoffs. Apodaca, who played five seasons for the New York Mets, is seen here in his fourth straight year as Columbia's pitching coach. Both men later gained big-league experience in their respective positions. (CCB, from *Columbia Record.*)

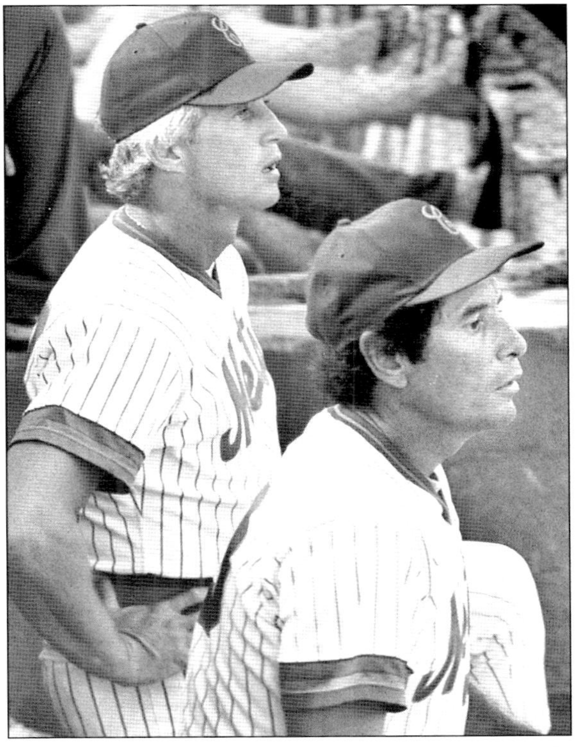

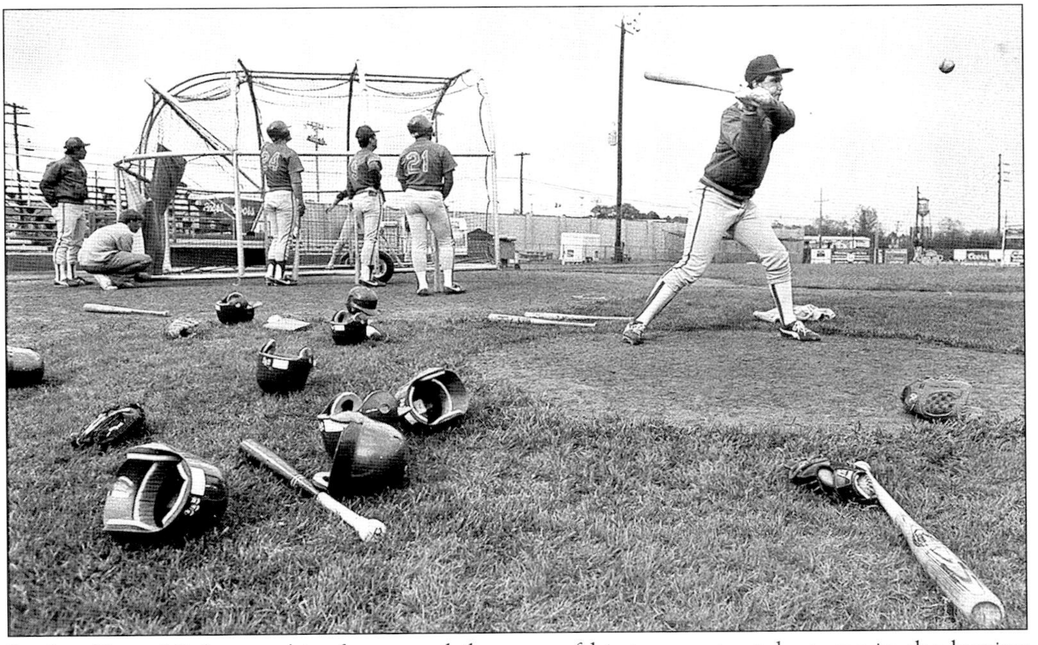

Pitcher Barry Hightower hits fungoes while some of his teammates take turns in the batting cage. Sometimes it is easy for fans to forget how many hours of practice the team puts in every day and every week, but it takes a lot of preparation and repetition to be ready for the myriad of possible game situations faced in the course of a season. (CCB, from *Columbia Record.*)

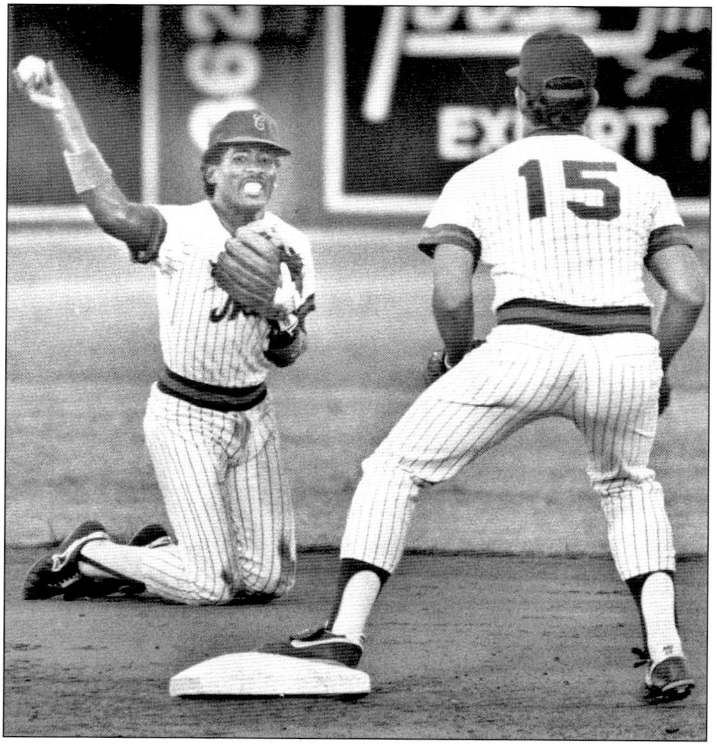

After snaring a grounder, Luis Natera throws to fellow infielder Adam Ging during a game in 1987. Natera played parts of two seasons in Columbia, but he was not done with the capital city. He returned as a coach for the 1999 Bombers, along with Mickey Weston, another former Columbia Met. Natera and Weston are just two examples of how an organization like the Mets keeps valued members of its family tree. (CCB, from *Columbia Record.*)

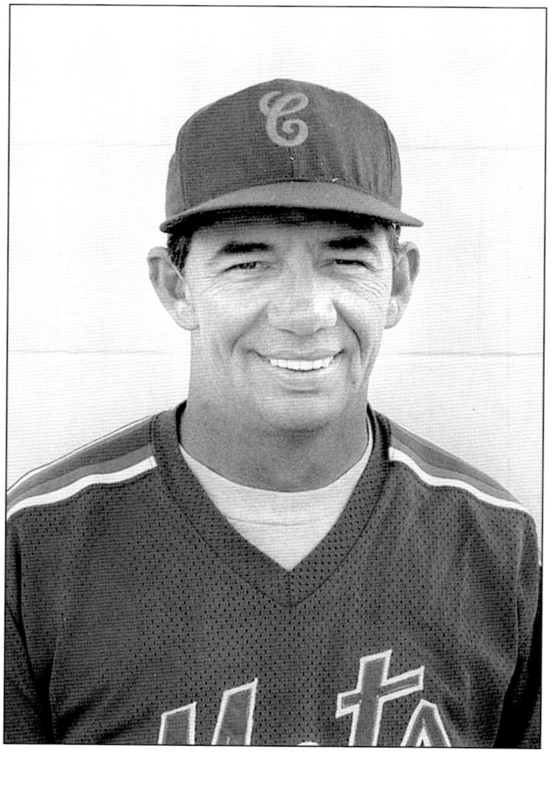

Bill Stein managed the Columbia Mets in 1989–1990. Managers often bring a wide array of experiences together to help teach their young players, and Stein certainly did that. In his 14 years in the majors, Stein spent time at every position outside the battery of pitcher and catcher. While in Columbia, he led the club to two winning seasons and one playoff berth. (CCB.)

An outfielder for the Columbia Mets during the 1987–1989 seasons, Rob Lemle never got the opportunity to play baseball again. In the fall of 1989, Lemle was shot and killed in gang-related violence in his hometown of Compton, California. (CCB.)

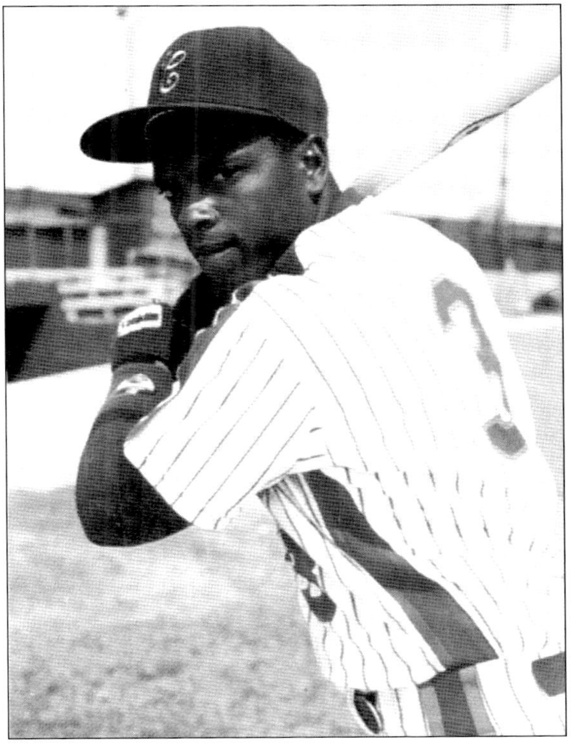

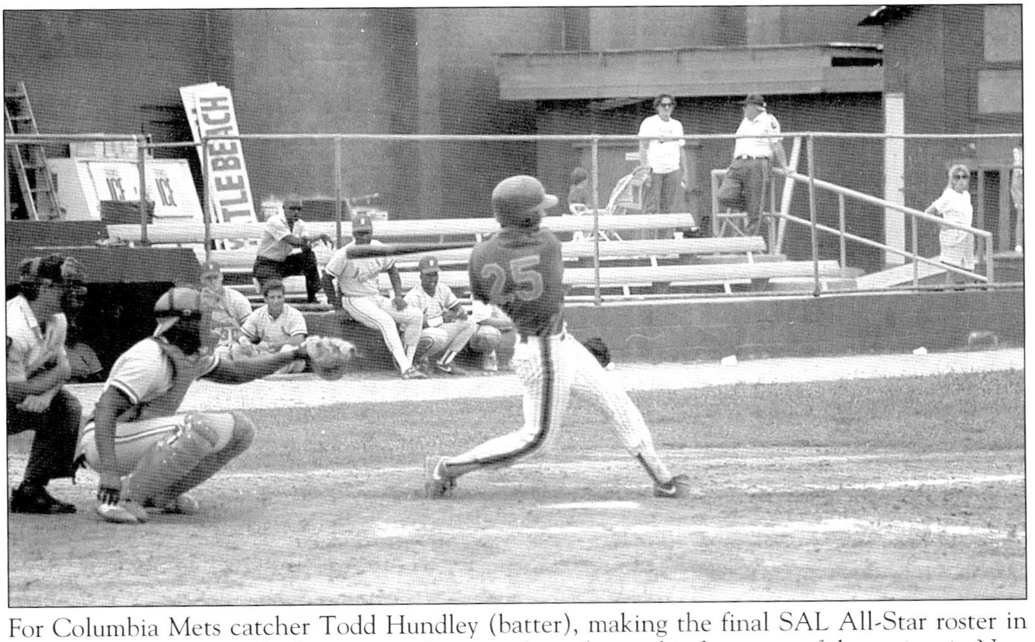

For Columbia Mets catcher Todd Hundley (batter), making the final SAL All-Star roster in 1989 proved to be just the beginning. One year later, he got his first taste of the majors in New York, and not long after that he established himself as a regular for the Mets, then the Cubs and Dodgers. His long and successful career included two selections to the Major League All-Star Game in 1996 and 1997. (CCB.)

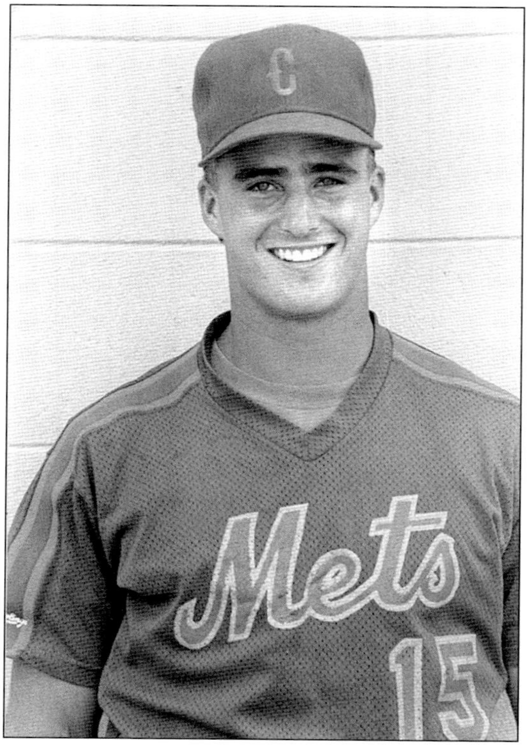

The backstop for the 1990 Columbia Mets, Brook Fordyce enjoyed a strong season. His selection to the final SAL All-Star Team marked the second straight year the Mets had the league's best catcher (following Hundley). For Fordyce, it was the second year of a three-year run of All-Star teams (Appalachian, South Atlantic, and Florida State Leagues). He went on to a productive career in the majors on several teams. (CCB.)

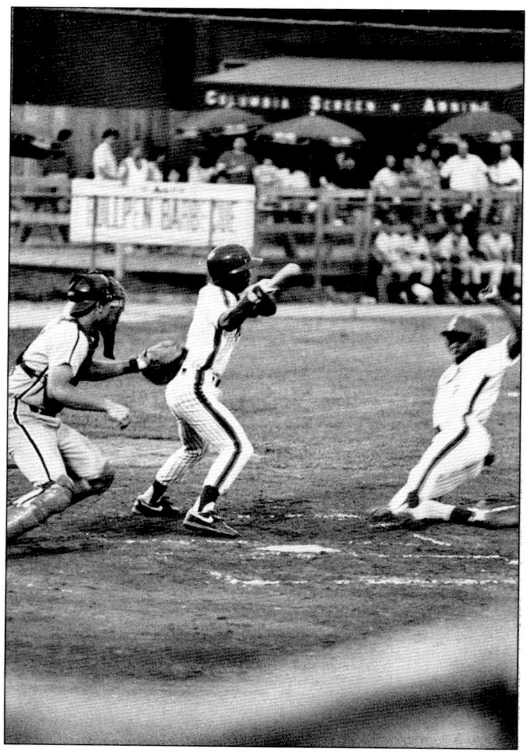

Here is a play that does not get captured on film very often: the suicide squeeze. The Columbia Mets executed the play perfectly, as the bunt is away (the ball can be seen above and to the left of the runner's head) and the catcher is helpless to stop the runner from scoring within a second of this snapshot from the 1990 season. (CCB.)

SEVEN

Welcome to Capital City Stadium

As baseball in Columbia entered the 1990s, new ownership looked at the team and took stock of what Capital City Park had to offer. What became obvious right away was that old wooden bleachers were not going to carry the team far into its future. A number of problems with the ballpark site needed to be addressed if both the city and the team owners were going to maintain a commitment to the health of professional baseball in town.

With those parties working together, Capital City Park became Capital City Stadium, a modern facility that brought Columbia closer to the sports standards of the time. Not much has changed to the structure of the ballpark since that major update, and Columbia's team has played in the same facility through the 2004 season. The significant transition from old ballpark to new one preceded another shift: from one team name to another. The early 1990s represented a time of change and growth for Columbia's minor league landscape. The team also won another South Atlantic League Championship, so plenty of things were looking up for Columbia's baseball fans.

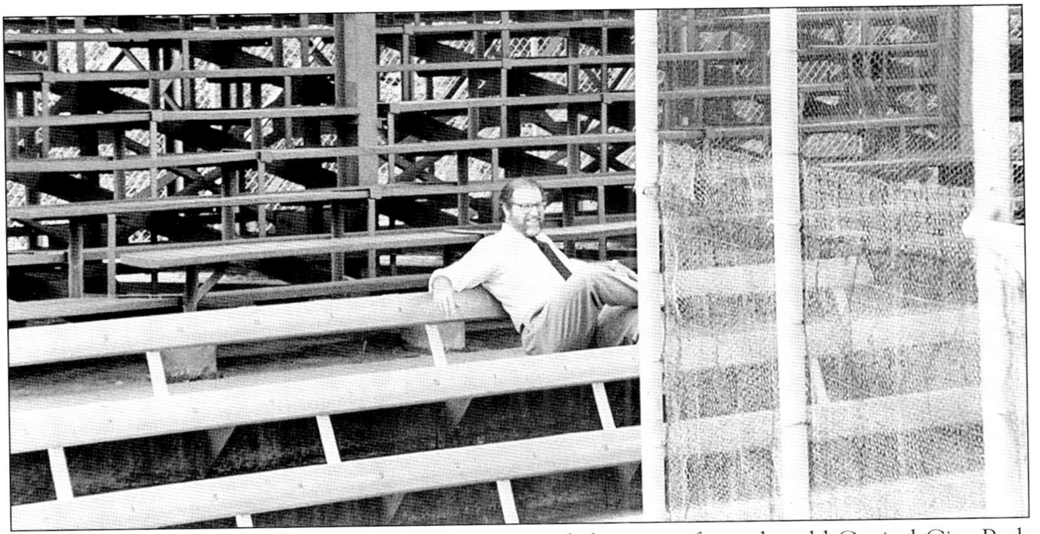

New York psychologist Dr. Eric Margenau surveyed the scene from the old Capital City Park bleachers during the 1990 season. Margenau headed the group of investors that would run the team for the next several years, but an update for the facility was necessary before his ownership could move the team forward. Margenau and his associates eventually owned several sports franchises. (CCB.)

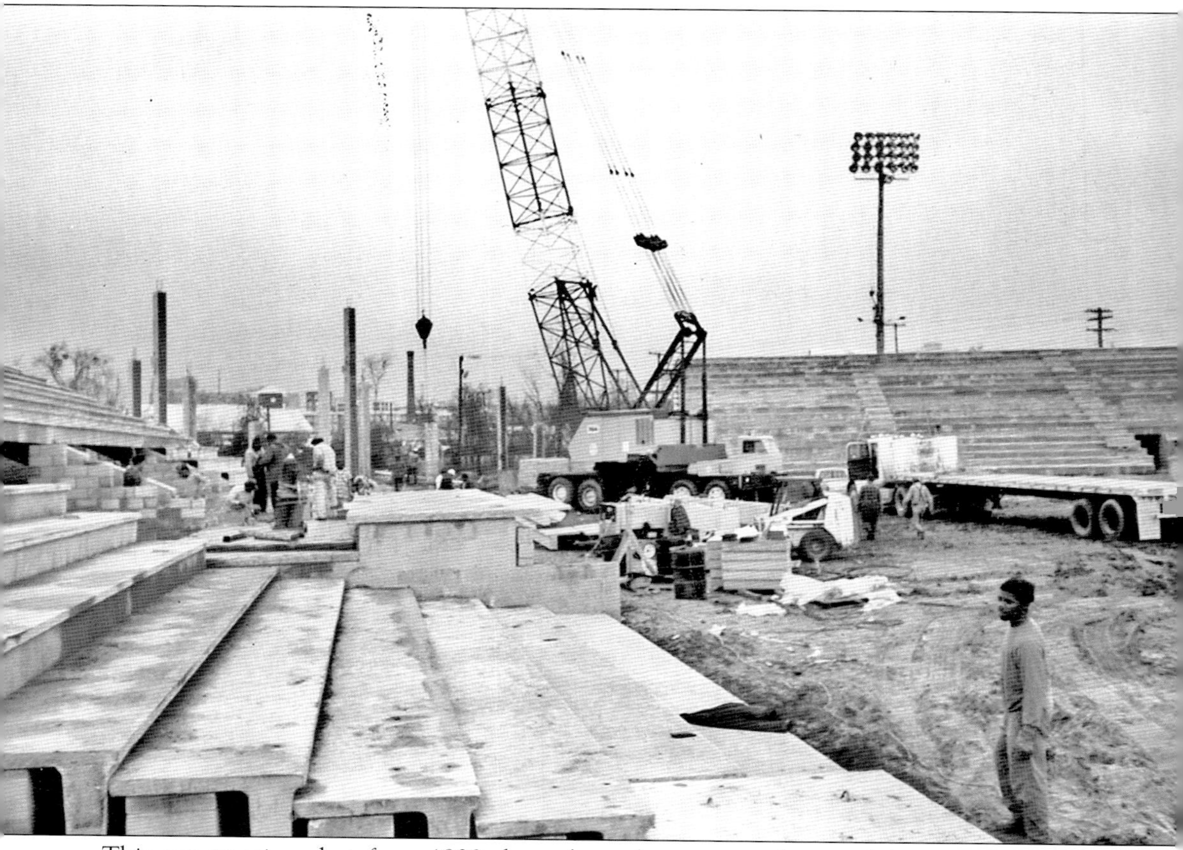

This construction shot from 1990 shows how the concrete forms of the new Capital City Stadium came together. Although on the same site, all traces of the old wooden bleachers were already gone by this point. Dreyfus Road and beyond are visible, as the center sections, including the press box and overhang, are only pilings waiting for more pieces of the puzzle to arrive. The design and construction were basic by modern standards. Not long after this facility was done, many teams in the minors started building much more elaborate ballparks. At the time, this new stadium's price tag came in around $1.5 million, quite a tame figure compared to parks in other towns. Capital City Stadium's owner is the City of Columbia, and the team has rented it from the city since the completion of construction for the 1991 season. (CCB.)

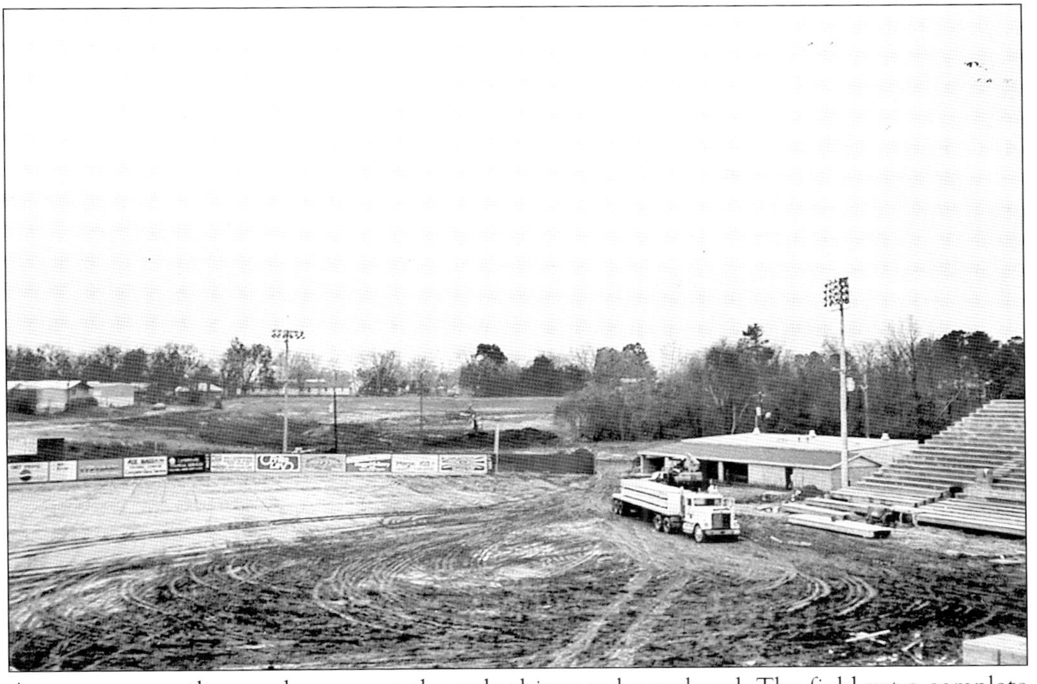

As you can see, the stands were not the only things to be replaced. The field got a complete resurfacing. Upgrades were also in store for parking areas at the ballpark (in background). Despite the upheaval all around, the outfield wall remained intact. Note the open area in front of the clubhouses in right field. The Pepsi Pavilion would not occupy this space until 1996. (CCB.)

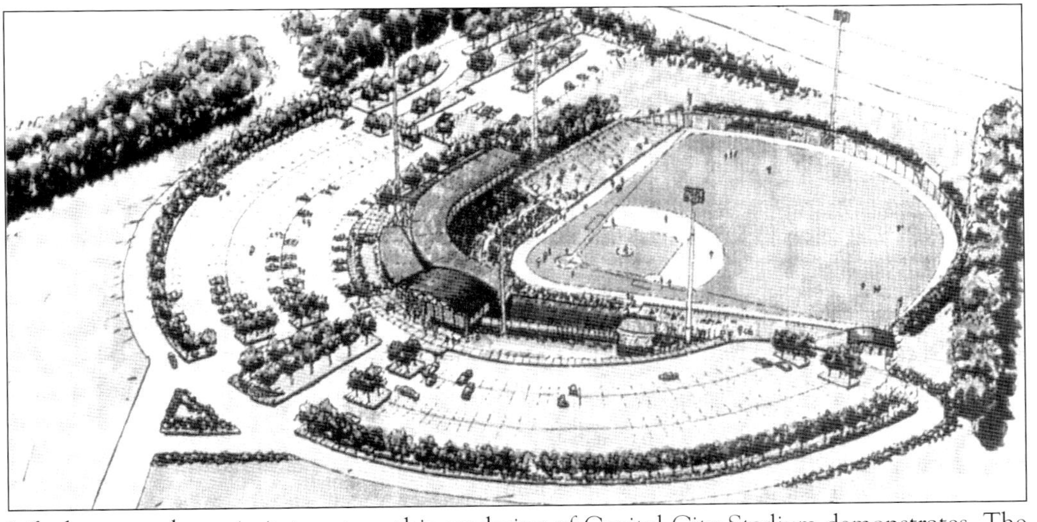

Life does not always imitate art, as this rendering of Capital City Stadium demonstrates. The ballpark and its surroundings did not turn out like the sketch, but a remodeled stadium did come about nonetheless. Just 10 years later, a new batch of even fancier designs cropped up as stadium talk was renewed for the new millennium. (CCB.)

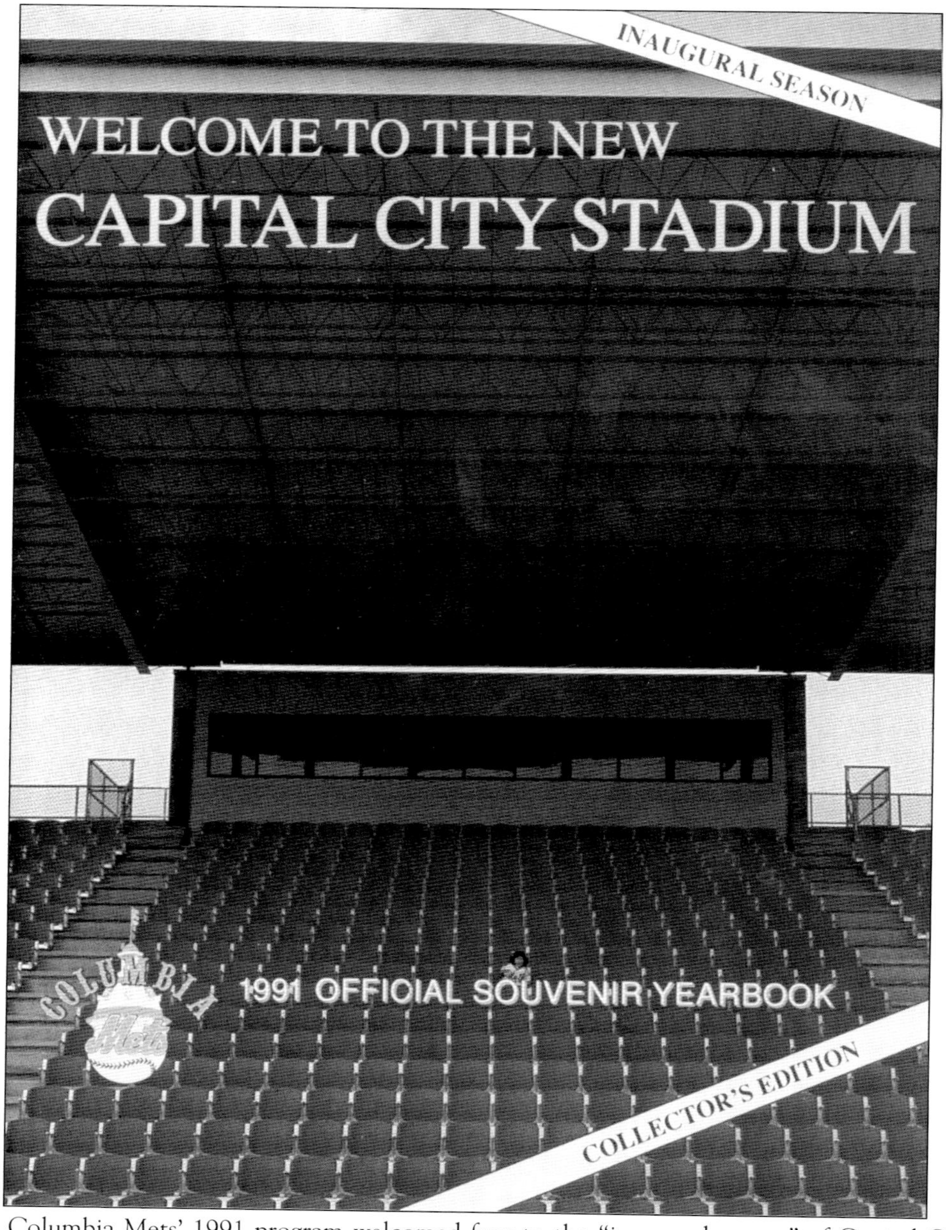

The Columbia Mets' 1991 program welcomed fans to the "inaugural season" of Capital City Stadium. That was true enough for the seating areas, but home plate was pretty much where it had been since the Dreyfuss Field dedication of 1927. Since this photo, many of the upper box seats pictured here were taken out to accommodate a camera deck and to allow for different types of seating. Other changes around the ballpark included a new scoreboard, new ticket office and staff offices, expanded clubhouses, and additional concession stands and restrooms. Even with all those updates, it became apparent after several years to many observers that the new ballpark had not been built sufficiently for long-term use, especially as significant changes arose in sports business and fan expectations. It remained an acceptable place to watch a game but offered few extras for attendees. (CCB.)

If the uniform did not give it away, you might have pegged Columbia Mets manager Tim Blackwell as part of a much older era in baseball. Blackwell, who played 10 big-league seasons as a catcher, led the 1991 Columbia Mets to the SAL title and the 1992 team to the league's best overall record. His 165 wins in two years have remained the most under any one manager in franchise history. (CCB.)

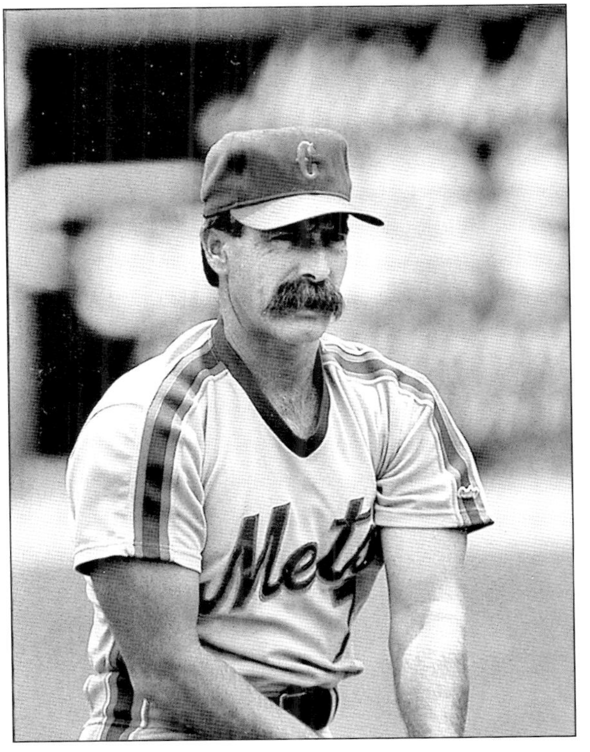

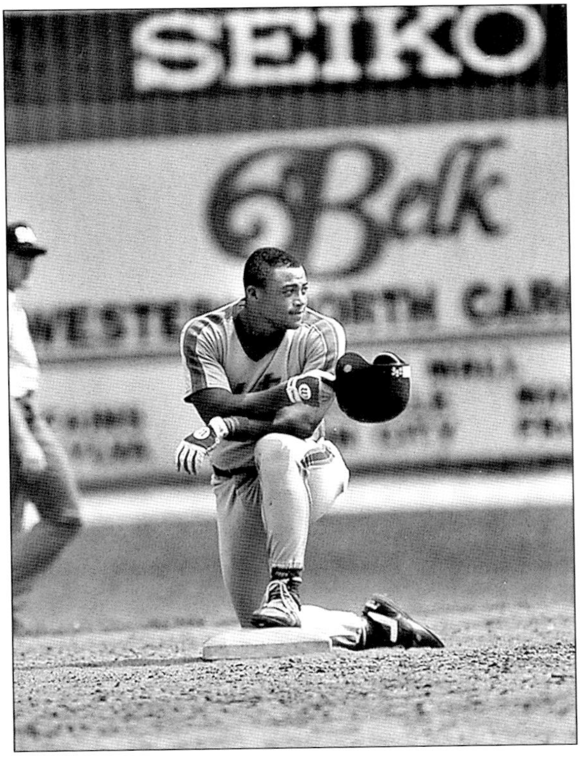

Columbia third-baseman Butch Huskey takes a breather at second base during a game in Asheville. Huskey had an outstanding season in 1991, batting .287 with 26 home runs and 99 RBIs. He also made the final SAL All-Star team that year. Huskey, who went on to a productive career in the majors, set a team home run record that stood for seven seasons. (CCB.)

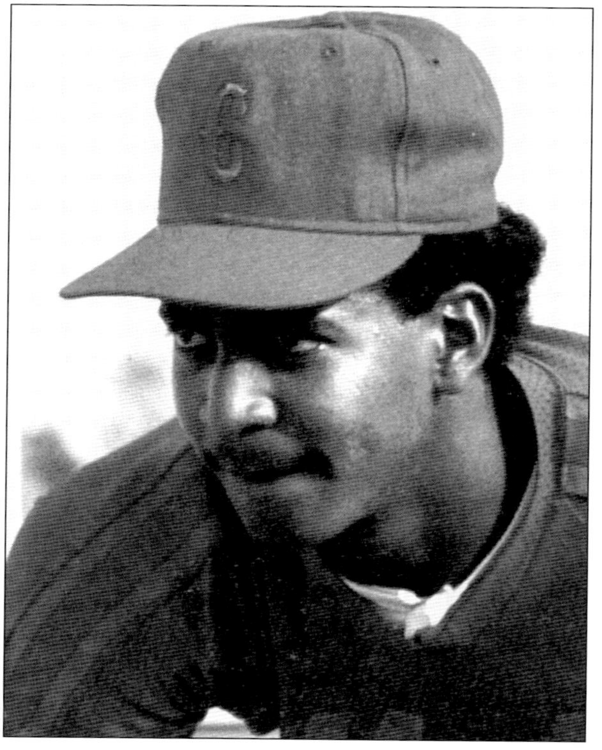

The ace of the 1991 Columbia Mets staff owned the league that year. Jose Martinez started 26 games and won 20 of them (20-4). He pitched 9 complete games (one shutout) and threw 158 strikeouts with only 30 walks. In 2004, Martinez still held franchise records for innings pitched (193) and for earned run average (1.49). He had only a brief taste of life in the majors. (CCB.)

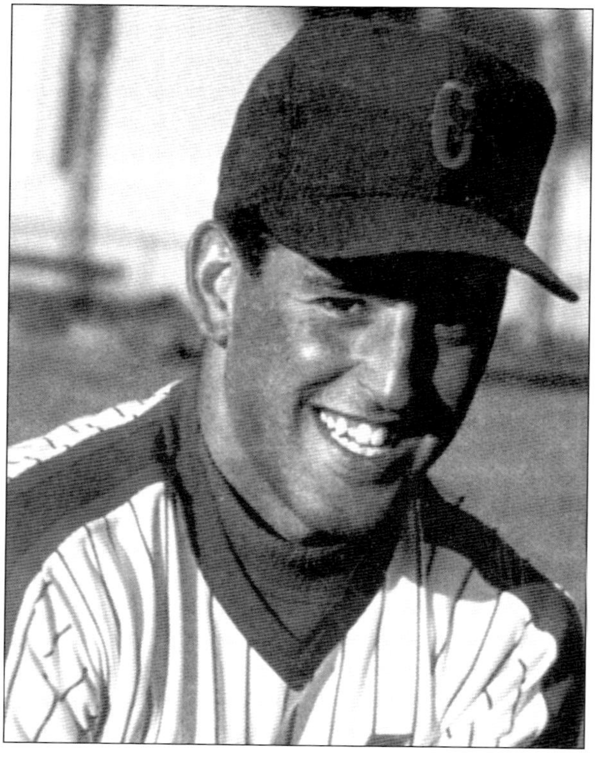

Infielder Fernando Vina played his first professional season in Columbia in 1991 and never looked back. Since making his big-league debut for the Mets in 1994, Vina became a regular for the Brewers, Cardinals, and Tigers, where he played in 2004. Vina remains one of the few Columbia Mets/Bombers selected to the Major League All-Star Game, along with Randy Myers, Gregg Jefferies, Todd Hundley, Bobby Jones, and Preston Wilson. (CCB.)

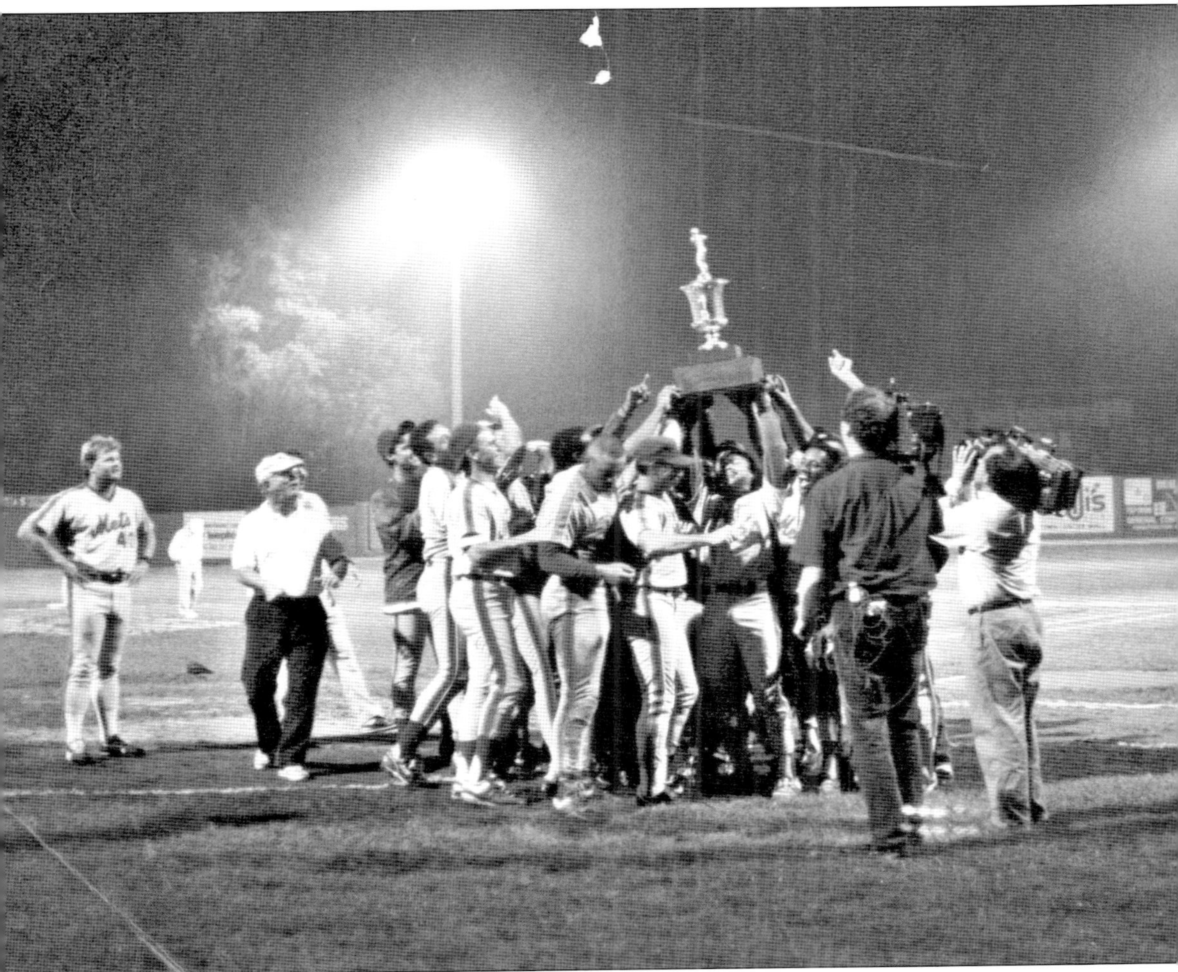

The Columbia Mets capped off the first season in their rebuilt ballpark by winning it all. Smart hitting may have had a lot to do with the team's success: the 1991 team set a franchise record for the fewest strikeouts in a season (782), which still held through 2003, and no Columbia team since 1992 had even kept its strikeout number under 1,000. The squad's record came to 86-54 at the end of the regular season, and then the team took care of all comers in the playoffs. Here we see the team savoring victory and raising the trophy for just the second time since baseball returned to South Carolina's capital city in 1983. (CCB.)

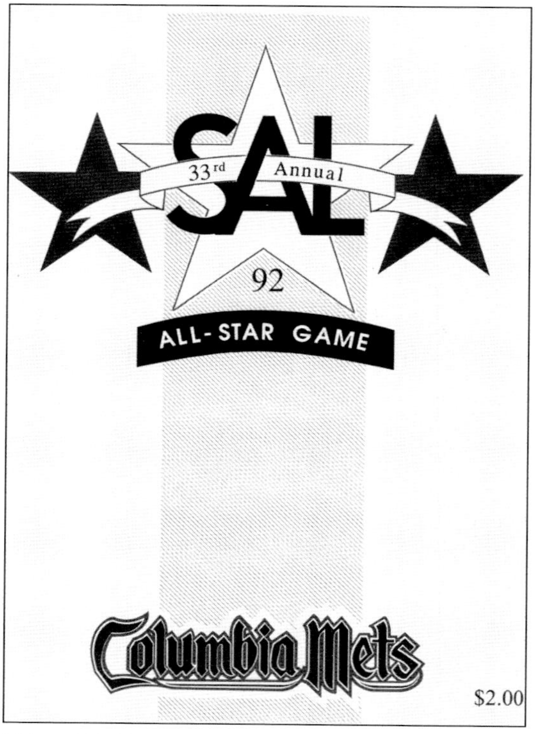

One of the rewards for a new or renovated ballpark often turns out to be a chance to show it off to the league with the mid-season All-Star Game, and Columbia had that chance in 1992. Three Mets made the North roster for the home crowd: Omar Garcia, Ricky Otero, and Quilvio Veras. Other notables in the game included Andy Pettitte, Pokey Reese, and Cliff Floyd. (CCB.)

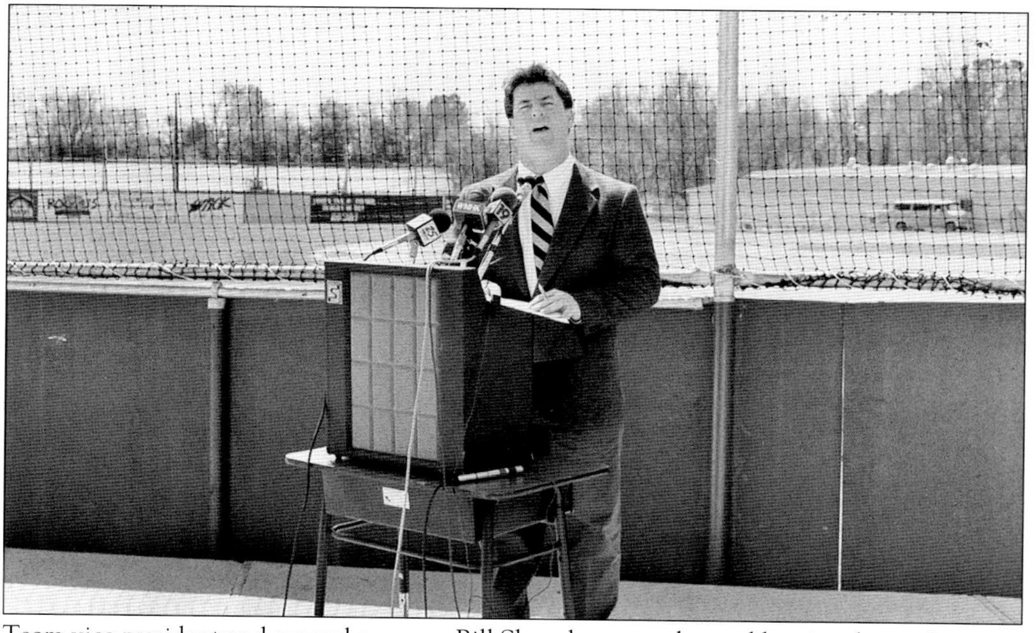

Team vice president and general manager Bill Shanahan, seen here addressing the media, came to Columbia in 1992 and quickly made his mark. A tireless promoter, Shanahan worked hard to build up the team's reputation for family fun and entertainment. He held his position with the team until leaving in 1996 to take the reins of the Mobile Bay Bears in the same ownership group. (CCB.)

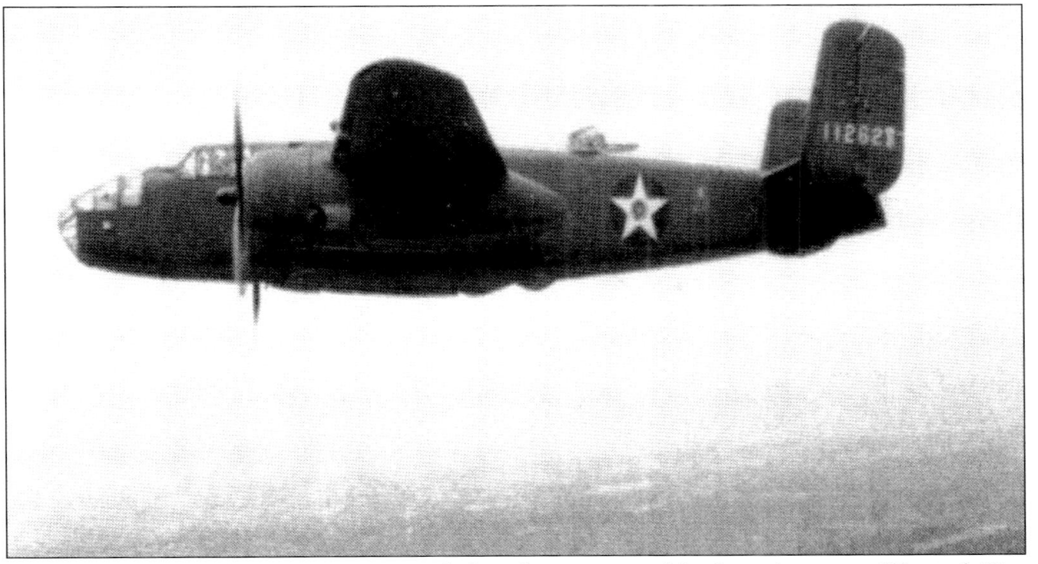

In 1992, the Columbia Mets announced that the team would adopt the name "Capital City Bombers" for the following season, honoring the famed Doolittle Raiders of World War II. Like the bomber seen here flying over the Midlands, Doolittle's B-25 crews trained for their assault on Japan from Columbia Army Air Field, now the Columbia Metropolitan Airport. (Flynn Bowie.)

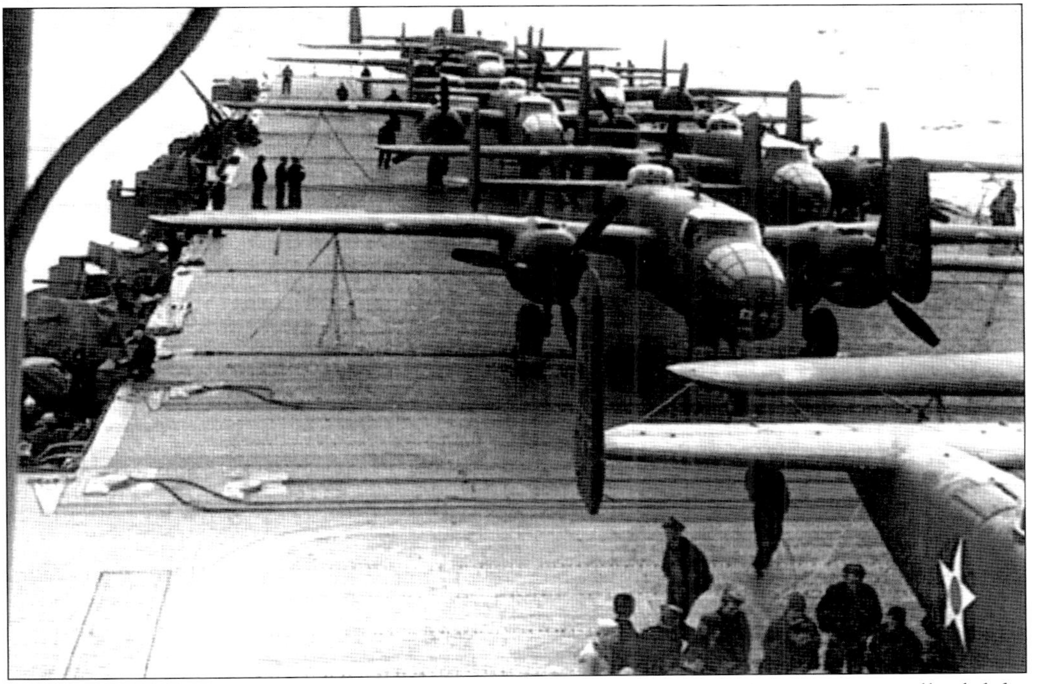

The Doolittle Raiders mission required amazing resolve, and what those men actually did for their country cannot be put into words. With no promise of return, the 16 five-man crews launched their B-25s from the deck of the USS *Hornet* aircraft carrier—something never done before with that aircraft—and struck targets in Japan. The physical damage done paled in comparison to the psychological victory achieved with the attack. (Flynn Bowie.)

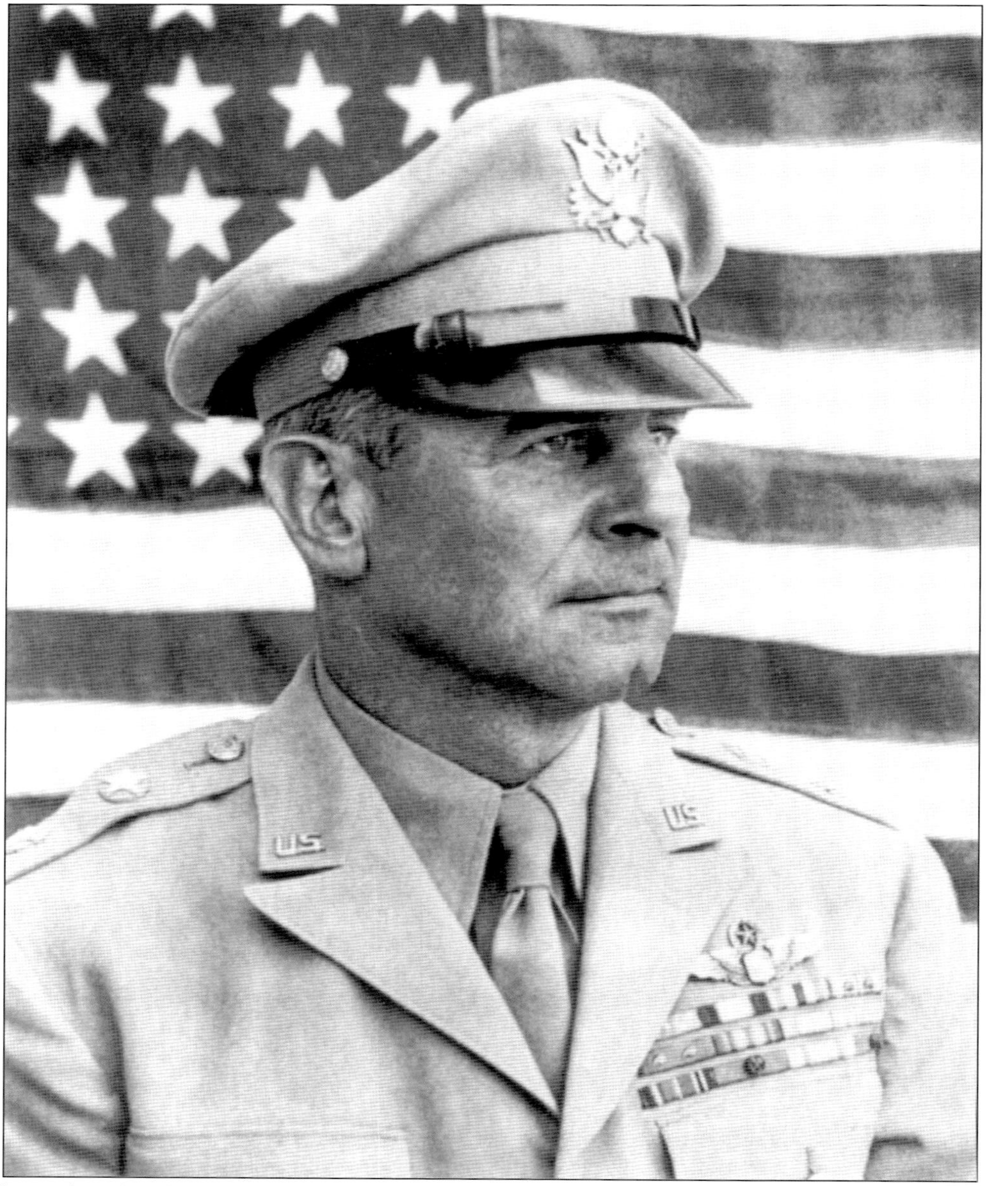

Obviously a baseball team can only aspire to the values of heroes like the Doolittle Raiders and their commander. Gen. James Doolittle served his country in many remarkable ways, most notably in military aviation. He was Lieutenant Colonel Doolittle when he took off from the USS *Hornet* with his men, bound for Japan. By that time, he already had quite a legacy: serving as a flight and gunnery instructor in World War I, working as a stunt flier in the 1920s, and setting a number of aviation records in the 1930s. Doolittle believed in the critical nature of the 1942 mission but knew better than anyone just how dangerous the assignment was going to be. After the mission, Doolittle received the Congressional Medal of Honor. He continued to lead campaigns through the remainder of World War II and then helped establish the post-war air force. The names of Columbia's airport and other area sites pay homage to Doolittle and his men, including the Capital City Bombers baseball team. (Flynn Bowie.)

EIGHT

Here Come the Bombers

With a new name that honored the past yet ushered the team into the future, the Columbia Mets were gone and the Capital City Bombers were born. Like many minor league teams, the Bombers retained their major league affiliation but shed the name of the parent club. A league that had recently fielded Mets, Pirates, Cardinals, Rangers, and other common names would soon find itself beset with Sand Gnats, Crawdads, GreenJackets, RiverDogs, and other bizarre creatures. The transformation of teams in the South Atlantic League and around the country had a great deal to do with the growing marketing power of minor-league baseball. Attendance was on the rise, and merchandising became a booming business. The value of having an individual team brand went from a luxury to a near necessity.

In 2004, the Capital City Bombers still took the field at Capital City Stadium and still played as an affiliate of the New York Mets, so some things have not changed. In 12 seasons as the Bombers, Columbia baseball enjoyed great prosperity with good attendance, crazy ballpark promotions, and wildly talented athletes. (CCB.)

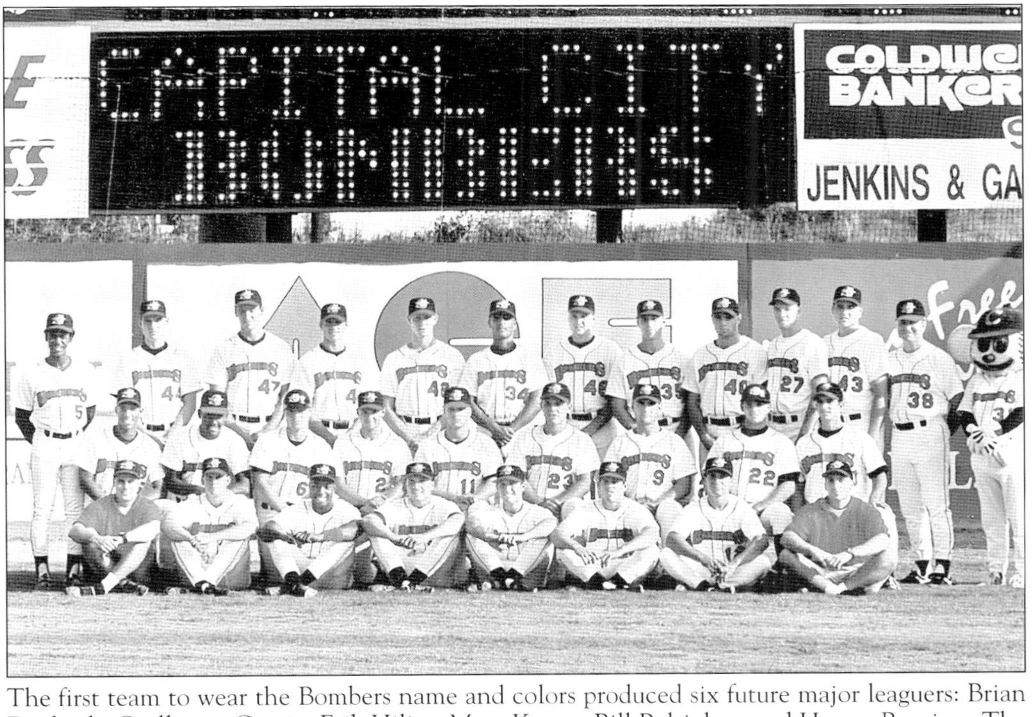

The first team to wear the Bombers name and colors produced six future major leaguers: Brian Daubach, Guillermo Garcia, Erik Hiljus, Marc Kroon, Bill Pulsipher, and Hector Ramirez. The squad also included the first Bomber to return as manager: catcher Tony Tijerina (#22). Note the early and awkward version of the mascot "Bomber the Mouse." (CCB.)

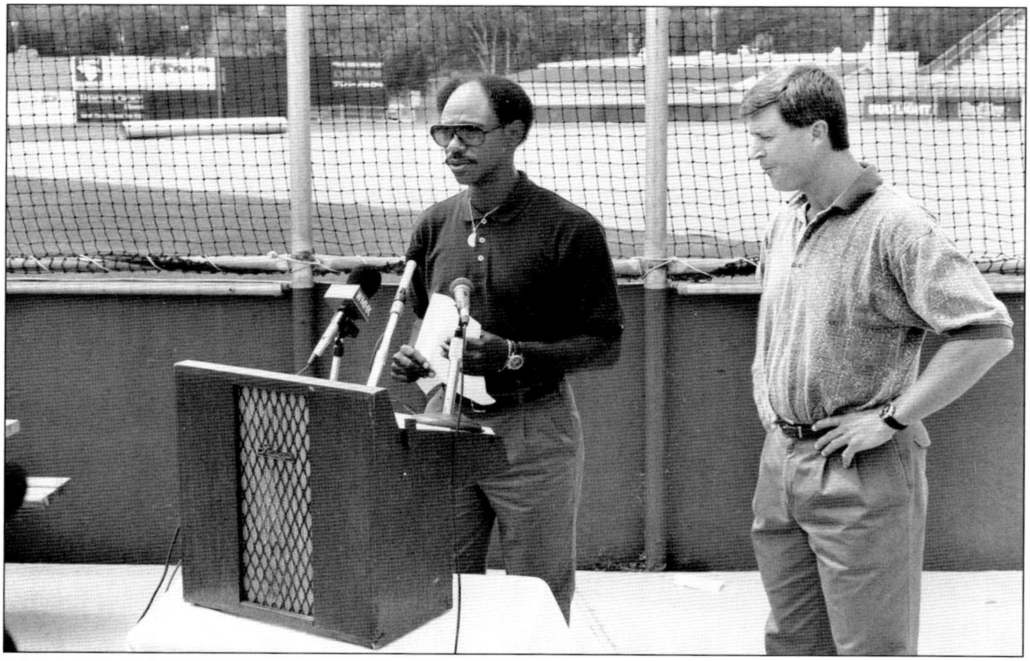

The New York Mets made local baseball history by naming Ron Washington (left) manager of the Capital City Bombers in 1993, as he was the first black manager in Columbia's minor league history. Washington, who played 10 seasons in the majors as an infielder for five different teams, returned to manage in 1994 and is seen here with pitching coach Dave Jorn. (CCB.)

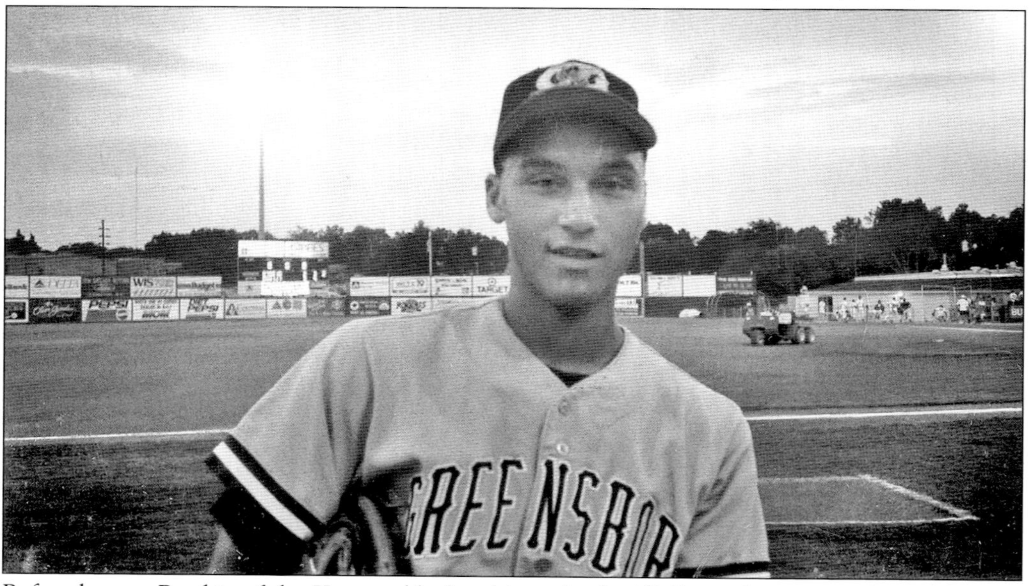

Before he was Rookie of the Year and before his multiple All-Star selections and World Series rings, Derek Jeter had to work past the minors like everyone else. Here we see him stopping in Columbia with the Greensboro Hornets, serving as a reminder that great players come through town on both sides every year. Every player on the field has that dream—and some of them will make it come true. (Bob and Fran Somogyi.)

Considered a high prospect for the Mets at the time, Al Shirley wound up proving how hard "A-ball" can be. Shirley played for the Bombers in 1993–1994. He demonstrated the power and speed expected of him, but his problem with strikeouts dogged him. Shirley struck out 208 times in 1994, setting a team record and tying the league record. (CCB.)

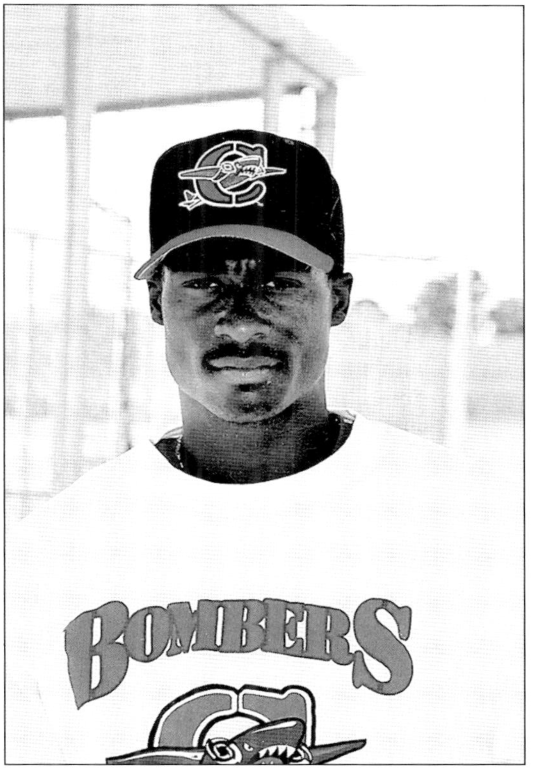

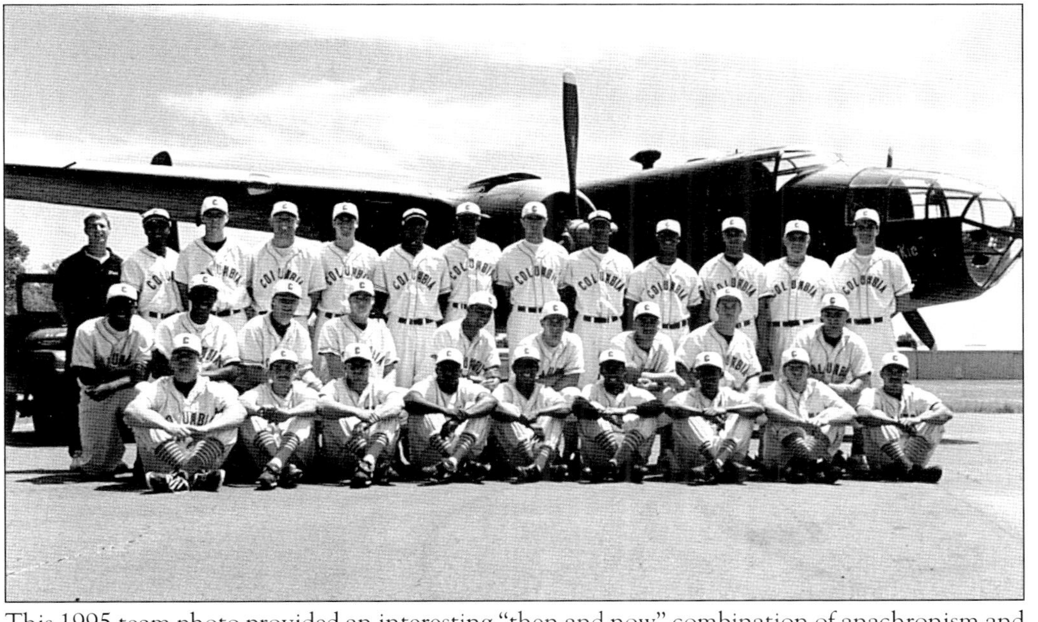

This 1995 team photo provided an interesting "then and now" combination of anachronism and nostalgia: the modern squad wore throwback uniforms designed to emulate teams of the 1950s while posing in front of a B-25, whose mission in the 1940s gave the team its name in the 1990s. Even with that confusing timeline, the combination created a handsome shot. (CCB.)

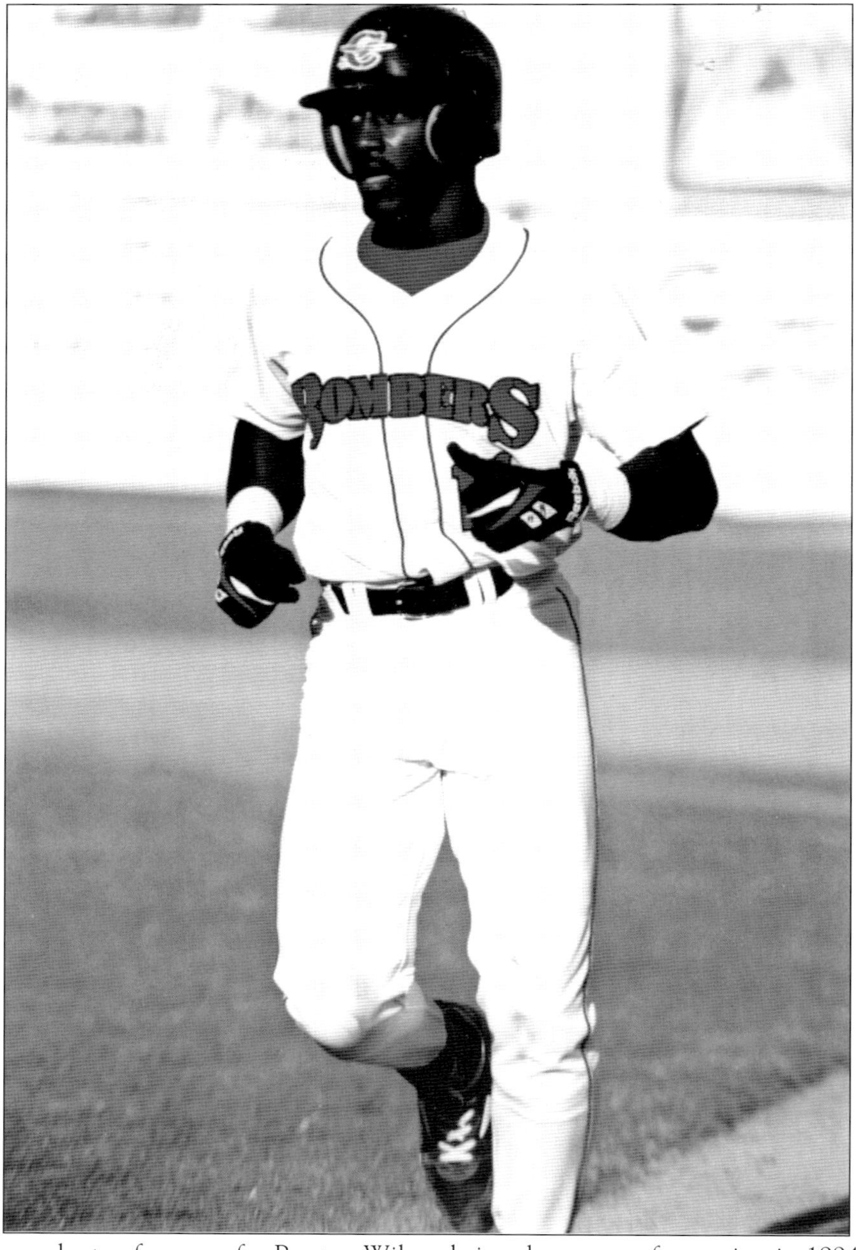

There were plenty of reasons for Preston Wilson being the center of attention in 1994–1995. The Mets selected him as a first rounder, ninth overall, in 1992; he had a baseball star as a stepfather in Mets World Series hero Mookie Wilson; and he was a native South Carolinian playing in his home state. Wilson took a while to deliver on the sky-high expectations, but he eventually blossomed into a big-league star. After moving from the Mets to the Marlins in the Mike Piazza trade in 1998, Wilson was runner-up for 1999 National League Rookie of the Year. He continued to contribute at the game's highest level, culminating in his selection to the 2003 All-Star Game while playing for the Colorado Rockies. The Bamberg native suited up for the Rockies again in 2004. (CCB.)

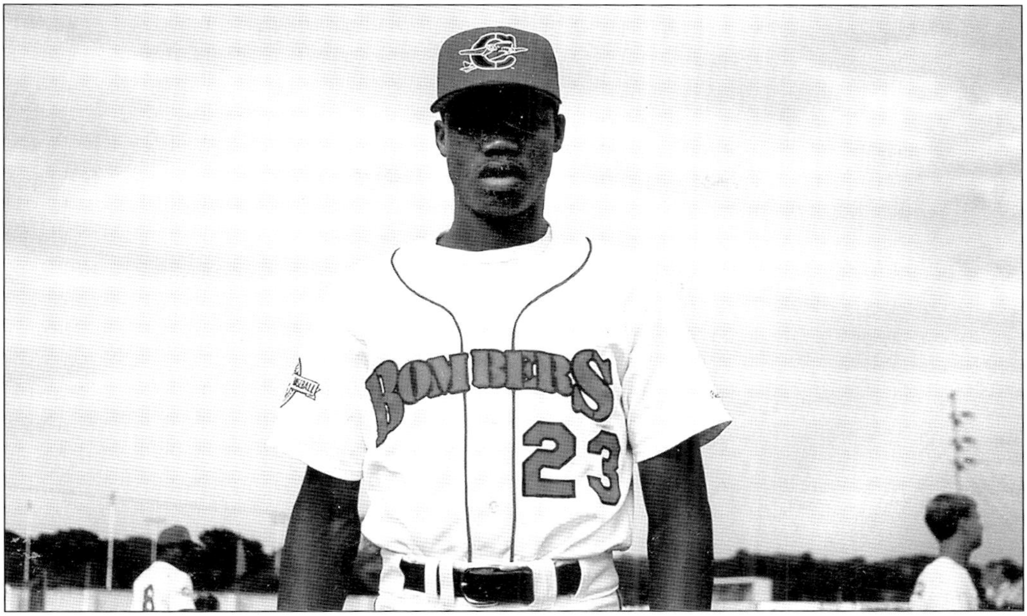

The case of Guillermo Mota is proof that you never know how a player will turn out. Mota played shortstop for the 1995 Bombers. He reappeared in the SAL in 1997 as a pitcher for the Cape Fear Crocs. The position change was the right move: Mota made his big-league debut on the mound in 1999 and has continued to contribute in the majors as a pitcher. (CCB.)

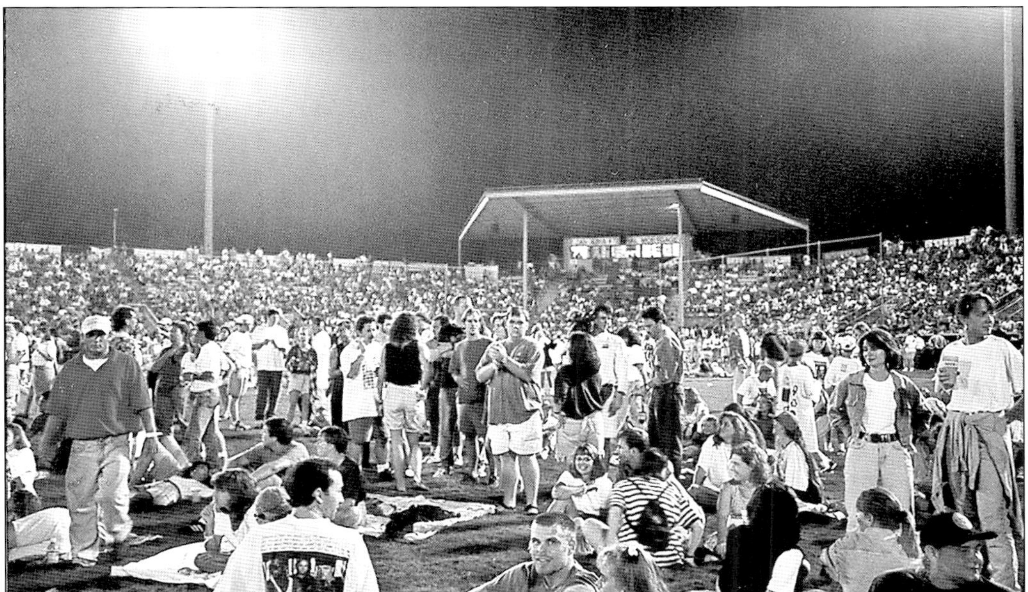

Baseball is not the only thing that has kept Capital City Stadium busy over the years. Here is a glimpse of the ballpark's biggest attendance night ever, without a bat or glove to be found. In 1995, the Columbia-based band Hootie and the Blowfish hosted a concert event that drew nearly 11,000 fans (filling the field and stands). There have been many other concerts in the stadium since then. (CCB.)

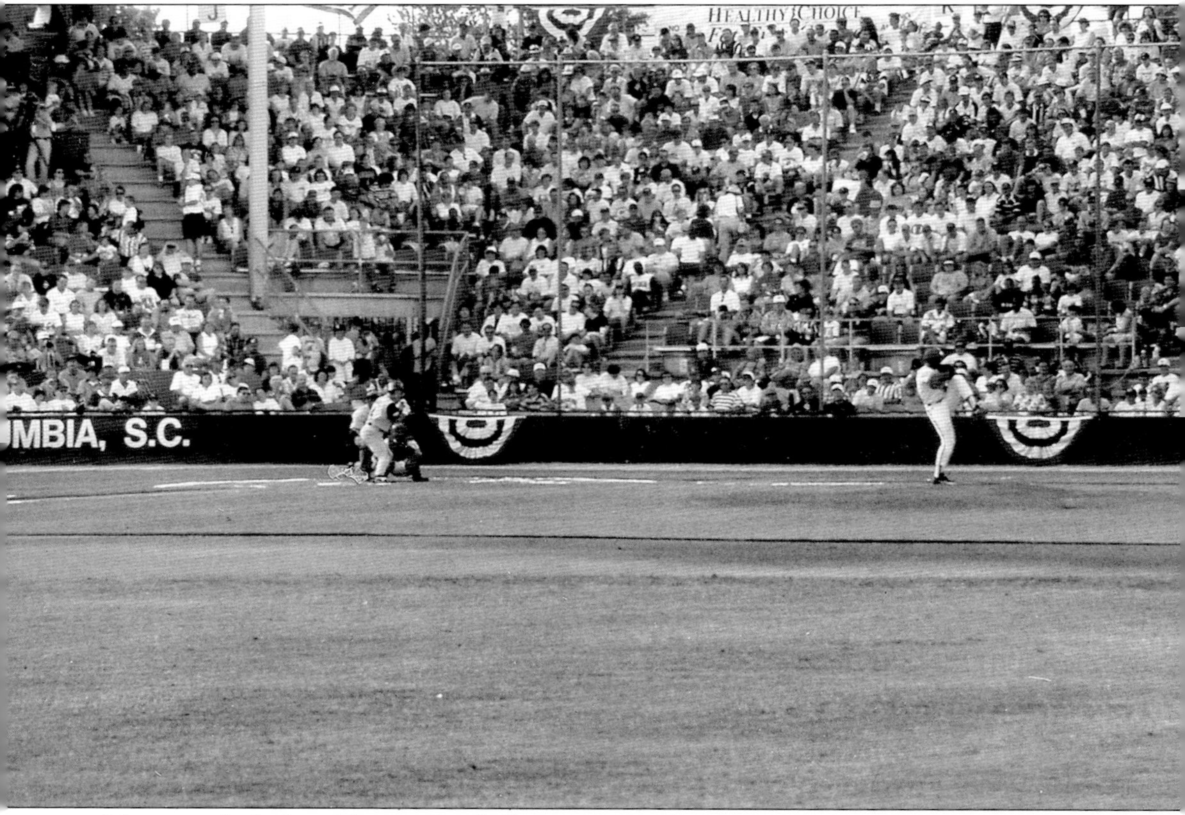

Three weeks before Olympic baseball competition began at the 1996 Atlanta Games, Team USA staged an exhibition against a tough Cuban team at Capital City Stadium. More than 6,500 fans crammed their way into the ballpark for a modern baseball attendance record in Columbia that still held up in 2004. The Bombers issued an impressive 60 media credentials for the event, as reporters came in from all around the country. Bombers vice president Bill Shanahan referred to the game as "the jewel in Capital City Stadium history." The game itself ended in a 4-2 Cuba win, but it kept the crowd excited and featured several future major leaguers as well. The starting lineup for Team USA was Chad Green LF, Warren Morris 2B, Mark Kotsay RF, Travis Lee 1B, J.D. Drew DH, Jacque Jones CF, Brian Loyd C, Casey Blake 3B, Augie Ojeda SS, and Billy Koch RHP. The starting lineup for Cuba was: Jose Estrada CF, Luis Alacia LF, Omar Linares 3B, Orestes Kindelan 1B, Antonio Pacheco DH, Rey Isaac RF, Eduardo Paret SS, Alberto Hernandez C, Juan Padilla 2B, and Omar Luis RHP. (CCB.)

Capital City's mascot took a fuzzy leap into modern times in the mid-1990s, putting the odd "Mr. Met"/Mouse hybrid look behind and taking on the cute and cuddly form you see here. Immensely popular with children around the Midlands, Bomber has always liked racing challengers around the bases but generally has not fared too well against his younger opponents. (CCB.)

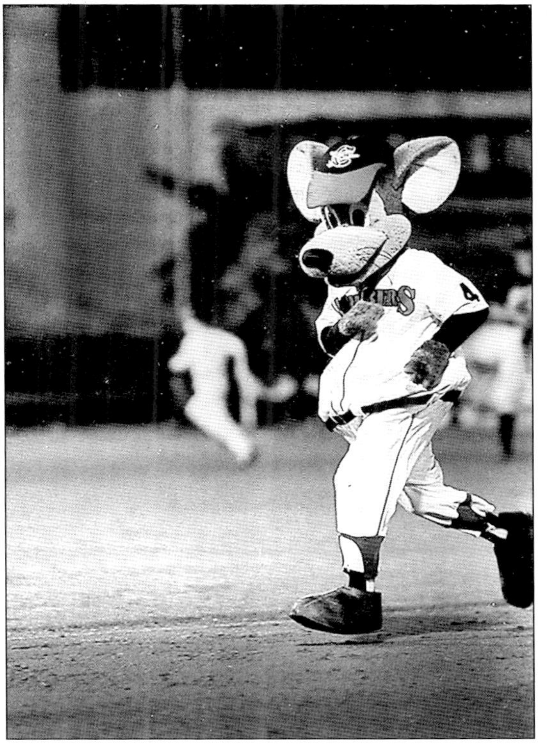

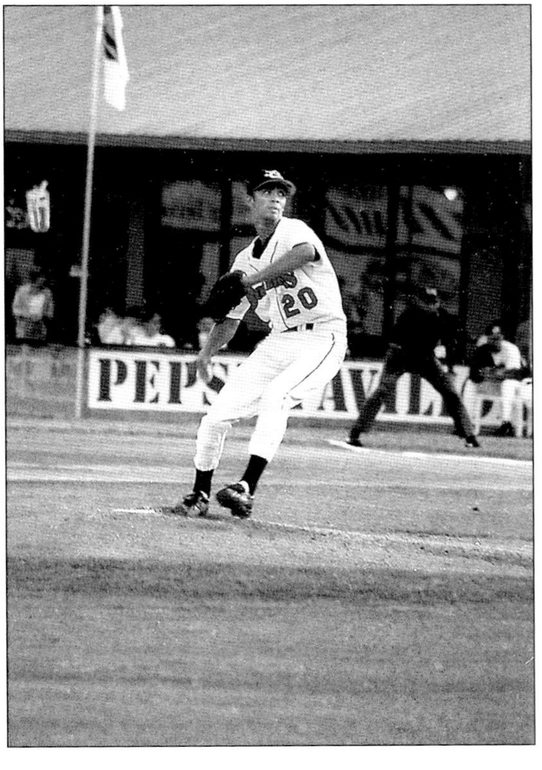

Superlatives litter the Capital City resume of right-hander Nelson Figueroa. The most dominant pitcher on the league's best staff in 1996, Figueroa left batters guessing all year. He posted a 14-7 record with 200 strikeouts and an amazing 2.04 ERA over 185 innings. "Figgy" tossed eight complete games (four shutouts) and made the final SAL All-Star team, earning the honor for Most Outstanding Pitcher. (CCB.)

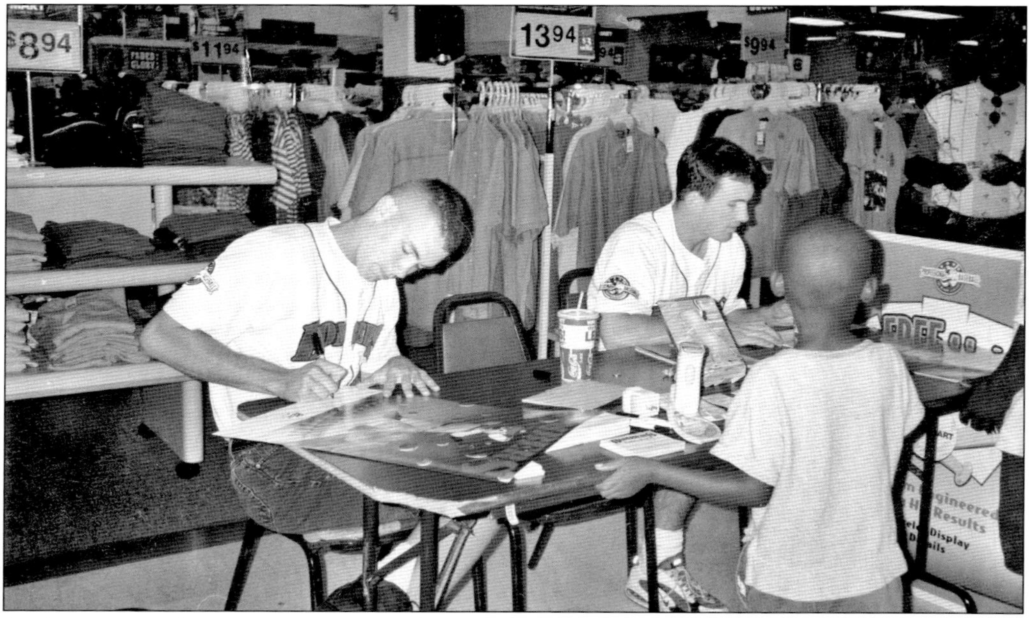

At this autograph session are two members of the modern franchise's best pitching staff—right-hander Andy Trumpour (left) and left-hander Ethan McEntire. Both pitchers joined Nelson Figueroa in the SAL's top five for earned run average. McEntire also made the league's final All-Star team. The 1996 staff had a franchise record 2.77 ERA and established marks for fewest hits (916) and fewest runs (451). (CCB.)

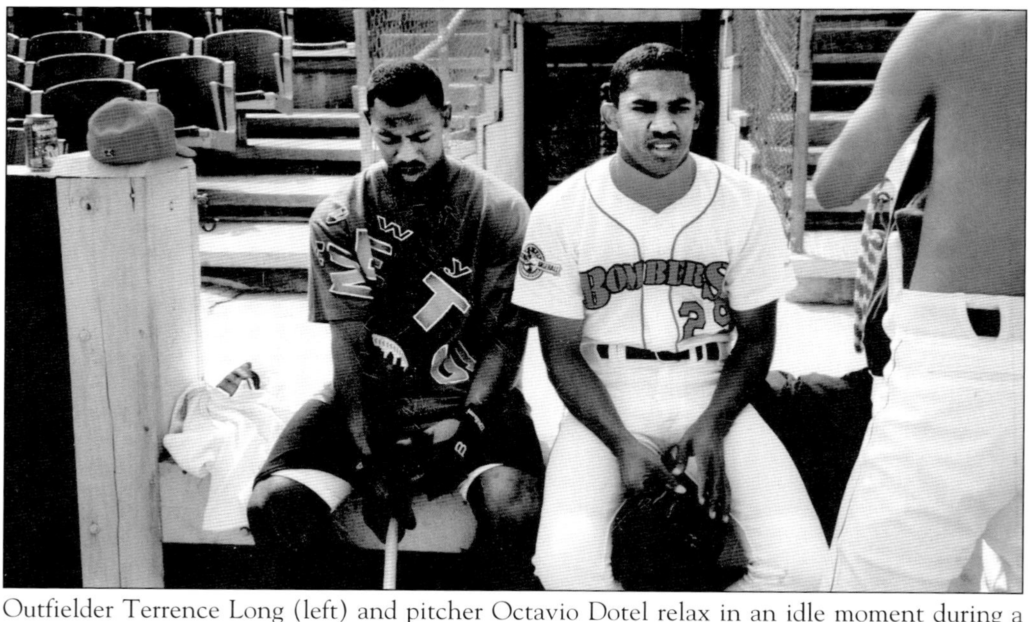

Outfielder Terrence Long (left) and pitcher Octavio Dotel relax in an idle moment during a photo shoot for Mets prospects. Both Long and Dotel later made their major league debuts for the New York Mets, but they soon became regulars for other clubs following trades, Long in Oakland, Dotel in Houston. By 2004, Long had switched to San Diego, but Dotel remained a mainstay in the Astros bullpen. (CCB.)

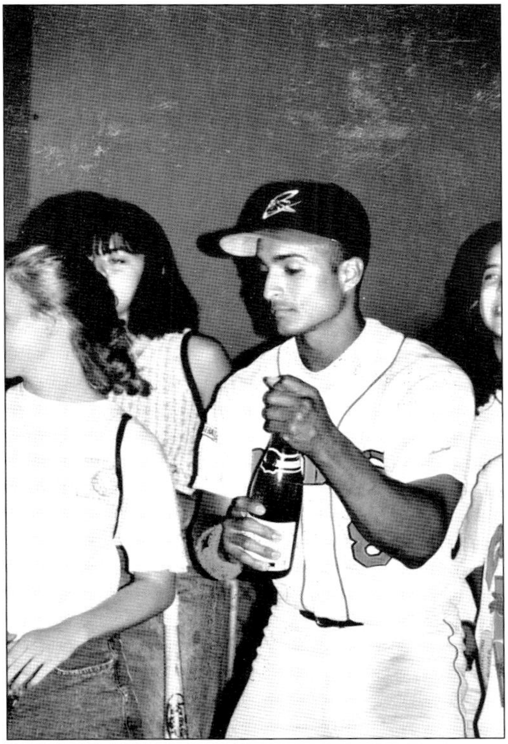

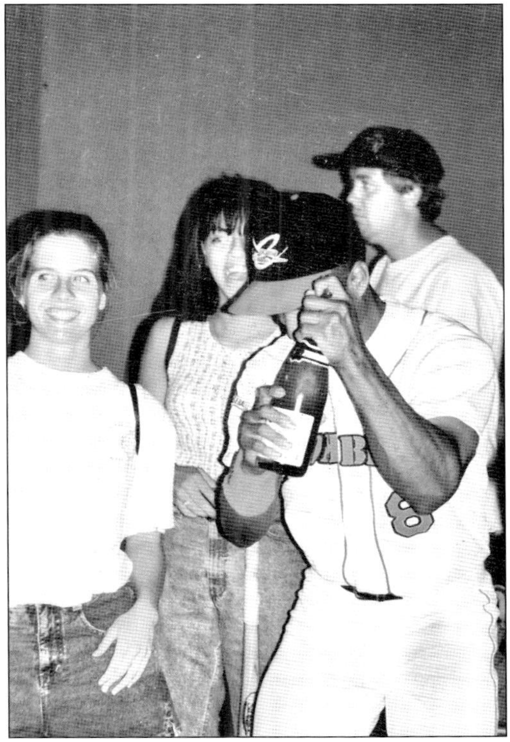

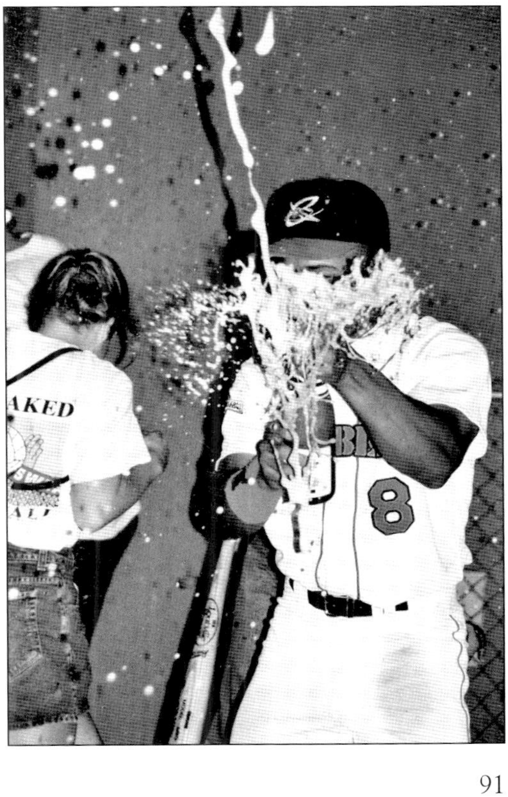

This sequence shows outfielder Carlos Mendoza getting caught up in the celebration of the 1996 team's playoff berth. Mendoza won the South Atlantic League batting title despite joining the team late in the season. A player who does not have enough plate appearances can still be crowned champion if he tops all others when given an "oh-for" in the required number of at-bats. Such was the case with Carlos Mendoza. Unfortunately, Capital City got bounced from the playoffs in the first round. They were eliminated in a rain-shortened game at Asheville after waiting through three days of bad weather. (CCB.)

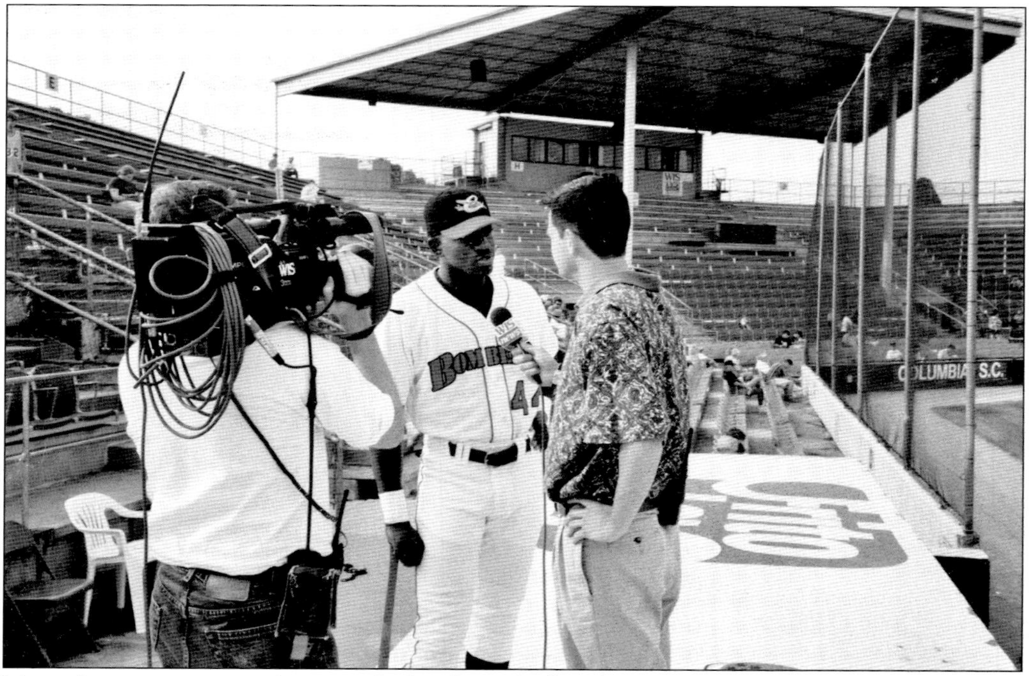

Many factors can get in the way of a local star finding his way onto his hometown's pro team, but that did not stop outfielder Garrick Haltiwanger. In 1996, the Mets drafted Haltiwanger, a baseball and football standout at Irmo High School and the Citadel, and they promoted him to Capital City for the 1997 season. Haltiwanger is seen here giving a pre-game interview for local television. (CCB.)

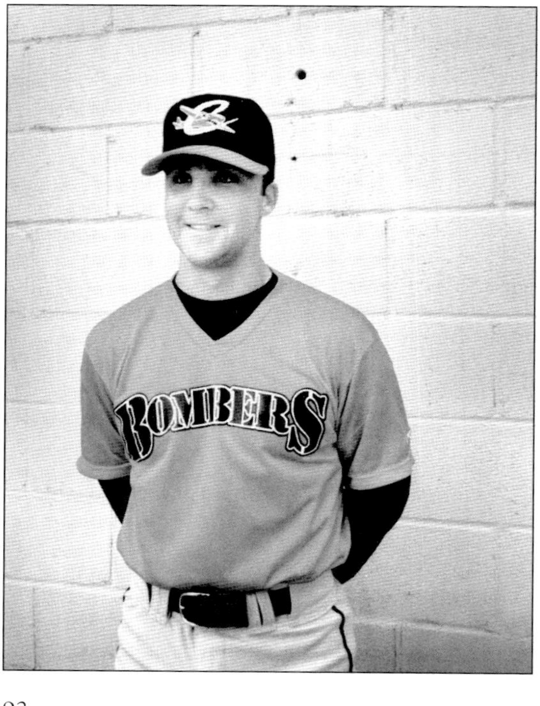

John Tamargo Jr. played for the Capital City Bombers in 1997, but the assignment was definitely not his first trip to Columbia. Tamargo was a batboy for the inaugural Columbia Mets of 1983, when his father was the manager. Fourteen years later, he hit .249 as an infielder for the Bombers. (CCB.)

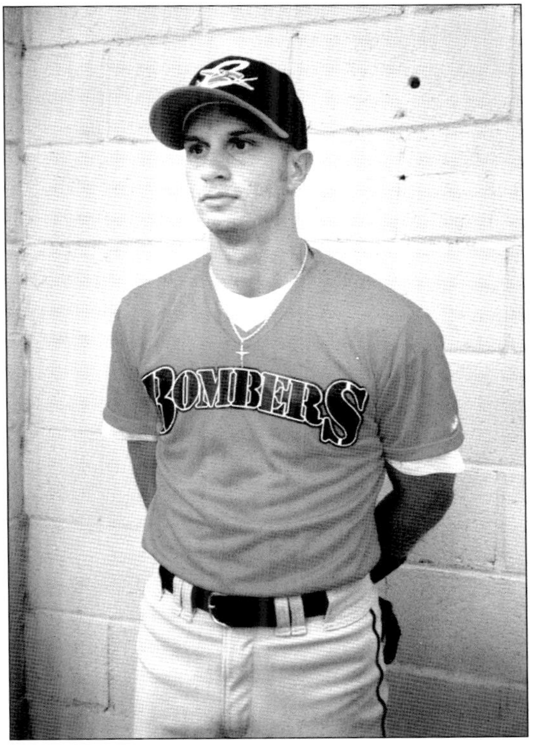

After the first road trip of the 1997 season, promising young outfielder Tim Bishop died in a car accident on a Columbia interstate. Bishop was driving from the ballpark to his apartment when the accident occurred. The Capital City Bombers retired his number (#4) and have kept a memorial on the outfield wall ever since. A street in Bishop's hometown of Valparaiso, Indiana, now bears his name. (CCB.)

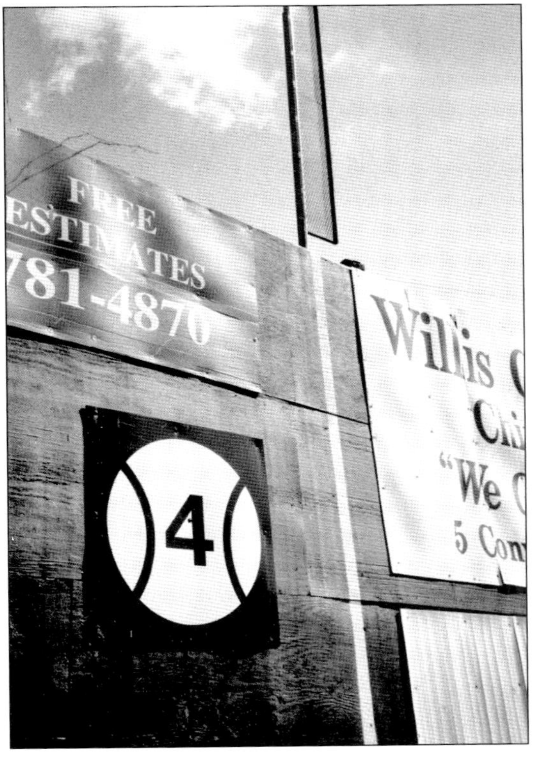

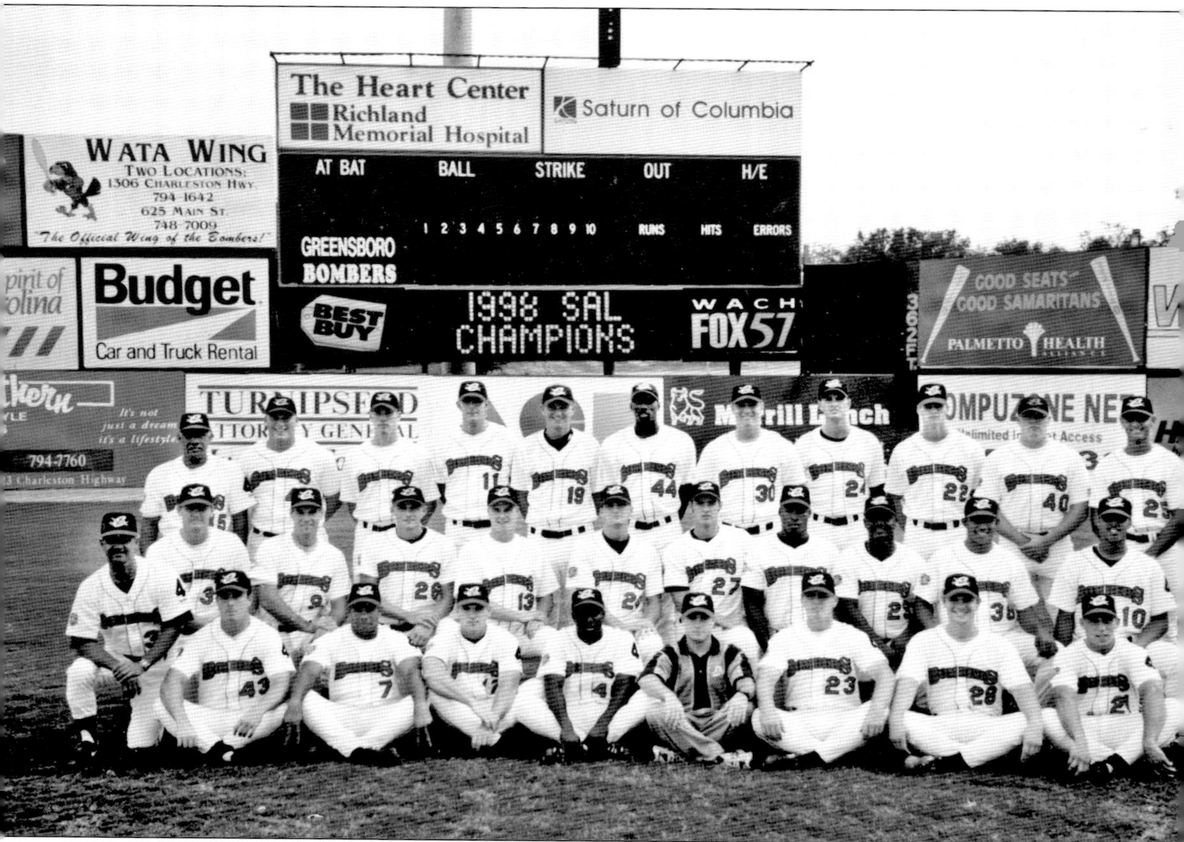

The 1998 South Atlantic League Championship team proved to be one of Columbia's finest squads. Nine players from that season had made the majors by the start of the 2004 season: Eric Cammack, Cesar Crespo, Alex Escobar, Leo Estrella, Dicky Gonzalez, Jason Phillips, Jerrod Riggan, Jason Roach, and Tyler Walker. The team set franchise highs for doubles (239), stolen bases (295), extra-base hits (399), and home runs (124), while winning the most games (90) and scoring the most runs (761) since the 1986 team. *Baseball America* listed a "Power Ranking" in each issue that season, seeding minor league teams regardless of classification, and the Capital City Bombers ended the regular season as the number one team in the country. (CCB.)

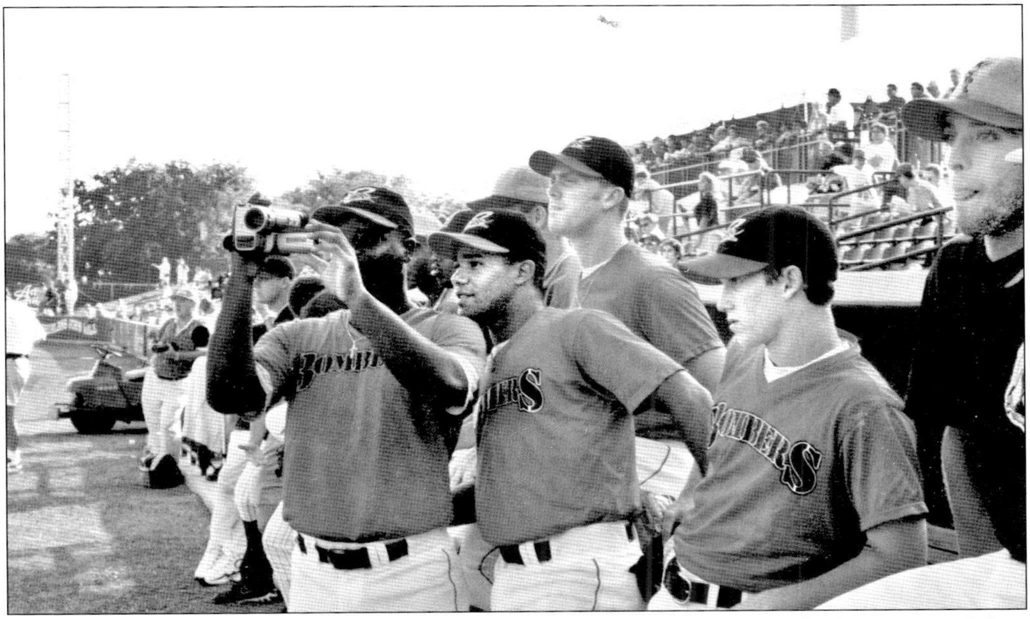

People sometimes forget that players can be fans, too. Here we see part of the large Capital City contingent at the 1998 South Atlantic League All-Star Game in Charleston, South Carolina, trying to capture some of the many pre-game events on camera. The Bombers seen here are, from left to right, Maurice Bruce, Jerson Perez, Shawn Barry, and Geoff Goetz. (CCB.)

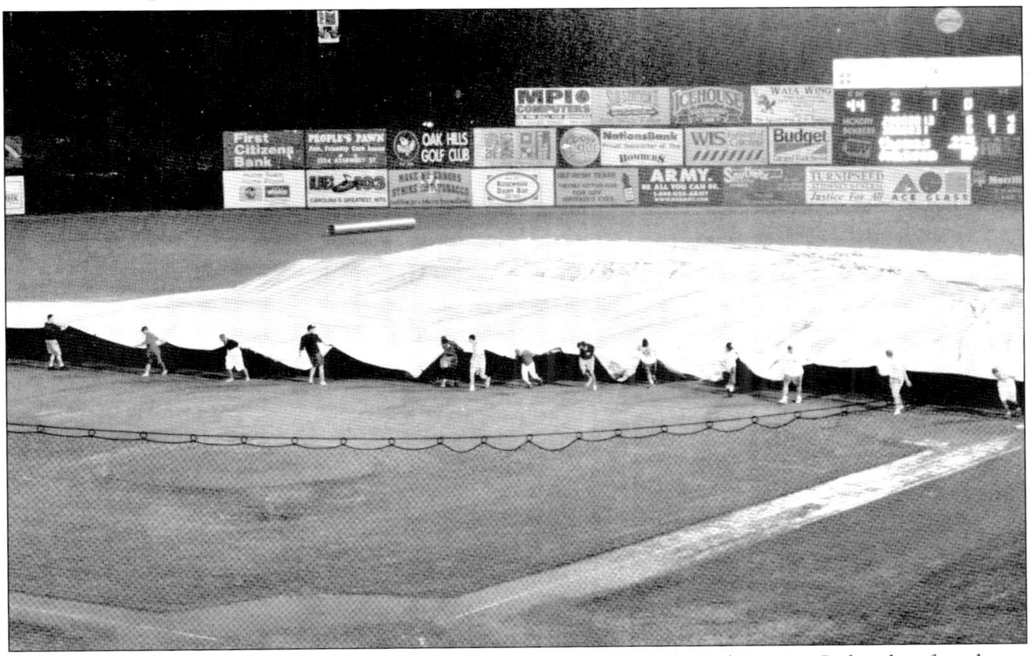

Rain and baseball do not mix, so when the rains come out, so does the tarp. Columbia fans have watched scenes like this too many times. As the scoreboard tells us, this particular tarp pull in 1998 came at a dramatic moment in the game: with the Bombers batting in the bottom of the eighth and the score tied 6-6 against Hickory. (CCB.)

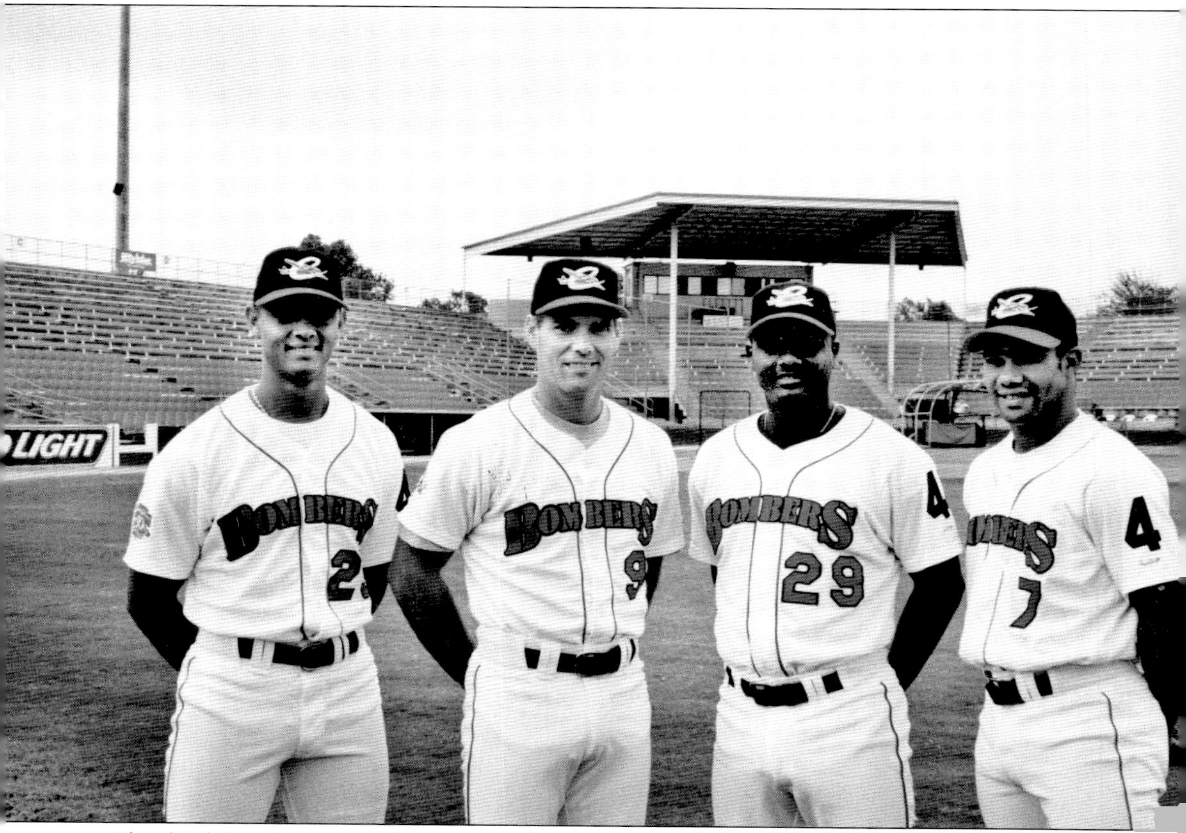

The final South Atlantic League All-Star team for 1998 reflected the dominance enjoyed by the Bombers that season. The list included, from left to right, outfielder Alex Escobar, manager Doug Davis, third-baseman Maurice Bruce, and shortstop Jerson Perez. Escobar also took the award for the league's Most Outstanding Major League Prospect and Davis soon added the Minor League Manager of the Year award from *The Sporting News*. Bruce won the SAL batting title for his franchise record .341 average. Perez tied for the league lead in triples with 10. By 2004, Bruce and Perez had not gotten the call to the majors, but Davis was a bench coach for the 2003 World Champion Florida Marlins and retained that post for 2004, and Escobar finally overcame a long battle with injuries to become an everyday outfielder for the Cleveland Indians in 2004. (CCB.)

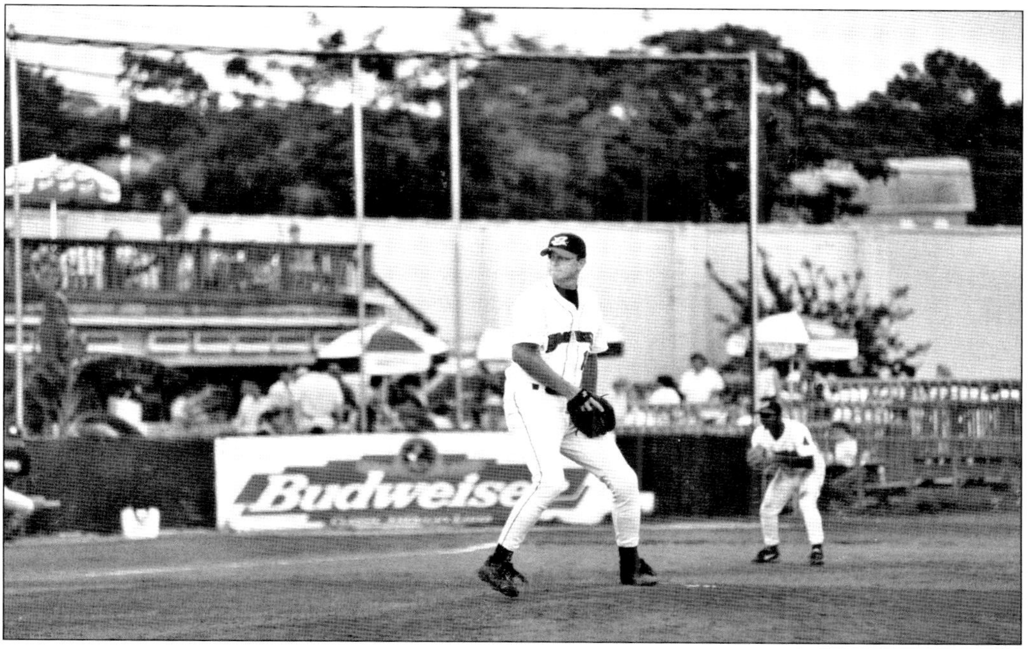

A good reason the 1998 Bombers never lost more than four in a row was that James Kevin Dougherty was in the five-man rotation. "Doc" started 20 games, going 15-2 with only three no-decisions and a 2.74 ERA. The left-hander's resume also included a complete-game shutout in the playoffs. (CCB.)

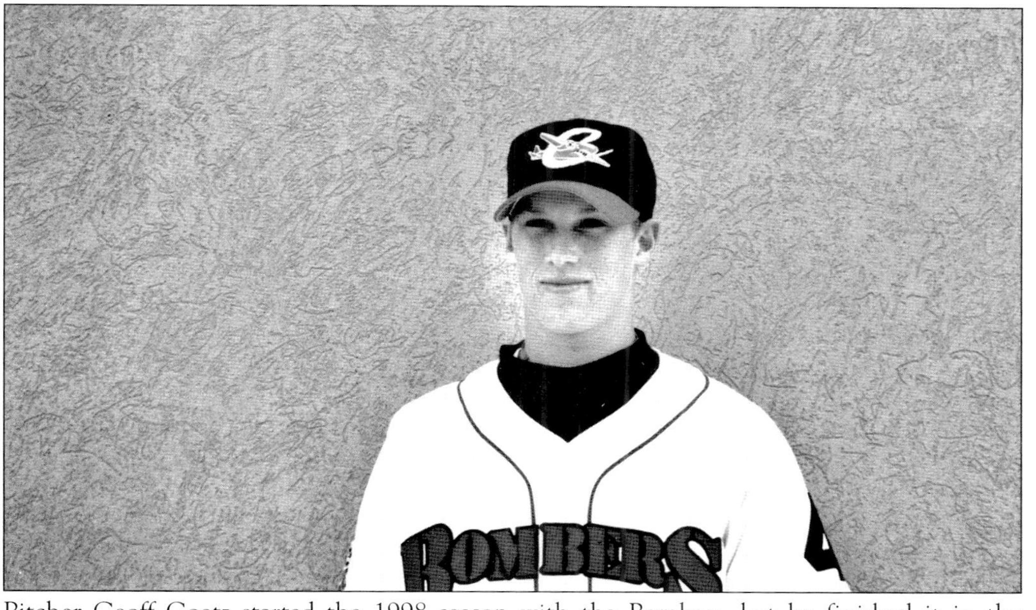

Pitcher Geoff Goetz started the 1998 season with the Bombers, but he finished it in the Marlins organization. Goetz was the "player to be named later" in the high-profile trade that sent Mike Piazza to the New York Mets. Even the minor league part of that deal attracted national attention, given that Goetz had been New York's top draft choice, sixth overall, the year before. (CCB.)

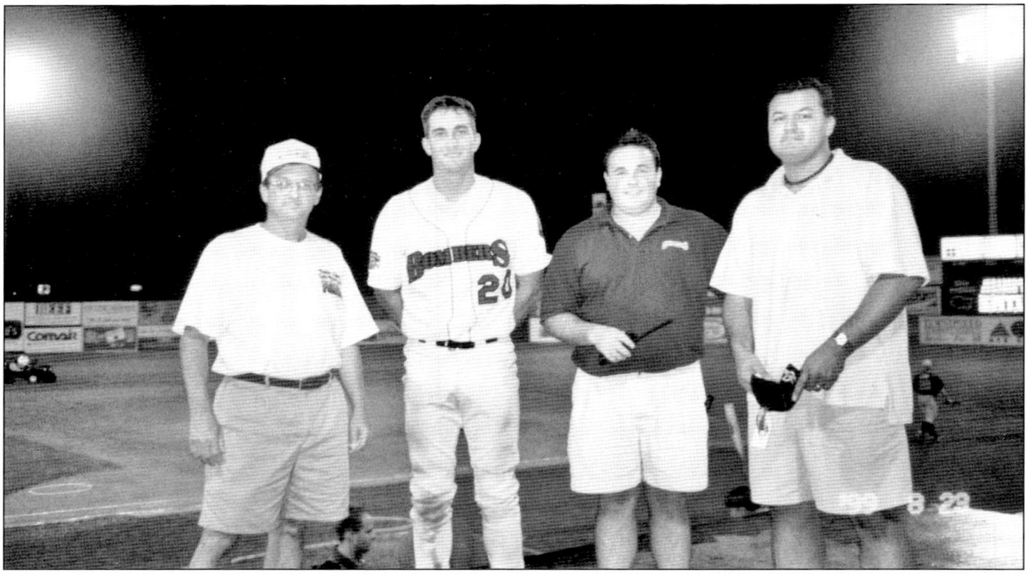

Bombers catcher Jason Phillips, who has since become a regular part of the lineup for the New York Mets, hit a special winning home run during a game in August 1998. The round-tripper did not win the game, but it did win Jim Kirkpatrick of Lexington, South Carolina, a new car! From left to right we see Kirkpatrick, Phillips, Bombers general manager Tim Swain, and Rick Dearden from Saturn of Columbia. (CCB.)

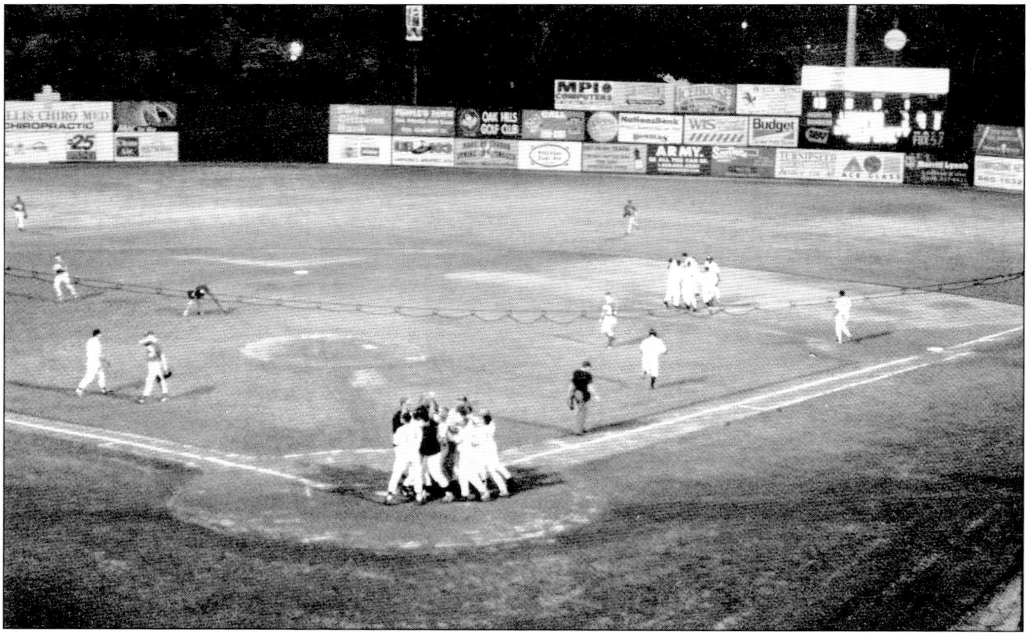

This press box view shows a special moment during the championship run for the 1998 Bombers. In game one of the SAL semi-finals against Hagerstown, catcher Ryan Bennett made the most of his only trip to the plate, driving Allen Dina home with a ninth-inning RBI single to win the game 8-7. Twin celebrations simultaneously engulf Bennett on the base path and Dina at the plate. (CCB.)

Facing elimination in the championship round of the 1998 playoffs, the Bombers put the ball in the hands of Tyler Walker. The big right-hander began the season in the bullpen, but he evolved into a starter when his team needed him. Walker responded with a sensational 16-strikeout performance against Greensboro, as the Bombers won 8-1 to force a deciding game three against the Bats. (CCB.)

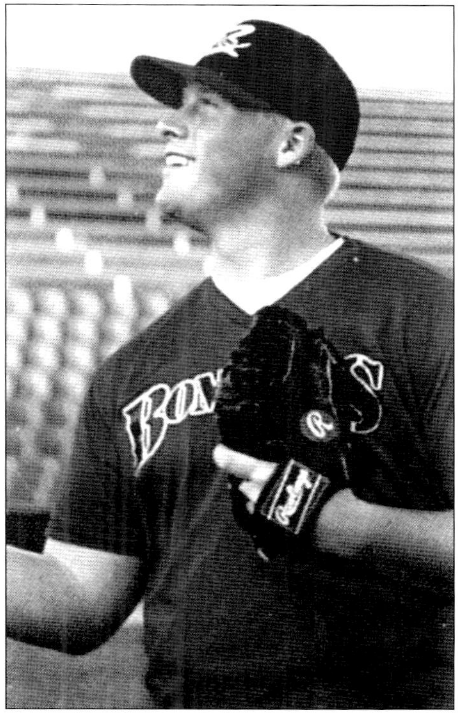

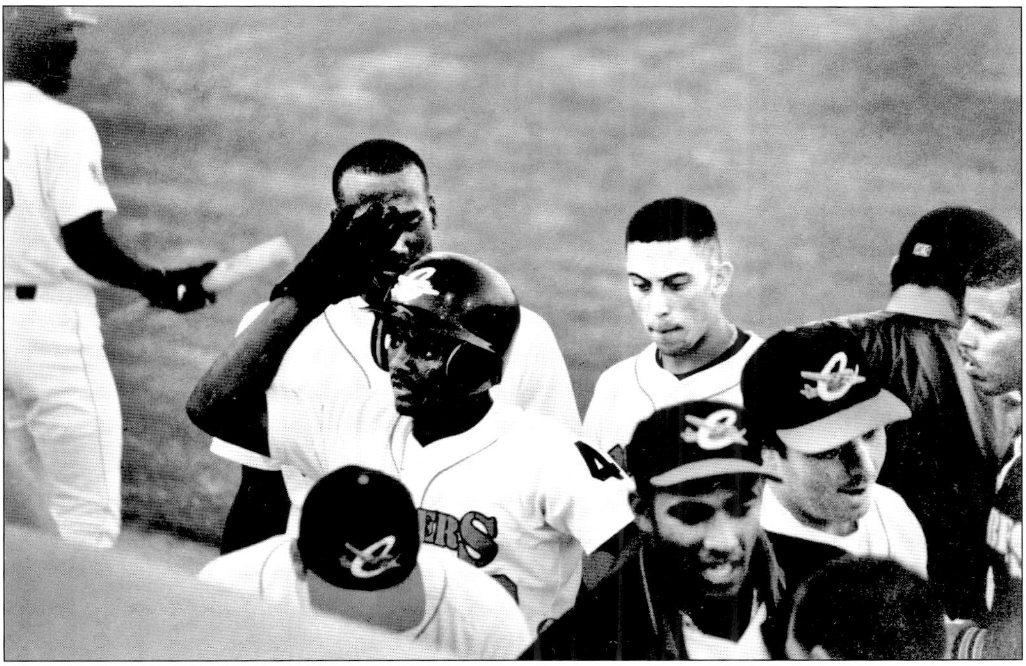

Capital City third-baseman Maurice Bruce celebrates with teammates after scoring in the championship-clinching game of the South Atlantic League finals. The Bombers put up a flurry of early runs and waited out the Greensboro Bats to win the game 10-2 and the title two games to one. (CCB.)

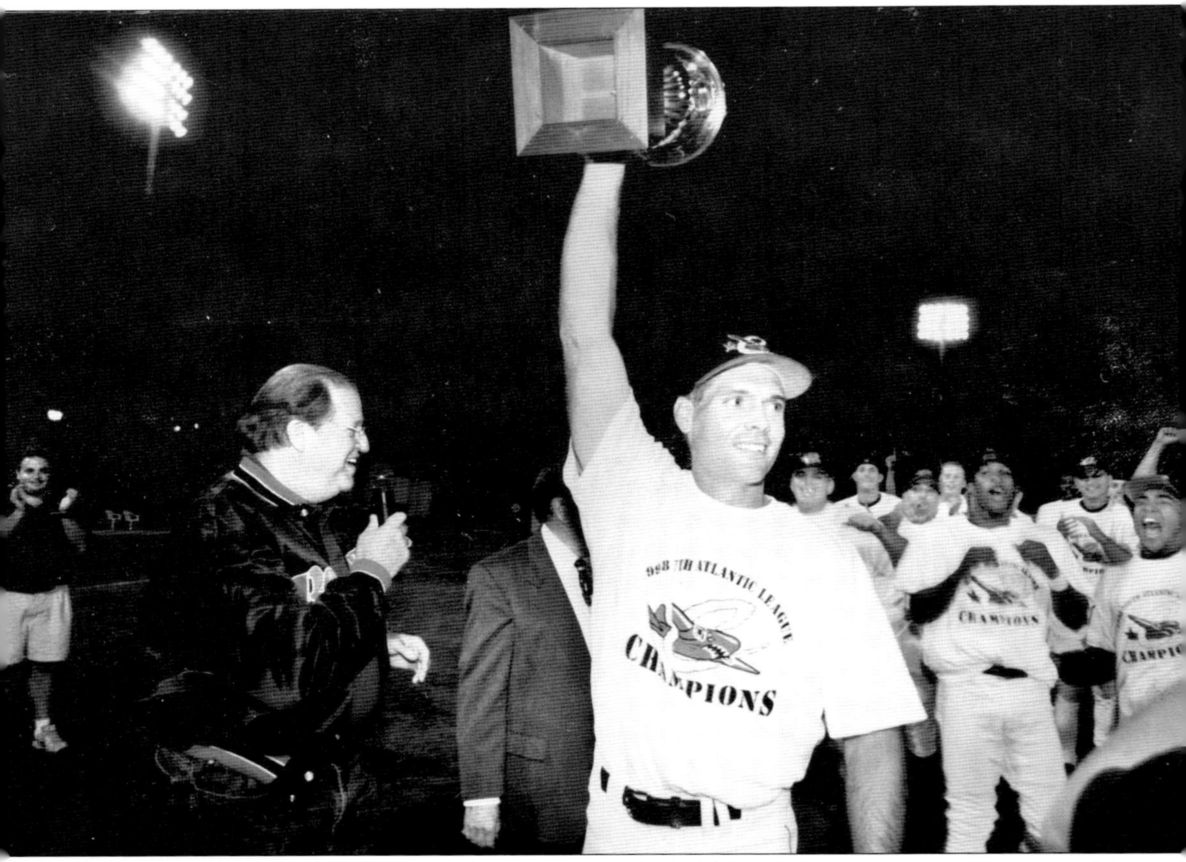

Bombers manager Doug Davis celebrates winning the 1998 South Atlantic League Championship by hoisting the trophy after defeating Greensboro at Capital City Stadium. The 1998 Bombers finished the regular season with a stellar 90-51 record, the only team in all the minors to win 90 games. They survived three rounds of playoffs to take the title—the third for the modern franchise, adding to the pennants taken in 1986 and 1991. The victory celebrated here remained the last time the Bombers had won the league through 2003. Team owner Eric Margenau (at left, with microphone) is seen here at his last Bombers game after eight seasons with the club. The team's sale to businessman Robert Cohen and his associates became official just months after this celebration. Cohen's group operated the Bombers for the next four seasons. (CCB.)

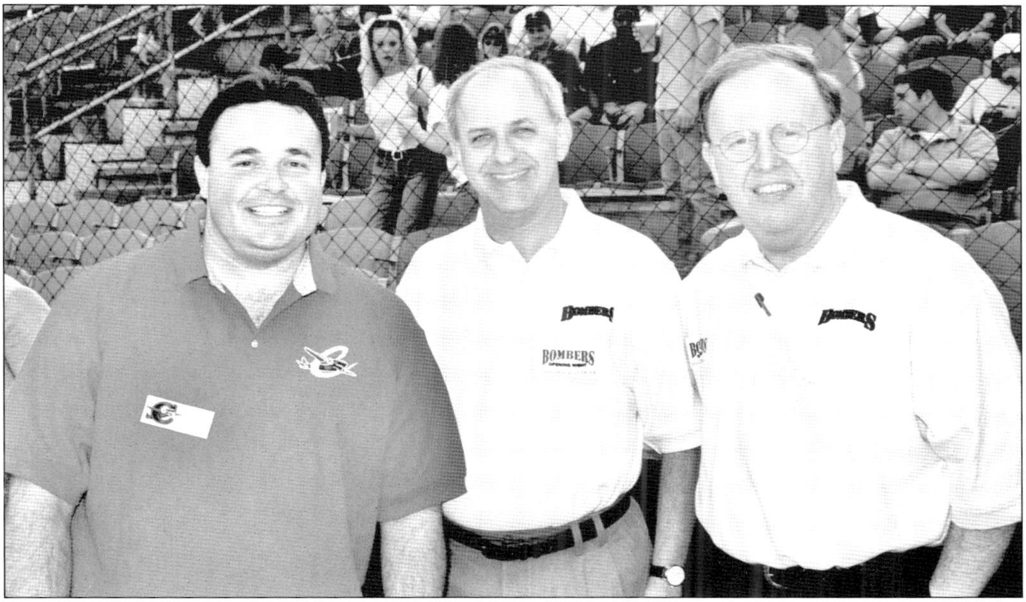

Bombers general manager Tim Swain (left) welcomed South Carolina governor Jim Hodges (center) and Columbia mayor Bob Coble to the ballpark for Opening Night 1999. Swain advanced to the GM position in 1996 and stayed there until leaving the team in 2004. Governor Hodges and his family were frequent ballpark visitors during his term. Mayor Coble has remained a strong advocate of baseball in the community throughout his time in office. (CCB.)

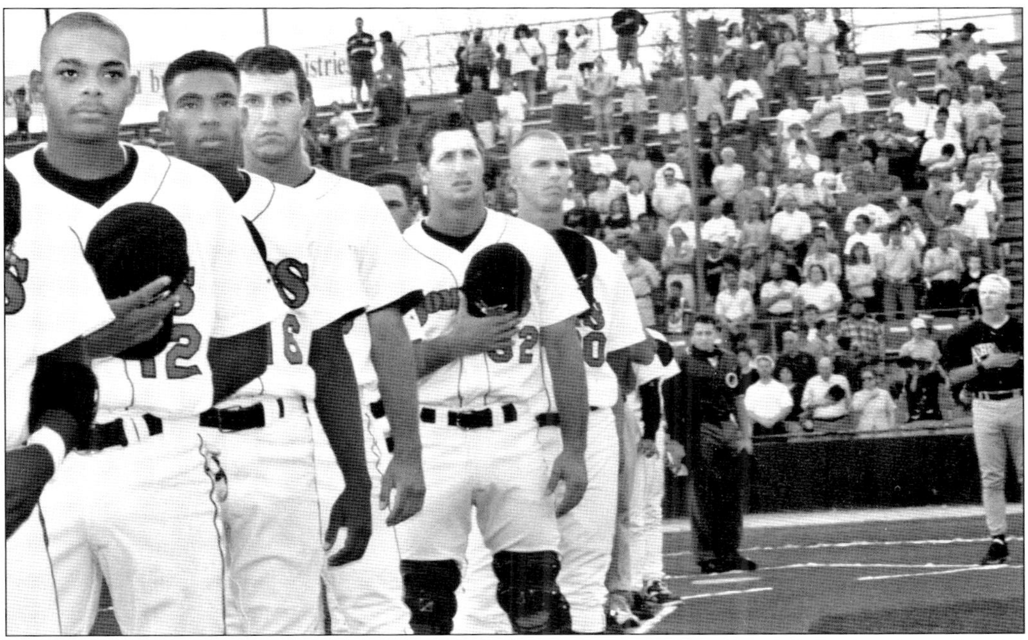

In a moment as American as they come, we see the Capital City Bombers lined up for the national anthem at the opening game of the 1999 season. The pre-game salute offers the team its final moments for reflection before facing the day's opponent, the Asheville Tourists in this case. (CCB.)

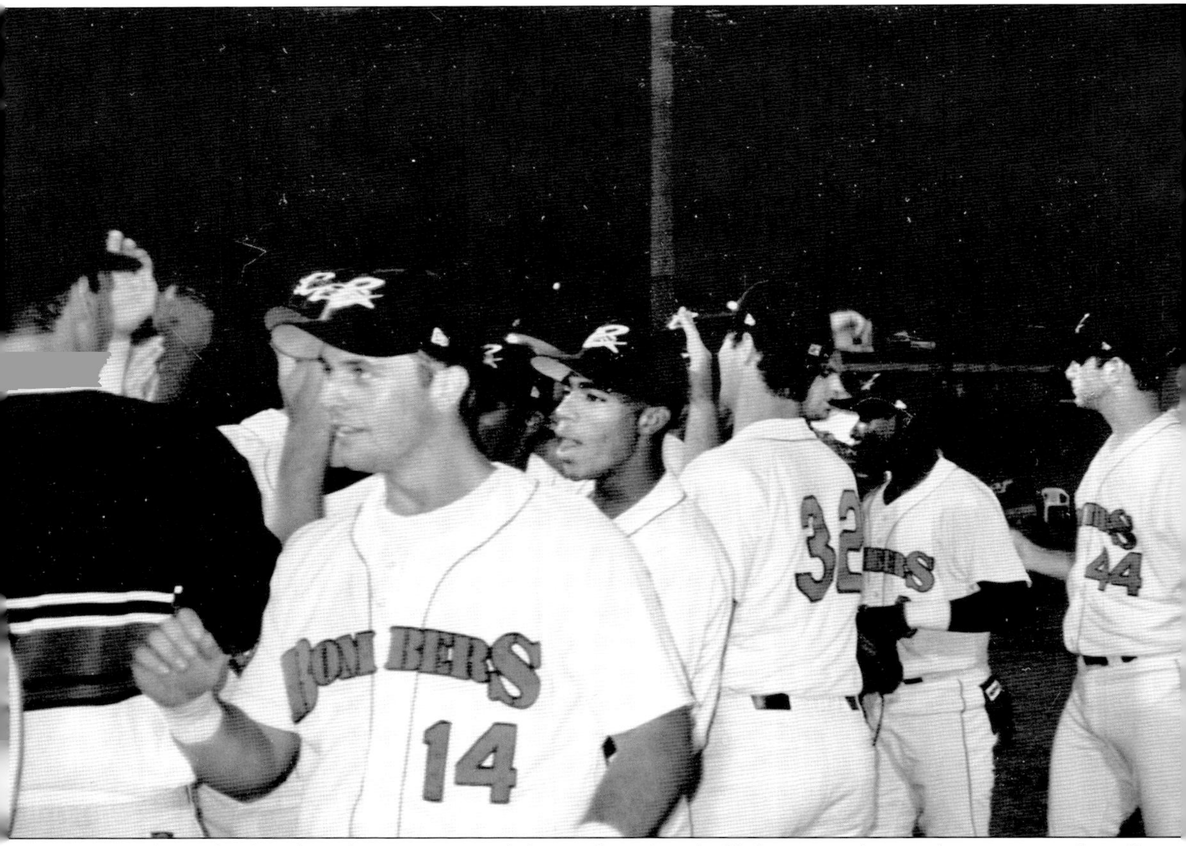

Earl Snyder (#14) and teammates celebrate their first-half championship and automatic playoff berth in 1999. That honor marked four straight half-seasons with the Bombers holding first place in their division. Although the team did not defend the pennant won in 1998 with another title, the club did produce the most powerful hitting numbers in franchise history. The home run records set for the team (155) and individual (Snyder, 28) categories still held up going into 2004. The 1999 team had four hitters with 20 or more home runs: Snyder, 28; Corey Erickson, 23; Robert Stratton, 21; and Brian Jenkins, 20. Manager Dave Engle soon advanced to the coaching staff of the parent club. (CCB.)

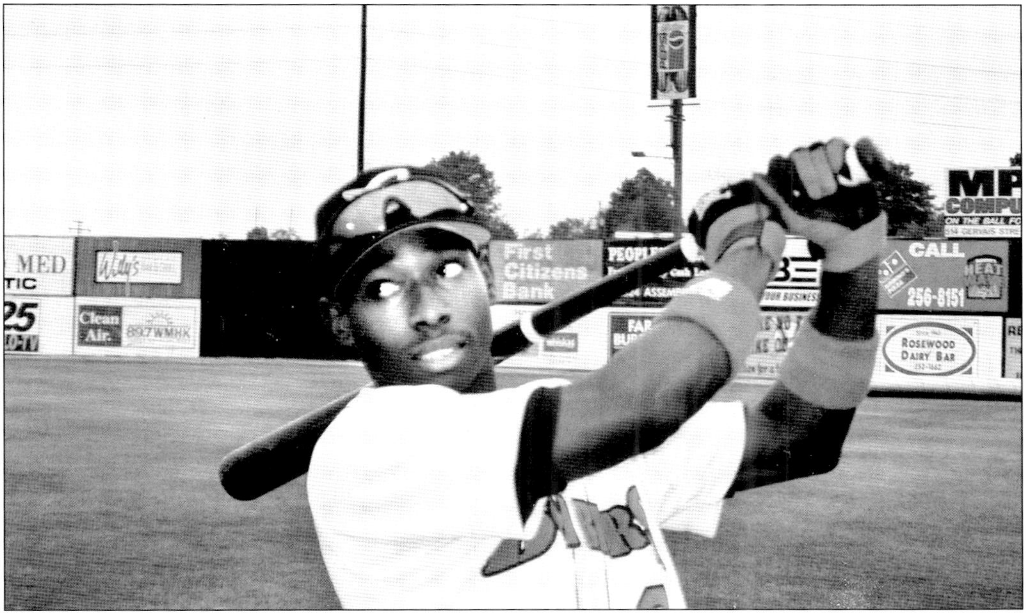

Outfielder Brian Cole hustled his way into prospect status when he proved to be one of the standouts of 1999. Cole, who set team records for doubles (41) and extra-base hits (63), displayed the variety of tools that could have made him a big-league star. Tragically, Cole only got the opportunity to play one more year. He died in a car accident immediately before the 2001 season was to begin. (CCB.)

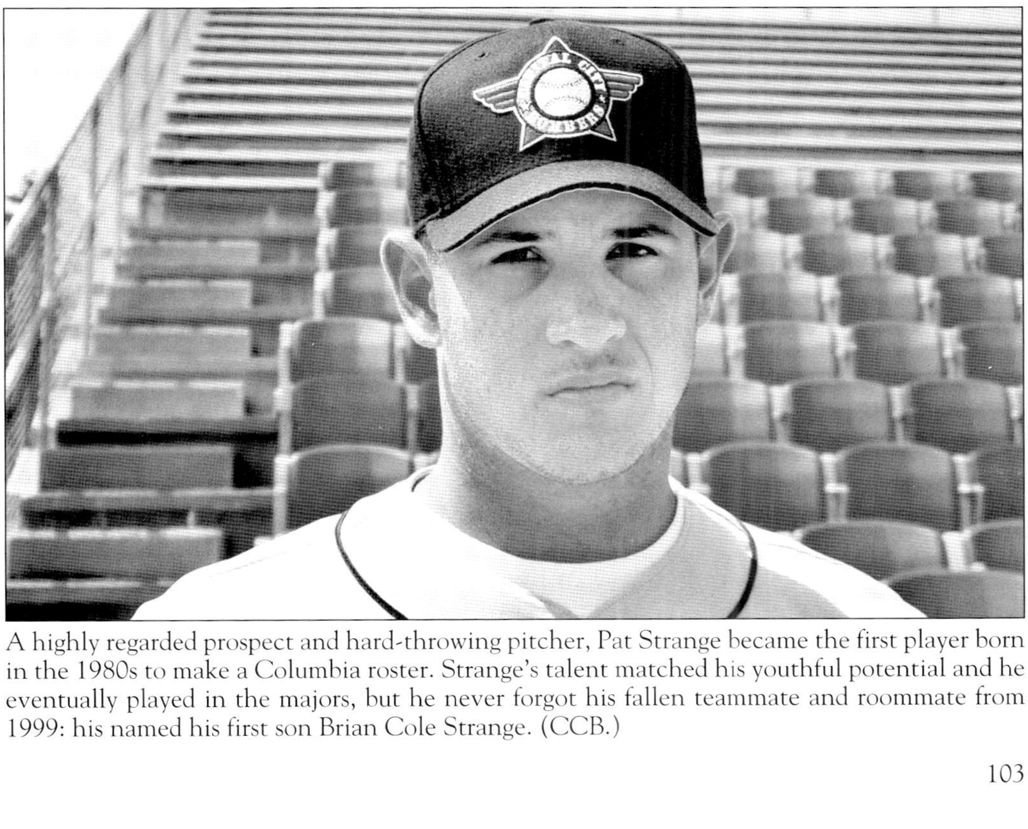

A highly regarded prospect and hard-throwing pitcher, Pat Strange became the first player born in the 1980s to make a Columbia roster. Strange's talent matched his youthful potential and he eventually played in the majors, but he never forgot his fallen teammate and roommate from 1999: his named his first son Brian Cole Strange. (CCB.)

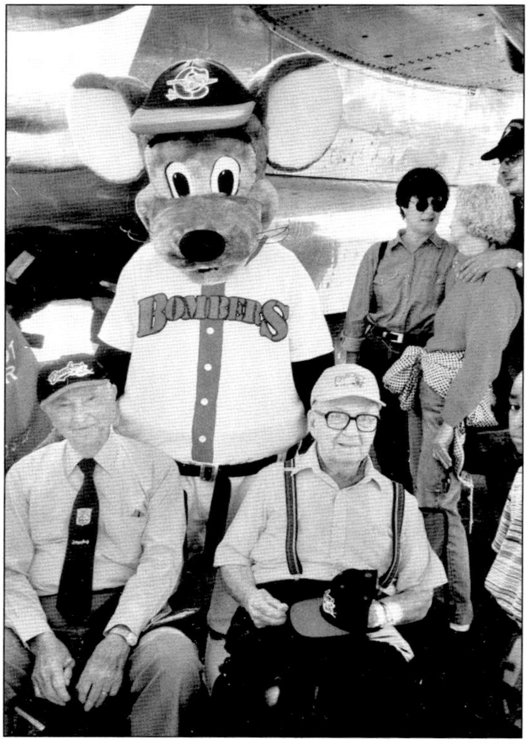

A special meeting took place in the shade of a B-25 bomber during a 1999 event at Owens Field in Columbia. Team mascot Bomber the Mouse met a pair of real Capital City Bombers: Maj. Nolan Herndon (left) and Col. Sally Crouch, members of the Doolittle Raiders and residents of South Carolina. (CCB.)

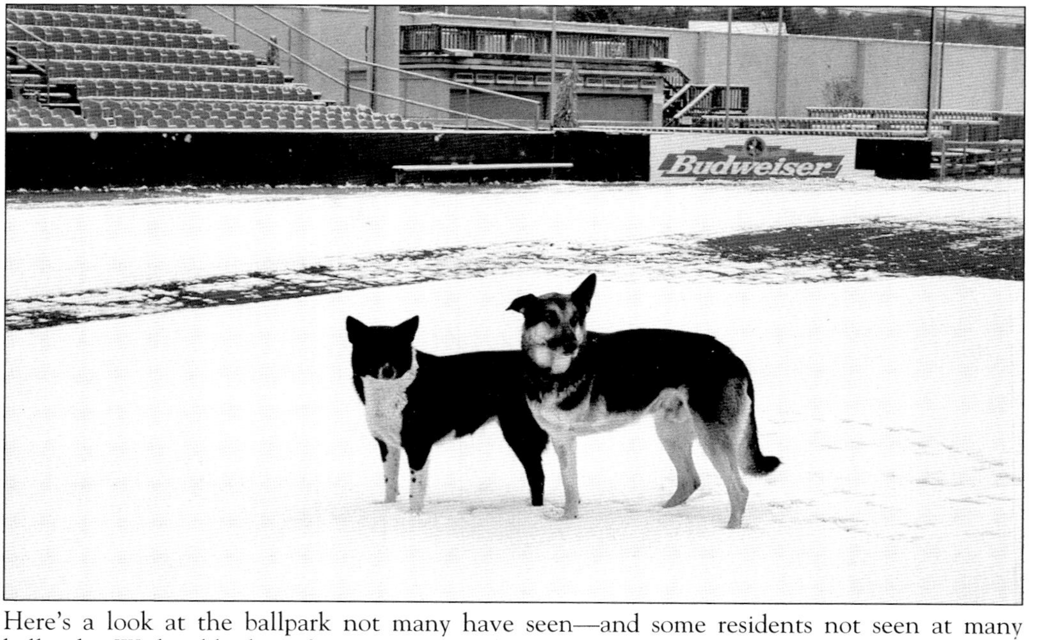

Here's a look at the ballpark not many have seen—and some residents not seen at many ballparks. With a blanket of snow covering the field, Sophie (left) and Bruno investigate the winter wonderland. The dogs have lived year-round at the stadium for most of their lives. Although this angle does not show it well, Sophie does have four legs; it's Bruno who only has three! (CCB.)

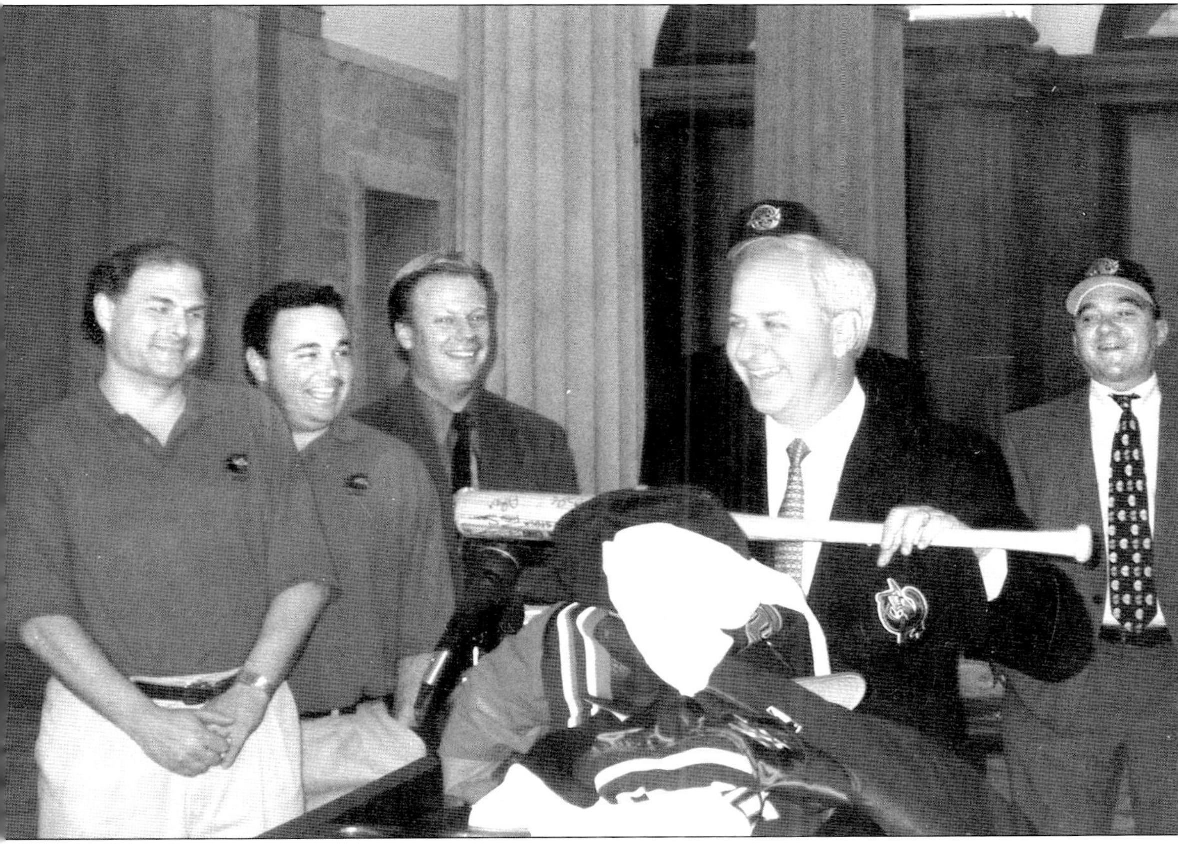

Gov. Jim Hodges proclaimed the week of April 24–28, 2000, as Minor League Baseball Week in the Palmetto State. The proclamation commended minor league teams for providing "fun, family-oriented recreation in an outdoor community setting." It also praised the players as fine role models, noted the attention brought to the state by its teams, and saluted those teams for the opportunities for fans to see baseball's "stars of tomorrow." Governor Hodges welcomed representatives from the five teams playing in the state and wound up buried in gifts from the teams. The five South Carolina clubs for that season were the Capital City Bombers, Myrtle Beach Pelicans, Charleston RiverDogs, Greenville Braves, and Charlotte Knights (from Rock Hill, South Carolina). The Bombers were represented at the ceremony by team president Robert Cohen (left) and general manager Tim Swain. (CCB.)

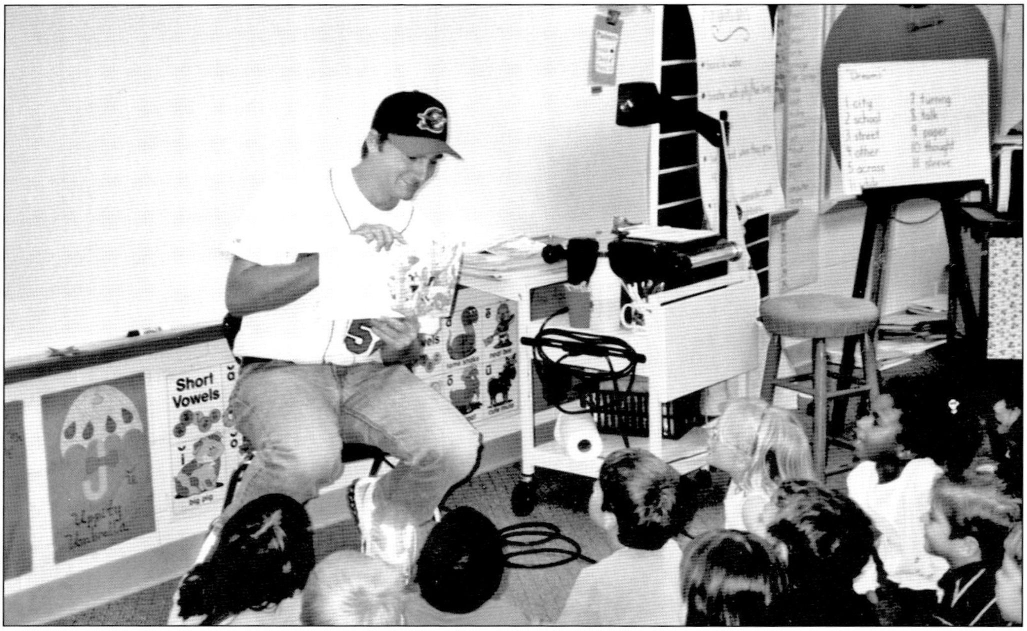

Pitcher Justin Dunning reads to children at River Springs Elementary School during the 2000 season. Dunning is just one of the many players who have volunteered over the years to reach out to the community and particularly to children. Whether participating in reading days, giving baseball clinics, answering questions, or offering autograph sessions, the players have always tried to return the support their fans have given them. (CCB.)

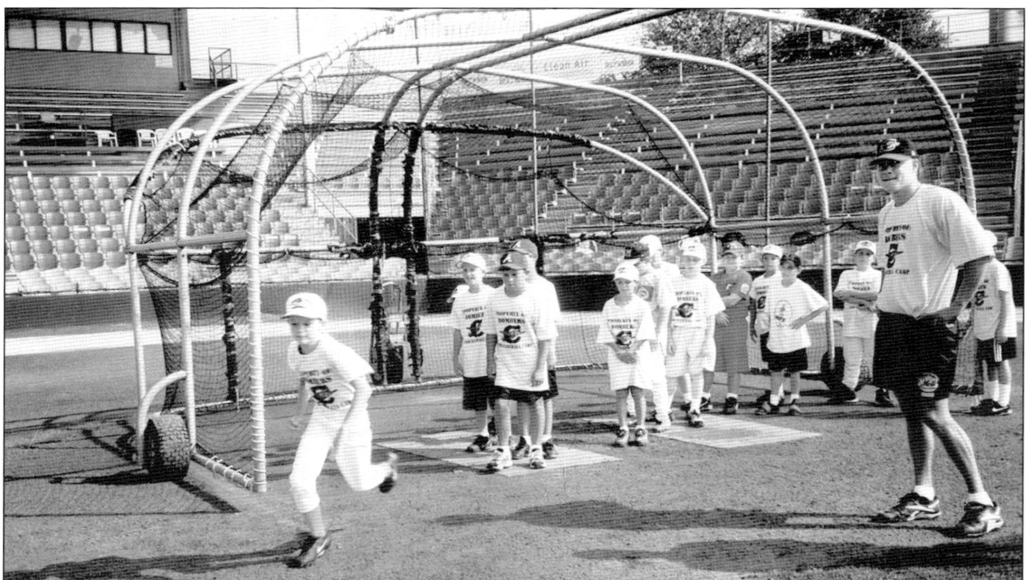

This scene comes from the annual Capital City Bombers Baseball Camp. The Bombers conduct a week-long day camp, in which the professional players and coaches teach fundamentals to children ages 7-14. The young campers make friends out of their heroes and the players reconnect to what made baseball fun in the first place. (CCB.)

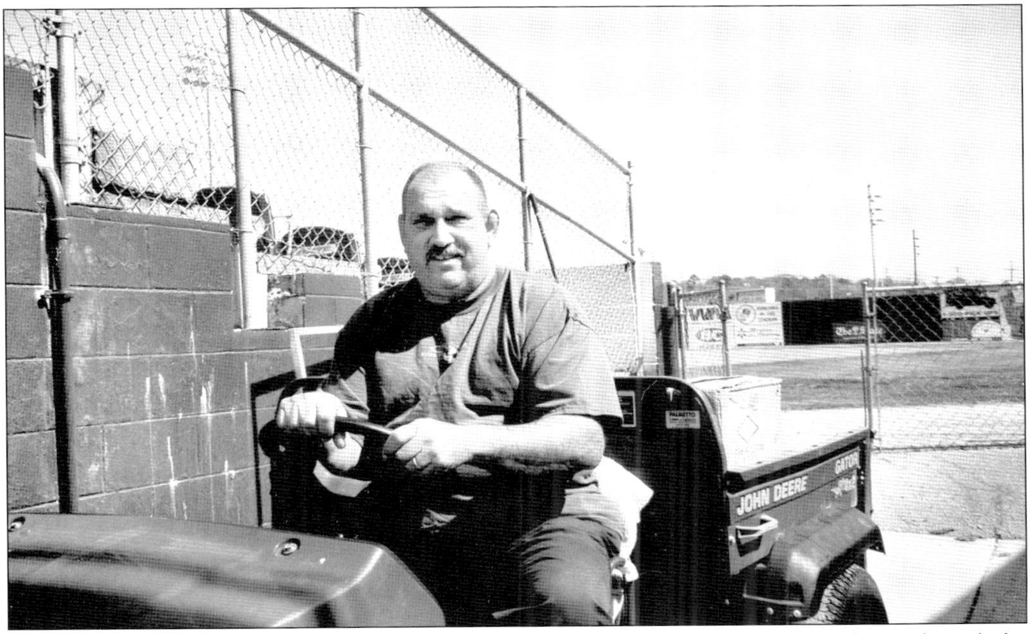

Keeping a field in baseball shape over many years can be tricky, but that has been the job for Bob Hook, Capital City Stadium groundskeeper for more than a dozen years. "Captain" Hook's background has a bit of everything: 25-year veteran of fire services, Clemson football player, minor league pitcher, and other varied experiences. (CCB.)

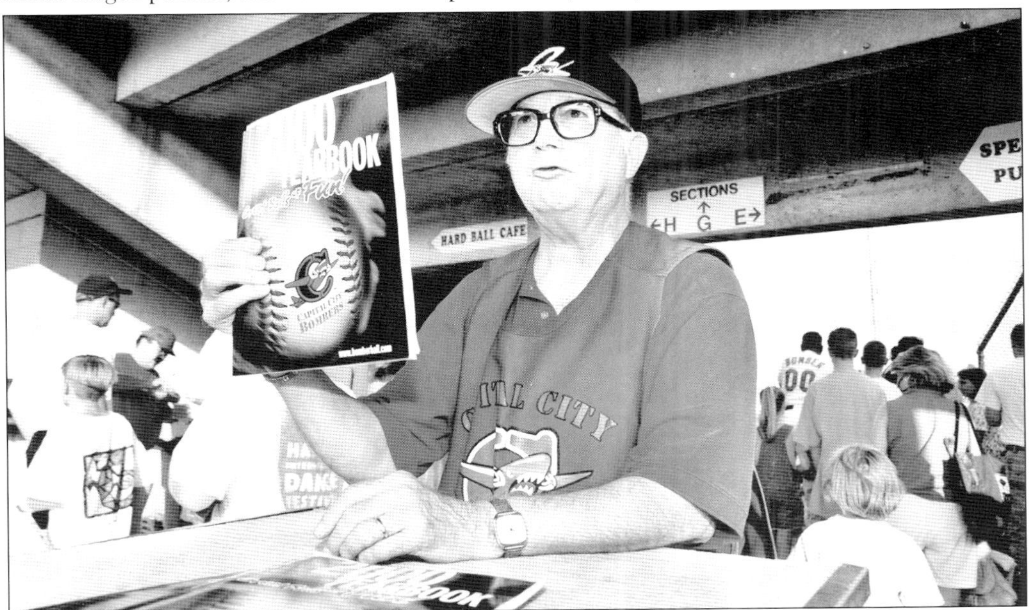

Whether you call it a program, a scorecard, or a yearbook, you expect a team to produce a special publication every season. The Bombers have maintained this ballpark staple over the years, seen here with vendor Waite Fulmer—known for his familiar call, "Get your program RIGHT HERE!" For 2004, the Bombers put a different spin on programs, giving them away for the first time. (CCB.)

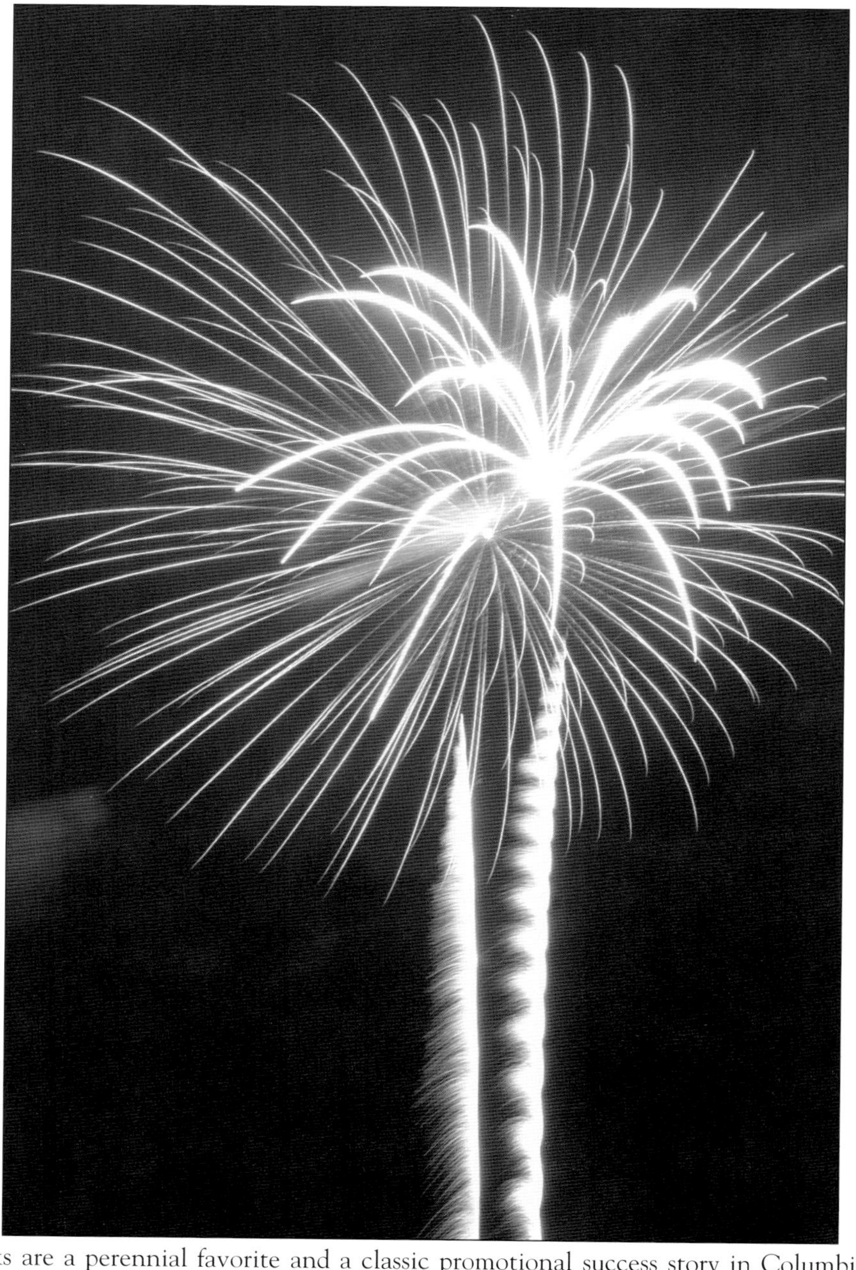

Fireworks are a perennial favorite and a classic promotional success story in Columbia. The Capital City Bombers became a part of central South Carolina's Independence Day tradition years ago, with sellouts common for games held on July 3 and 4 thanks to these pyrotechnic spectaculars. Pairing a good display with good music turned any given show into a "Concert in the Sky," a marketing hook that the Bombers used for years. The surrounding Olympia Mills neighborhood reverberates with the booms and blasts about a half dozen times per season on average. This particular gem of a photo was taken by noted local photographer Allen Sharpe at a Capital City Stadium fireworks show and was dubbed the "Pyrotechnic Palmetto" for its resemblance to the state tree, thanks to an open shutter and good timing. (CCB.)

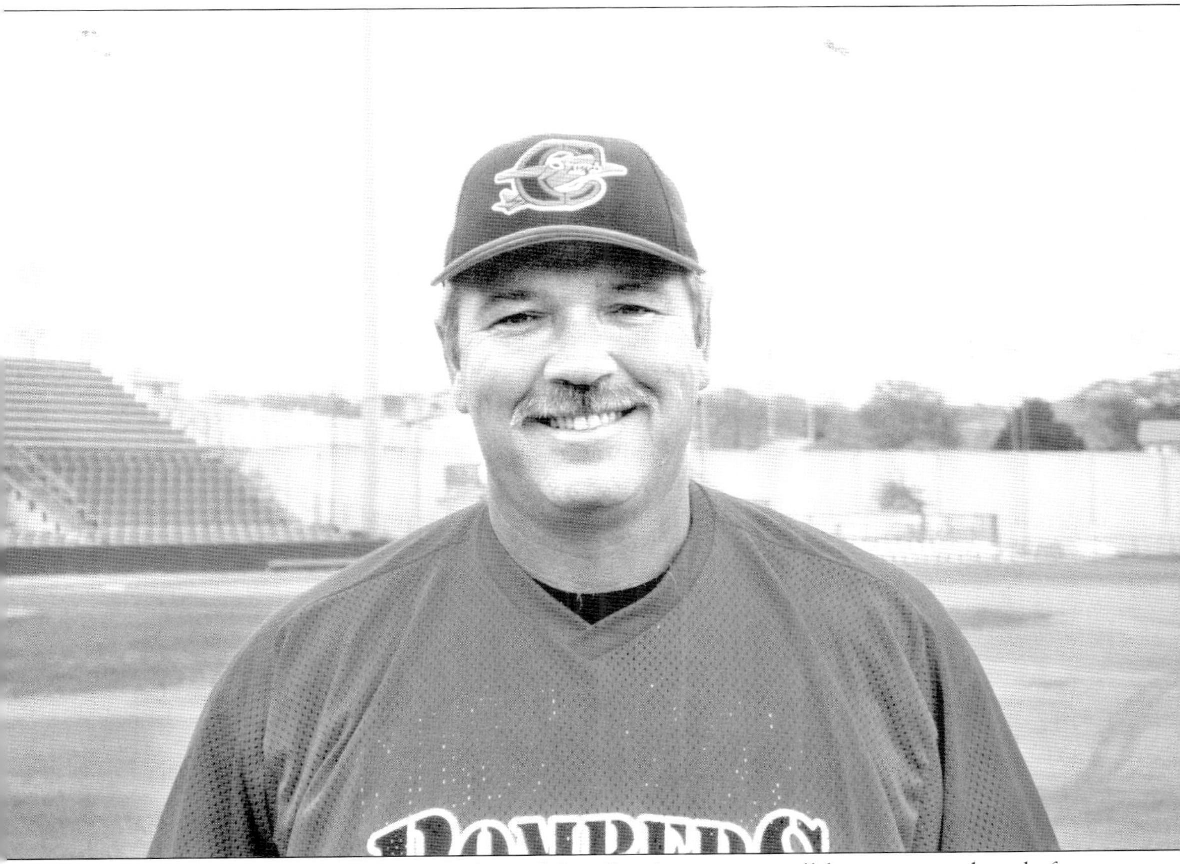

Ken Oberkfell, manager for the 2001 Capital City Bombers, was a well-known name long before his arrival in Columbia. "Obie" had earned a World Series ring as a member of the spectacular St. Louis Cardinals infield in 1982. He had also spent significant time with Atlanta, which endeared him to the many Braves fans in Columbia and around South Carolina. Oberkfell's career included other stops, and toward the end of his playing days he got one more crack at the World Series. He played for San Francisco in 1989 and was at Candlestick Park for the famed Earthquake Series, won by Oakland after being delayed. His stint with the Bombers was not his first trip through the South Atlantic League. Oberkfell had already passed through town as a manager with the Piedmont Boll Weevils, Philadelphia's affiliate in the SAL at the time. (CCB.)

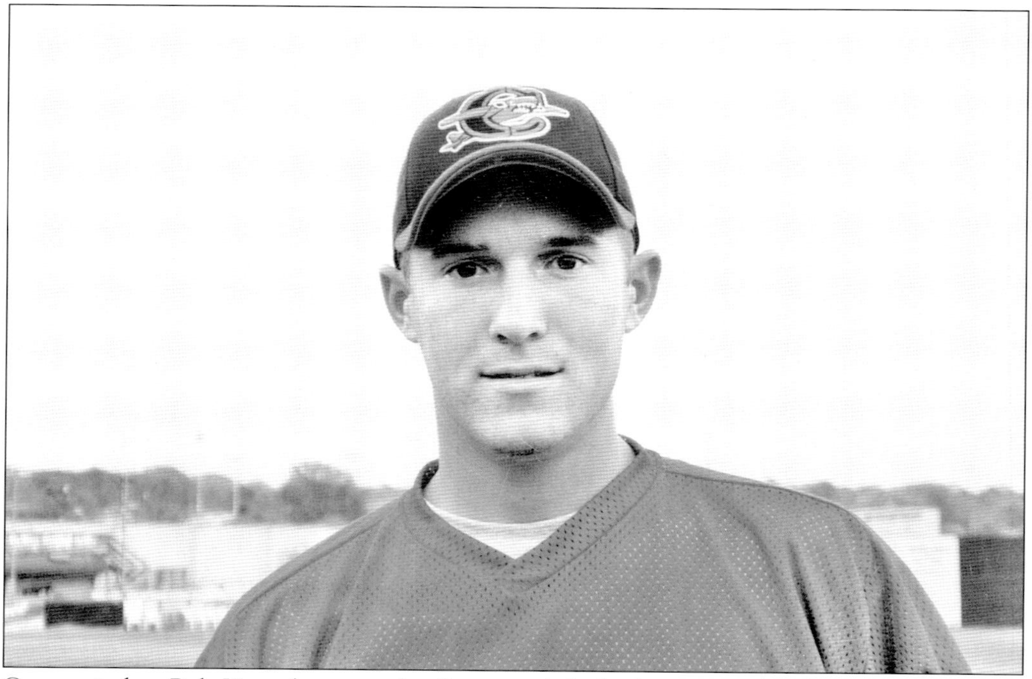

Count pitcher Bob Keppel among the first-round draft choices to play for the Capital City Bombers. He had a losing record in 2001 (6–7) but kept his earned run average down to a solid 3.11 on the year. The Mets grabbed Keppel 36th overall in the 2000 draft, a supplemental pick following the regular first round taken as compensation after losing John Olerud. (CCB.)

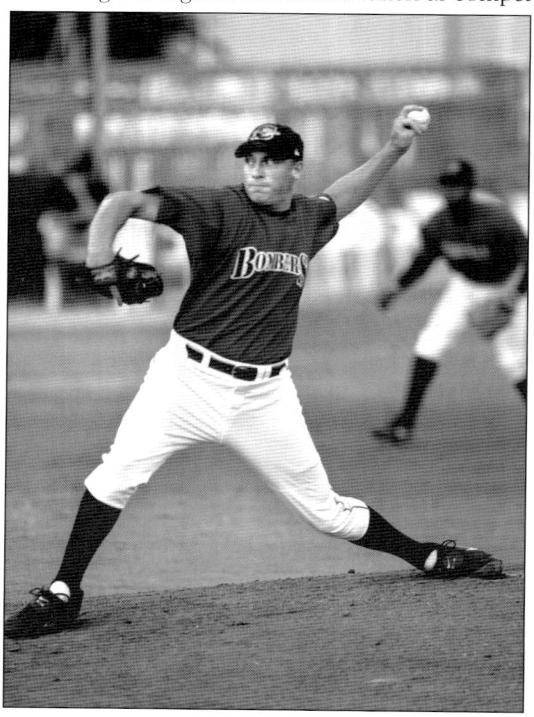

Left-hander Neal Musser was another highly regarded player to take the mound for the Bombers in 2001. The Mets selected Musser in the second round of the 1999 draft, but it was the first pick New York had available (their opening selection went to the White Sox as compensation for free agent Robin Ventura). Musser had a strong season for Capital City: 7–4, 2.84 ERA, 98 strikeouts, and 18 walks. (CCB.)

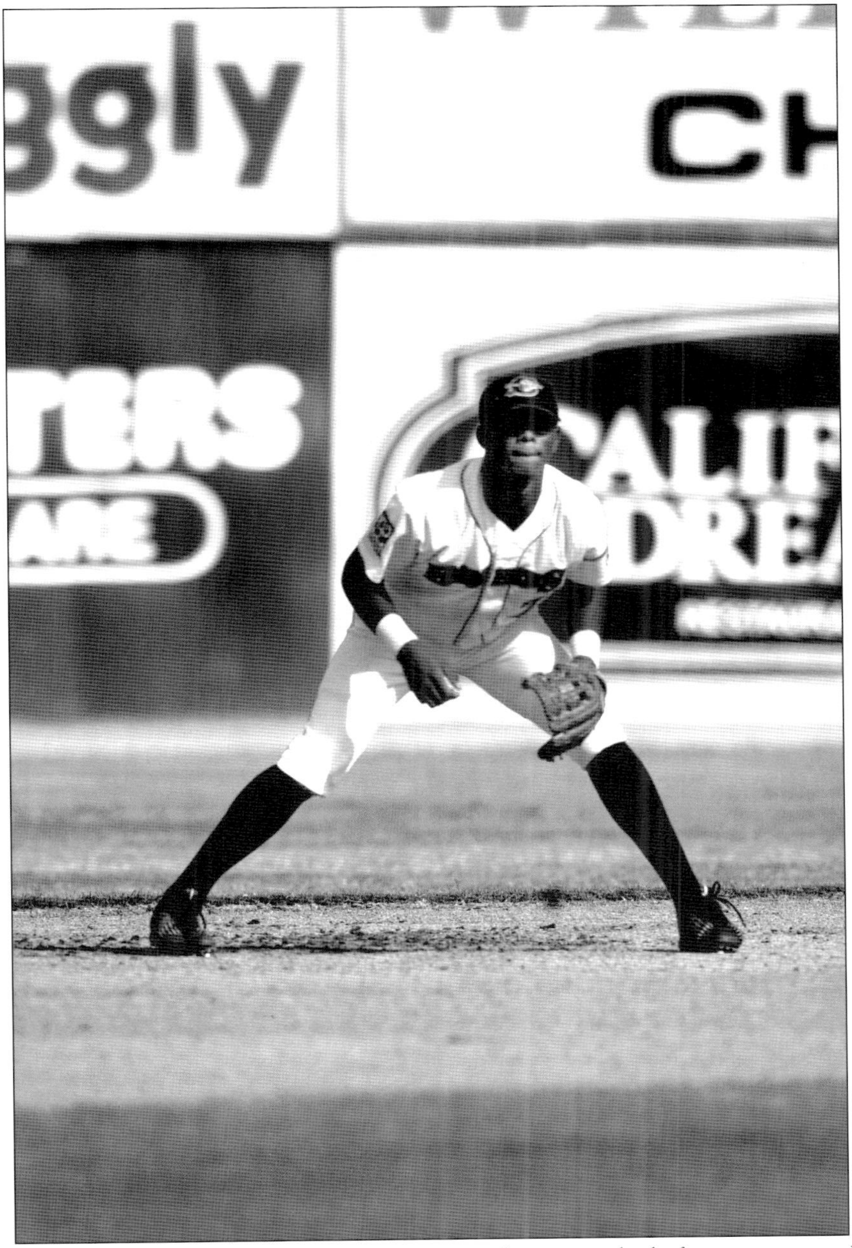

Proving that sometimes a baseball phenomenon can happen right before your eyes, shortstop Jose Reyes had jaws dropping during 2001. The Dominican teenager put on a performance that seemed to get better with every at-bat. Reyes went from almost being a secret to becoming an absolute sensation that year. He earned a cascade of awards and an avalanche of attention from national publications: *Baseball America* named Reyes the Mets Minor League Player of the Year and marked him as having the organization's Best Infield Arm and being the Best Defensive Infielder, *USA Today* labeled him the Top Hitter for the Mets, and some prospect services moved him to the top of their lists. He made his big-league debut in 2003, and if he can remain healthy, Reyes is expected to be an infielder in the majors for many years to come. (CCB.)

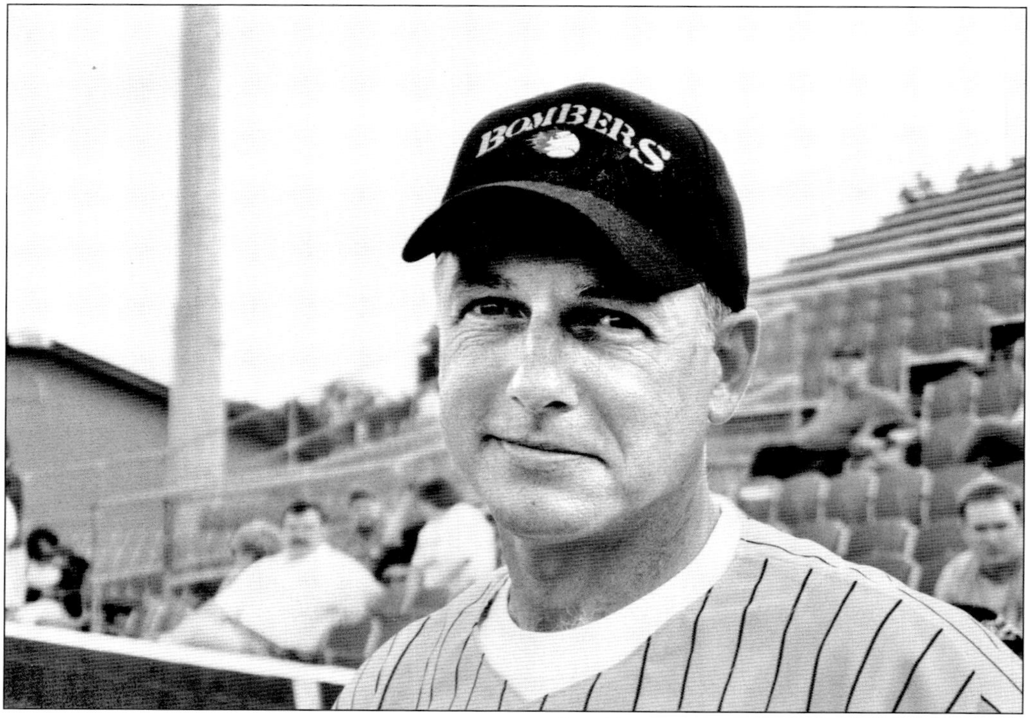

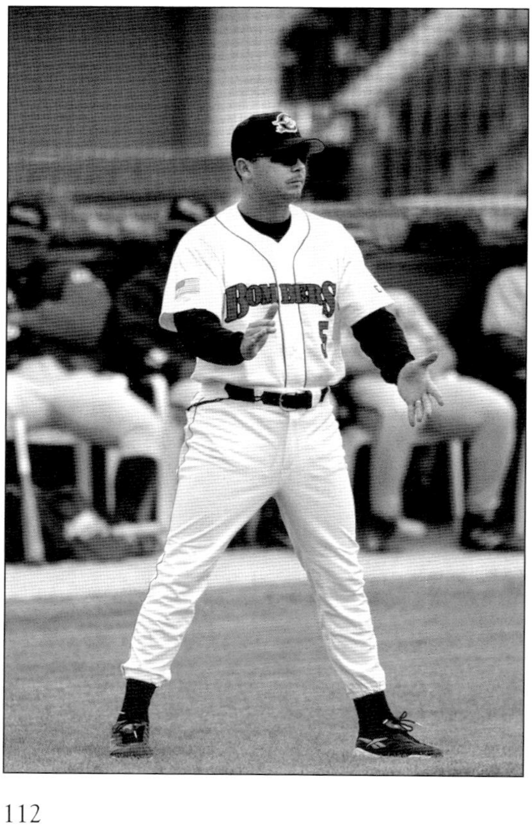

For 10 years, actor Mark Harmon headlined a Celebrity Baseball Game at Capital City Stadium. A fun idea and a friendly association with Bombers general manager Bill Shanahan from his California League days led to the start of the game in 1992, and it continued all the way through 2001. Harmon, known for his work in television and film, brought in a team of friends to play against local media celebrities. (CCB.)

Manager Tony Tijerina became the first former Bomber to take the job as manager. "TJ" had found success elsewhere in the Mets organization, and he wanted to add the SAL ring to his collection. Although his Bombers did qualify for the playoffs, a first round exit kept him short of his goal. Tijerina returned to manage in 2003, but that team fell short of post-season play. (CCB.)

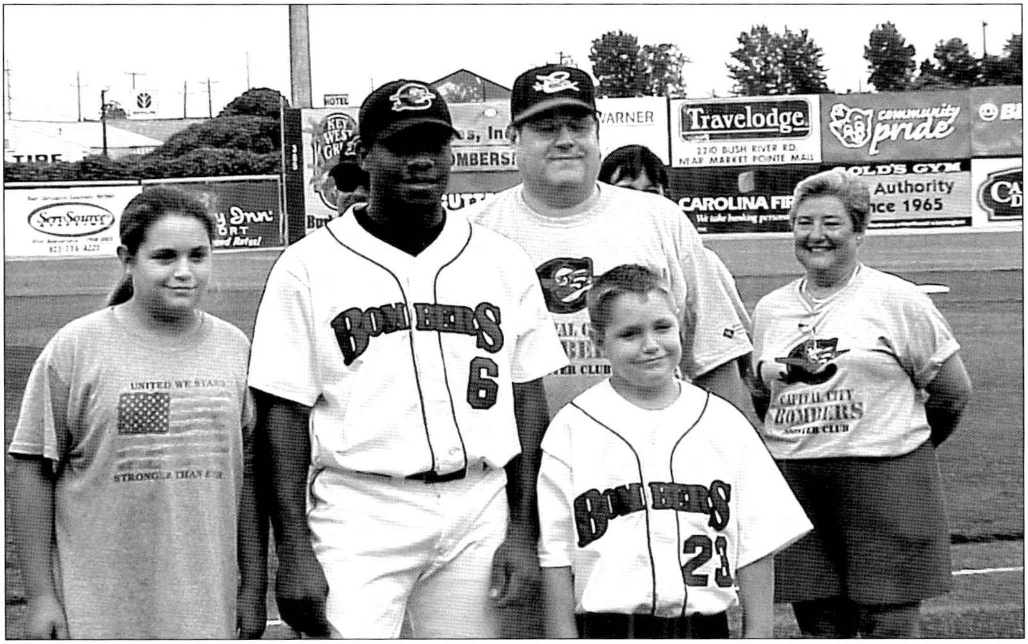

The Bombers Booster Club acts as both fan group and support network. While the Bombers are professional ballplayers, they are still young men on their own, often quite far from home. The Boosters try to make Columbia more of a home by welcoming players, helping them find things they need, providing them with some home-cooked meals, and rewarding them for their best performances. (CCB.)

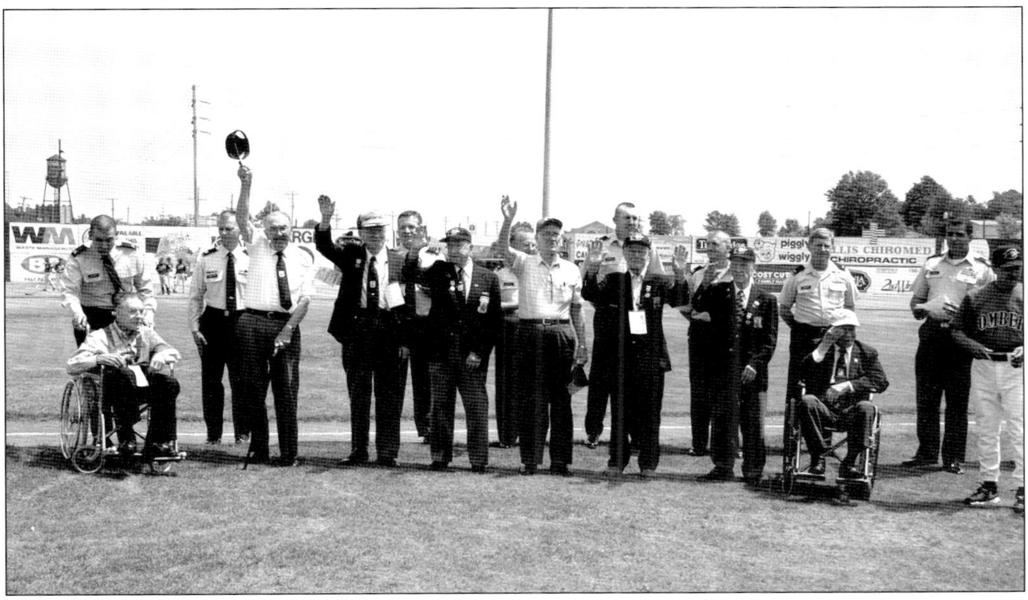

In April 2002, 60 years after their historic World War II mission, the Doolittle Raiders came back to Columbia for a week of special events in their honor. Most of the 23 surviving Raiders attended the reunion, which included a stop at the ballpark for a special salute from the team. (CCB.)

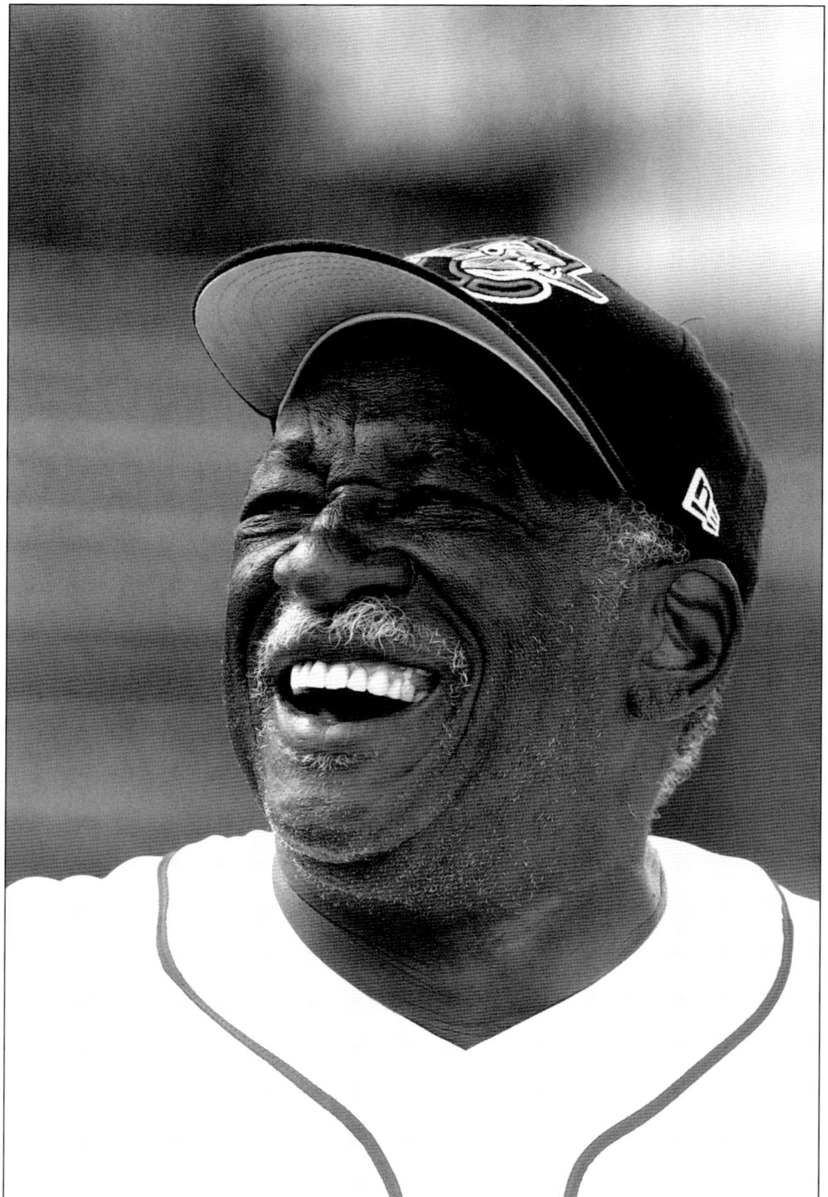

He has been called a fan, friend, and cheerleader for the team, but what David Williams has really meant to everyone goes well beyond that. A fixture at Capital City Stadium for more than 20 years (and at Gamecock athletics as well), David has become a Columbia icon. His days of leading cheers for the Columbia Mets evolved into a role as the ballpark's official singer for "Take Me Out to the Ballgame," and the seventh-inning stretch simply would not be the same without him. The nightly mystery at the ballpark has always been the question of what tune David would choose as his second song for the inning break. David achieved one of the true hallmarks of baseball popularity and celebrity: the bobble-head doll. The Bombers gave away 1,000 David Williams bobble-head dolls to fans who anxiously grabbed the souvenirs in what was one of the most talked-about giveaways in team history. (CCB.)

A skilled outfielder, Wayne Lydon was at his most dangerous on the base paths. In 2002, he racked up a total of 87 stolen bases, second-best in franchise history. Lydon is the only player to even get within 25 steals of Marcus Lawton's 1985 record of 111 stolen bases. His exceptional season earned him a spot on the final SAL All-Star roster for 2002. (CCB.)

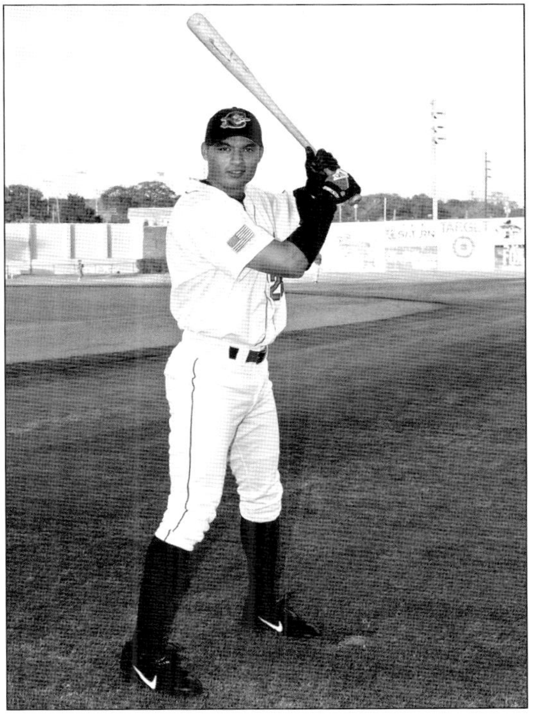

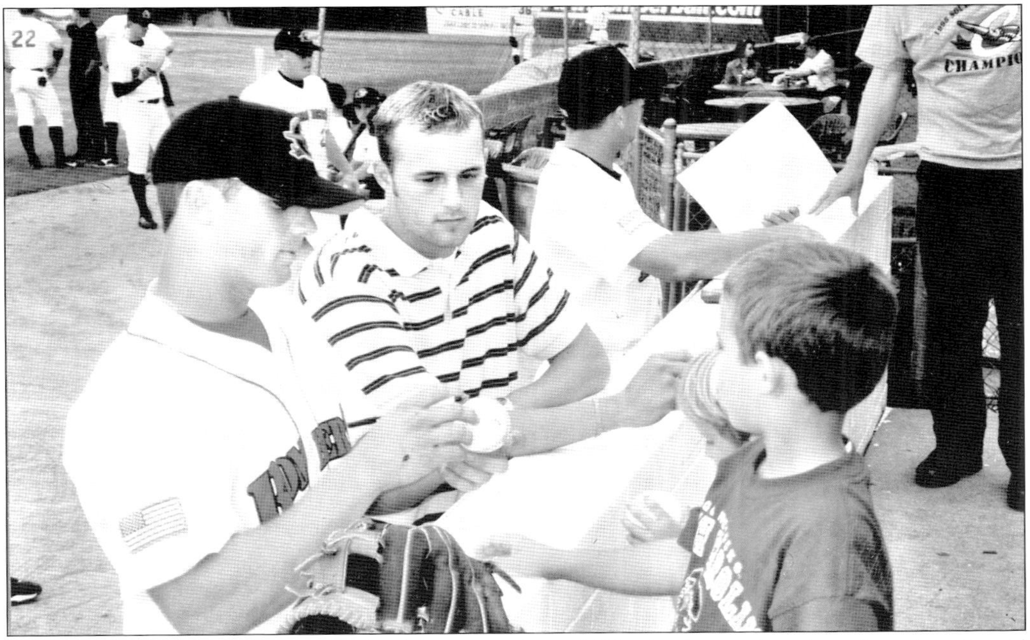

Young fans get a moment with third-baseman David Wright (in uniform) and pitcher David Mattox. In 2002, both players used their time in Columbia to further their status as prospects. Wright, a first-round draft pick, earned his label as the Mets third-baseman of the future. Mattox, one of the few Bombers to be born in the South Carolina Midlands, was the organization's Pitcher of the Year. (CCB.)

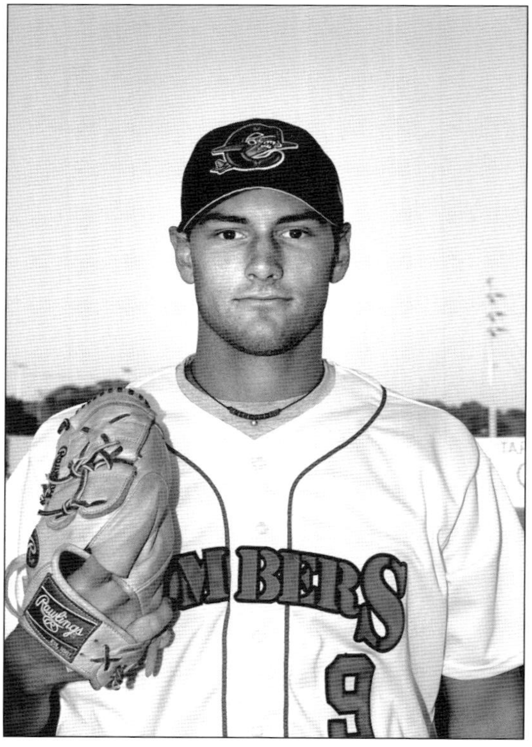

A third-round draft pick of the Mets, Lenny Dinardo pitched well but without much fanfare for the 2002 Bombers. Two years later, he made his big-league debut for the Boston Red Sox. Dinardo became the 99th Columbia Met or Capital City Bomber alumnus to make the majors, leading to speculation over who would have the distinction of being number 100 on the list. (CCB.)

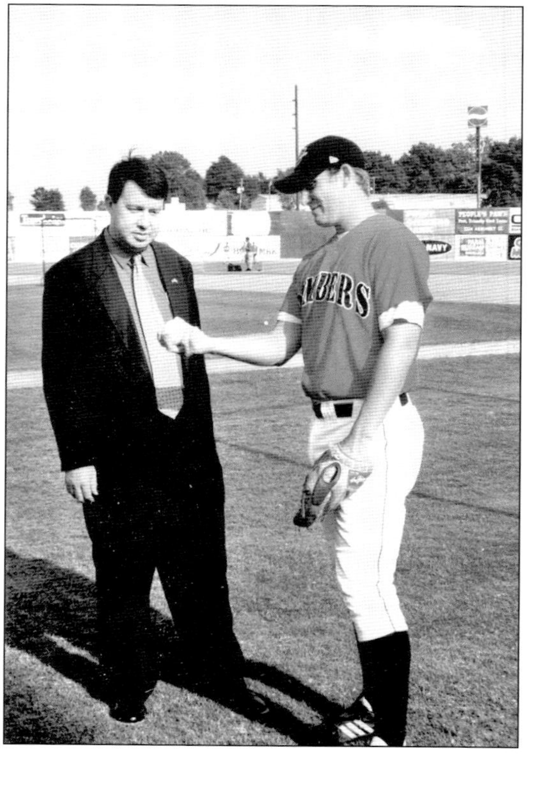

South Carolina has had a "sister state" relationship with Queensland, Australia, for years. That connection has produced a number of cultural exchanges. Coincidentally, the 2002 Bombers had a Queensland native on the roster in pitcher Wayne Ough. Here we see Ough demonstrating pitching grips to an unidentified member of the Queensland government on a visit to Columbia. (CCB.)

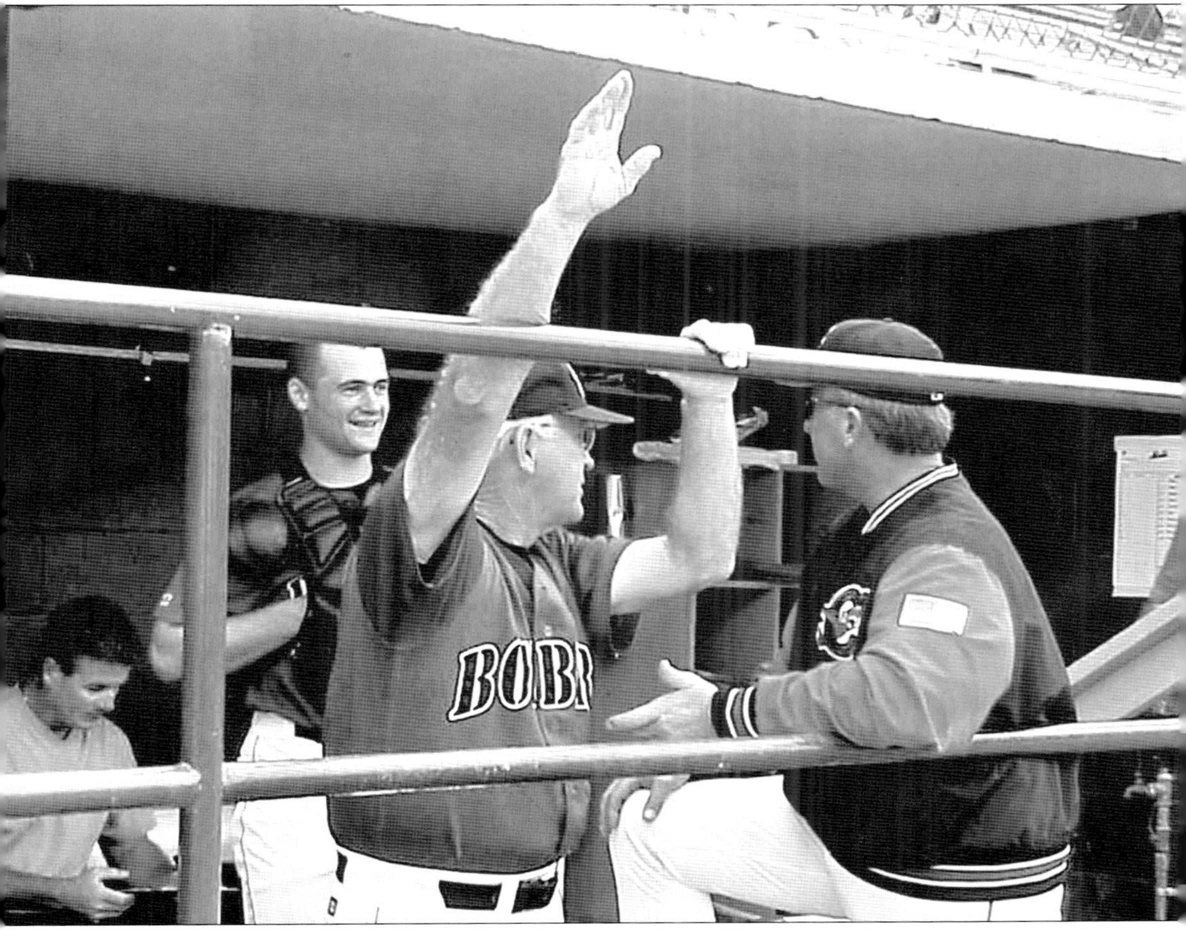

This picture from the 2002 season captured a rare baseball moment: three generations of major-league caliber catchers talking about their trade. Bombers catcher Justin Huber (left) developed into a highly regarded prospect, expected by many to see big-league playing time. Huber, an Australian, also provided another example of successful global scouting in the Mets organization. Capital City hitting coach (and former manager) John Stephenson (center) had a 10-year career in the majors. His days behind the plate included catching the first big-league strikeouts thrown by Nolan Ryan. Gary Carter (right) came through Columbia on several occasions as a roving instructor for the New York Mets. Carter's sensational playing career in the majors merited induction in the Baseball Hall of Fame. (CCB.)

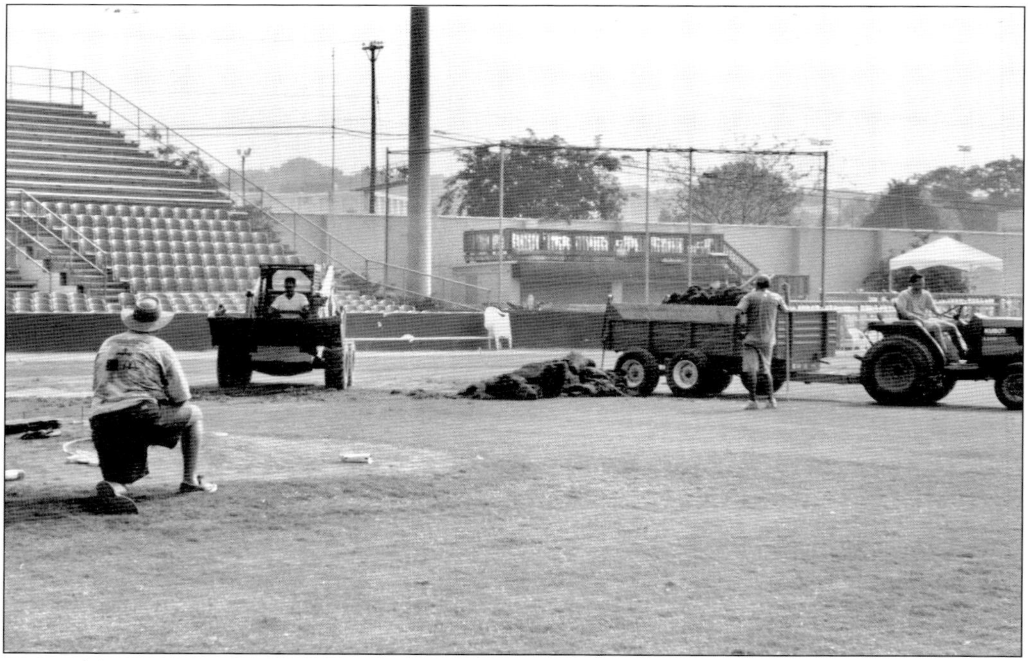

Groundskeeper Bob Hook watches on one knee for a moment as workers literally dig into the process of resodding and reshaping the entire infield in 2002. New owners for the team paid for the improvements before the club's sale was complete, demonstrating a strong commitment to making sure the facility provided the best place it could to play or watch a game. (CCB.)

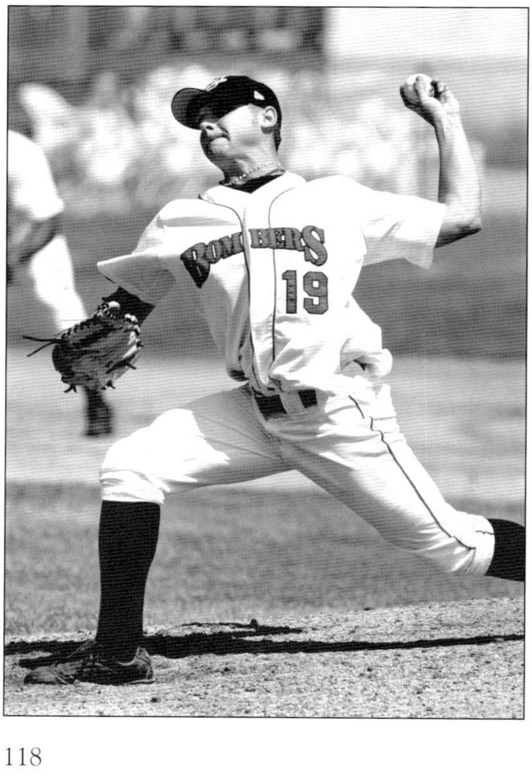

The personification of a modern-day top prospect, Scott Kazmir got drafted in the first round out of high school in Houston—the Mets were wowed by the left-hander's 97-mile-per-hour fastball. Kazmir got right to work for the 2003 Bombers and sufficiently impressed the organization, getting a midseason promotion to St. Lucie of the Florida State League. Kazmir entered the 2004 season as the Mets' number one prospect. (CCB.)

A staple promotion of the Bombers for several years had the ballpark population howling. "Bring Your Dog Night" was as simple as it sounds, and the result brought an amazing change to the atmosphere of the game. About 200 dogs in a minor league stadium can do that—after all, how can you not smile? (CCB.)

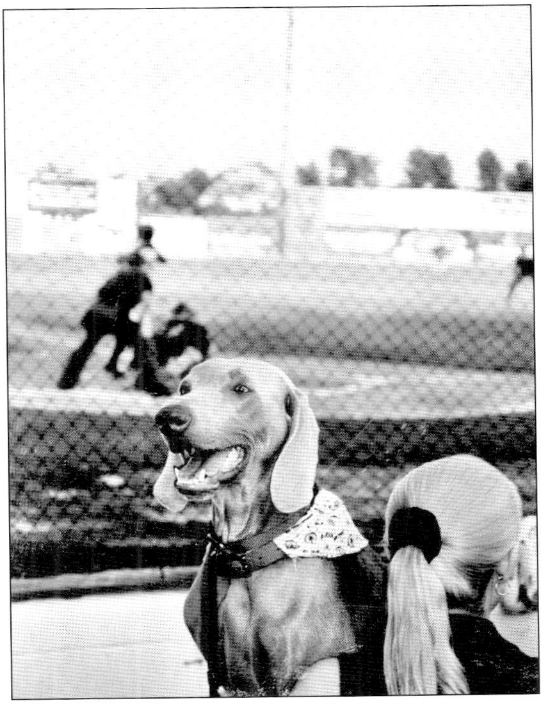

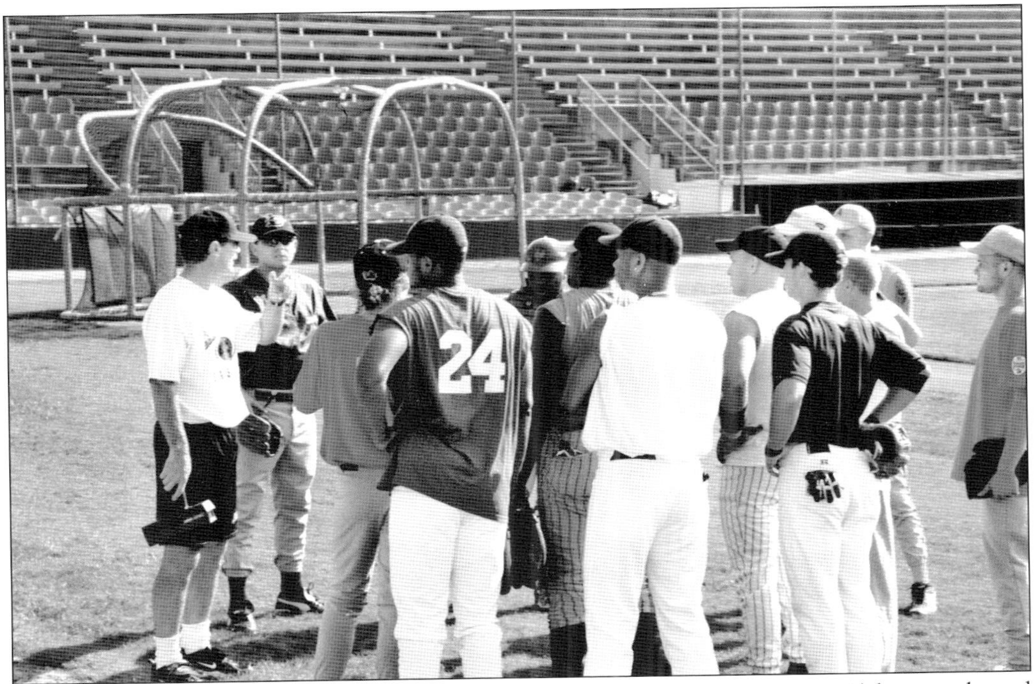

Mets area scout Marlin McPhail (far left, with manager Tony Tijerina in 2003) has conducted an open tryout at Capital City Stadium for many years. Scouts hold these events to seek out any players that might have been overlooked by pro teams. Although staging tryouts is a long-standing tradition for baseball scouts, a player truly worth signing can be a rare find. (CCB.)

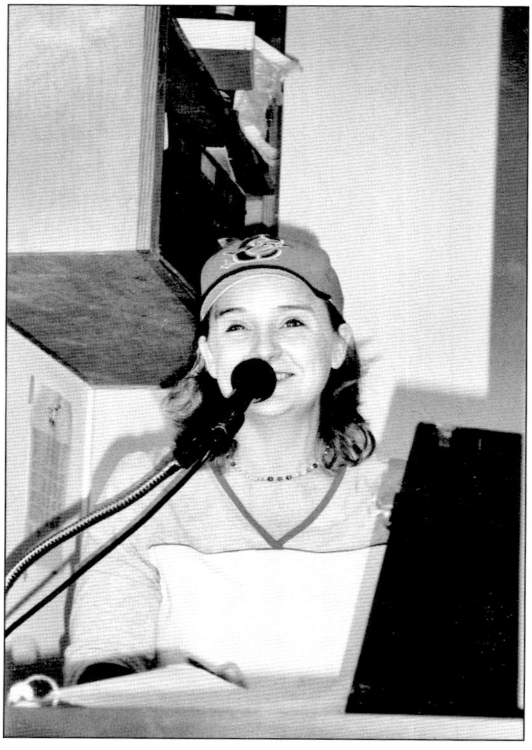

Capital City Stadium featured a different sound in the 2003 season with the voice of public address announcer Ashley Byrd. Although female PA announcers are not unheard of, they are quite rare in baseball. Byrd, a long-time Bombers fan, described the opportunity as "a dream job." Prior to her stint in the press box, she had played concerts at the ballpark as singer and guitarist for the band She Says. (CCB.)

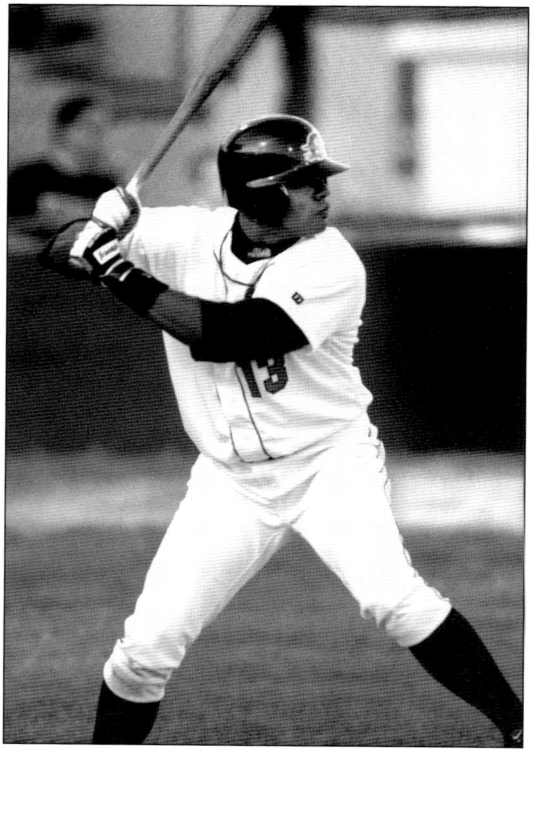

The lone All-Star on the final list for 2003 was third-baseman Aarom Baldiris. His strong season also earned him recognition from *Baseball America* as a national all-star for Class A baseball. Strangely enough, Baldiris did not finish the year with the Bombers, as the Mets actually sent him down a level to help the Brooklyn Cyclones in their push to the New York–Penn League playoffs. (CCB.)

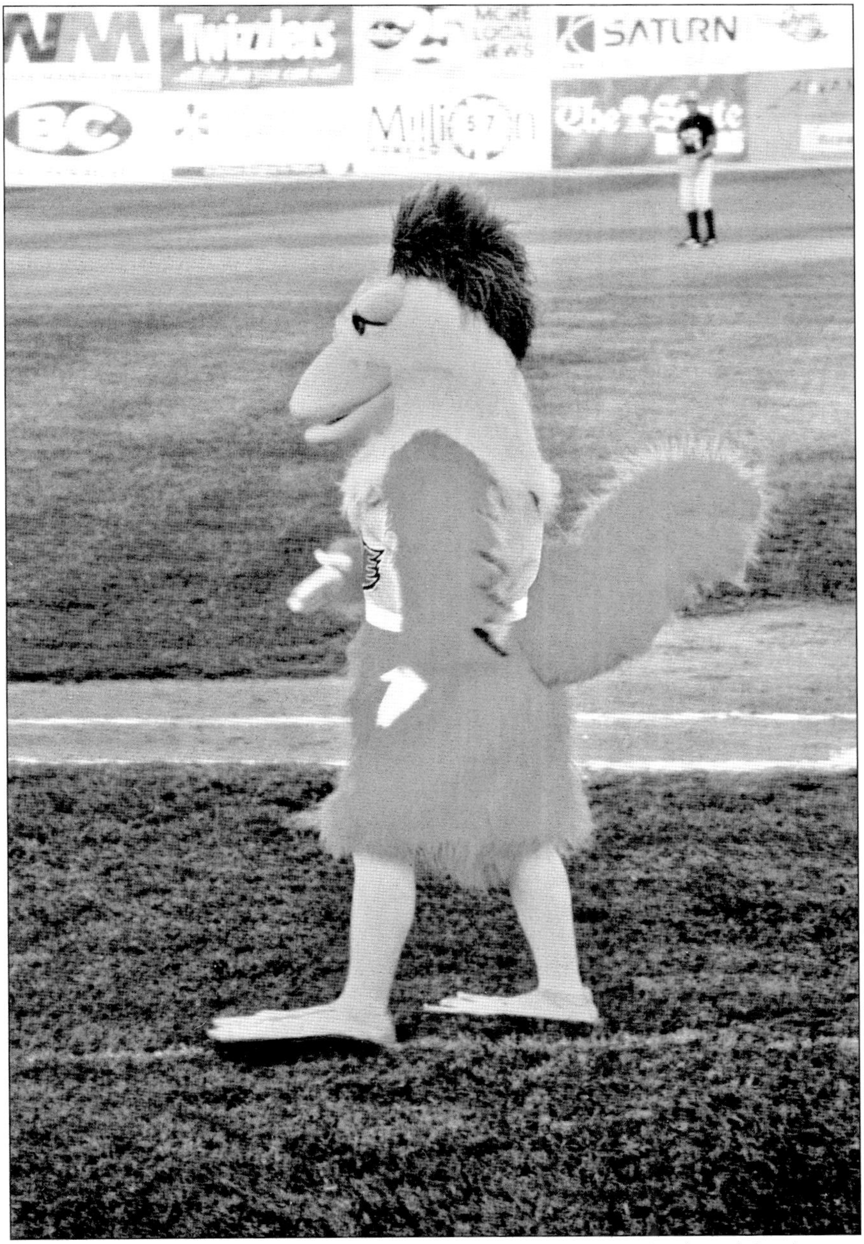

The original costumed character and super-mascot, the Famous Chicken (also known as Ted Giannoulas), has visited the Columbia Mets and Capital City Bombers several times and is seen here in his 2003 visit. Promotional appearances by touring entertainers have been found all over the schedule throughout the years, but only a few other acts have approached the popularity or the humor of the original Famous Chicken. Some of the other acts seen at the ballpark over the years include the Zooperstars, World Famous Monkey Boy, the Blues Brothers, the Mayberry Deputy, Little E, Krazy George, Myron Noodleman, Jurassic All-Stars, Sport, Flying Elvises, Skyy Dogs USA, and the Phillie Phanatic. Copyrighted characters like the Rugrats, Veggie Tales, and Scooby-Doo have also checked in to entertain fans. (CCB.)

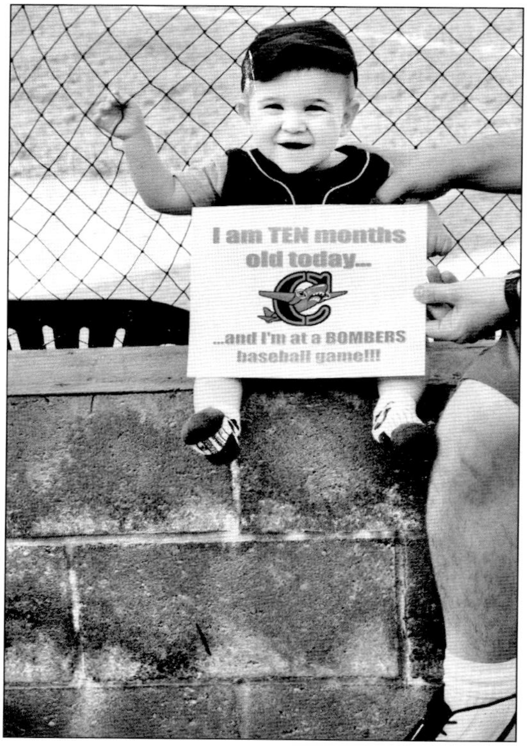

Countless young fans have celebrated birthdays at the ballpark over the years, but apparently some cannot even wait for their first birthday to celebrate with the Bombers, like Griffin Bryant in 2003. The family aspect of baseball extends not only to fans, but to the children of team staff, coaches, and players as well. The game gets repeatedly handed off to new generations that have grown up in ballparks. (CCB.)

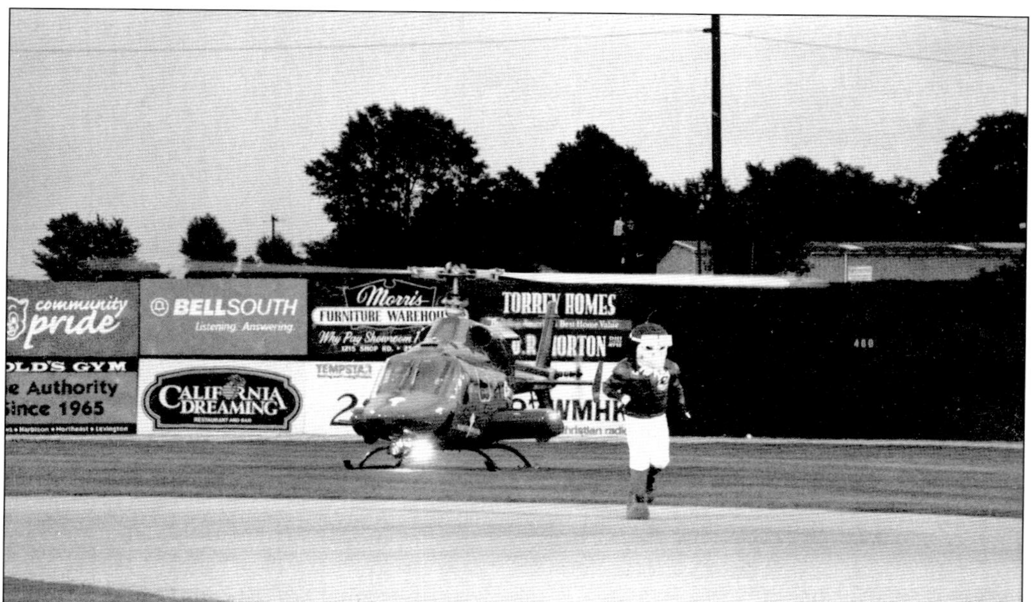

When the Bombers decided to add a second mascot character in 2003, they found the perfect way to introduce him. "Ace the Eagle" flew into Capital City Stadium via helicopter between games of a Memorial Day Weekend doubleheader! Long-time batboy and mascot performer Kevin Chastain got the thrilling ride on the Palmetto Health CareForce chopper for Ace's debut. "Ace" was chosen for referring to the best of both pilots and pitchers. (CCB.)

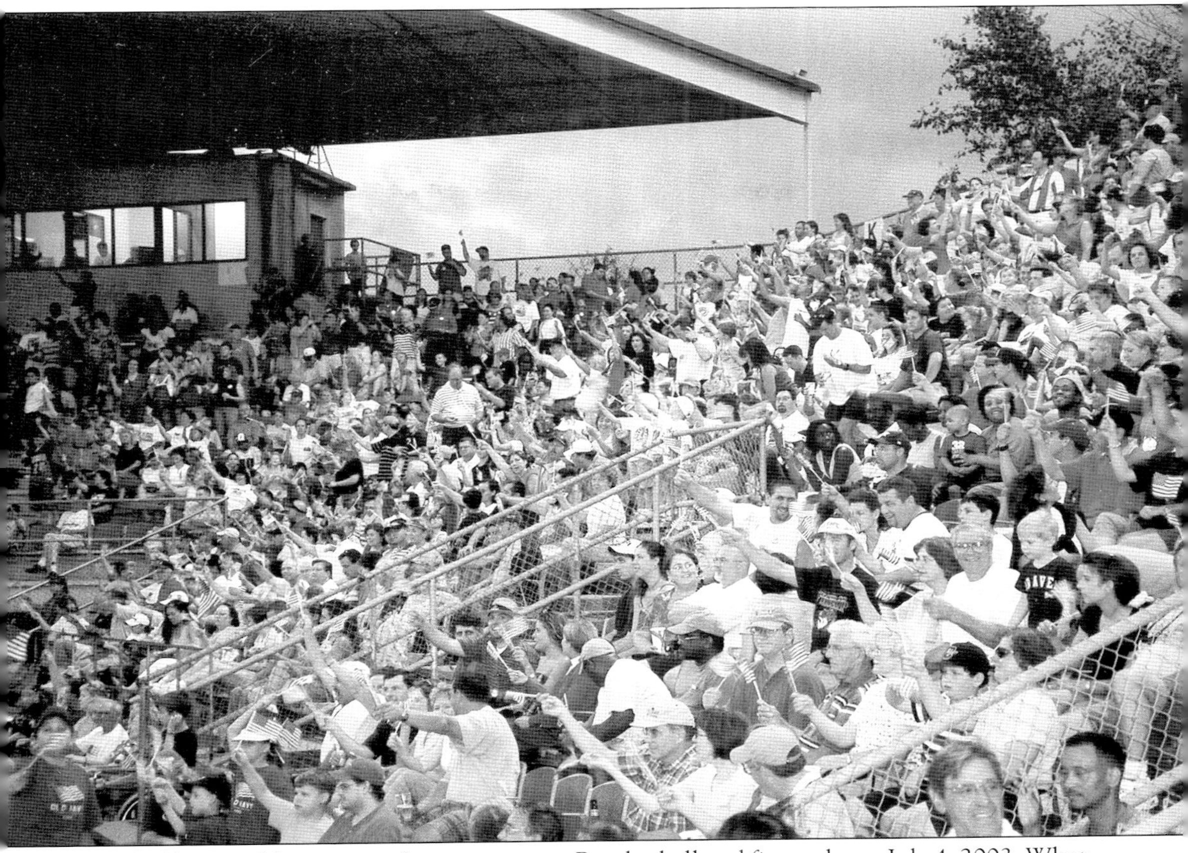

A packed house of flag-waving fans came to see Bomberball and fireworks on July 4, 2003. What they got instead was an unwanted piece of history. The Bombers and Asheville Tourists got trapped in a game seemingly without end. It took Asheville 19 innings to defeat the home team, coming two innings shy of the league record for longest game. The marathon was the longest for any Columbia pro team since the Comers went 20 innings in 1919. Making matters worse, the team got trapped in an unexpected bind: it could not stop the game to launch the expected fireworks, but it also could not legally shoot the fireworks after midnight. Add in rain showers that came and went during the game, and you have a recipe for all-around disappointment. The game ended shortly before 2:00 a.m., with a few hundred dedicated (or crazy) fans still in the house to see the Tourists win. (CCB.)

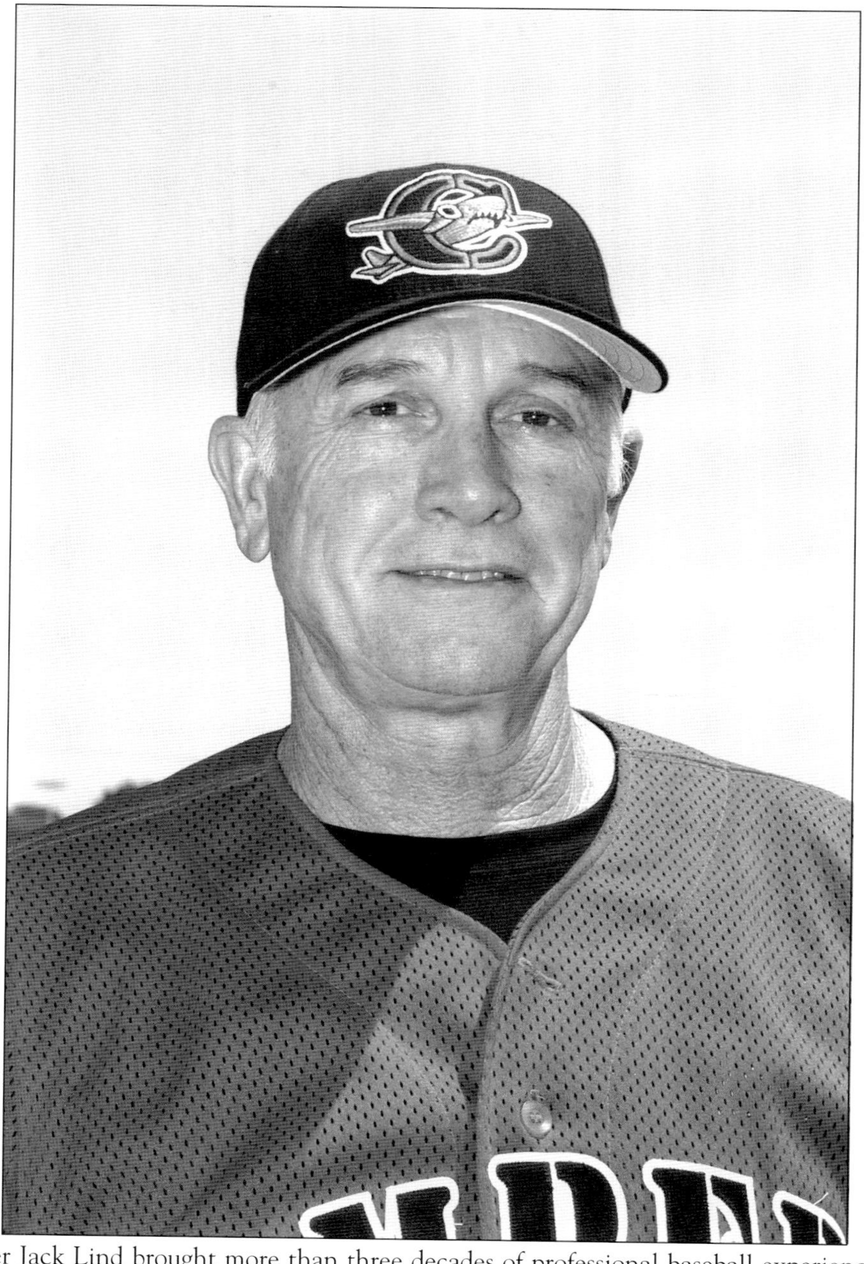

Manager Jack Lind brought more than three decades of professional baseball experience with him when he arrived to take the spot as Capital City's skipper for the 2004 season. The Arizona native starred at shortstop for the 1967 National Champion Arizona State baseball team and moved on to a pro career that peaked with a big-league stint in Milwaukee. Before he finished playing, he not only suited up for the Brewers but also for the Yomiuri Giants, which gave him a very unusual distinction: Lind is one of only two players to be teammates with Home Run Kings Hank Aaron and Saduharu Oh (the other is Davey Johnson). Lind logged more time in the majors as a coach for the Pittsburgh Pirates. He has had other stops as a manager in the minors, but his first year with the Mets organization brought him to Columbia. (CCB.)

Dave Hollins joined the Bombers coaching staff in 2004, but he already had connections to the area. His brother Paul played for the 1983 Columbia Mets, and both brothers played college ball at USC, where Dave was a standout in the mid- to late 1980s. Hollins's career in the majors included a trip to the 1993 All-Star Game when he was a member of the National League champion Phillies. (CCB.)

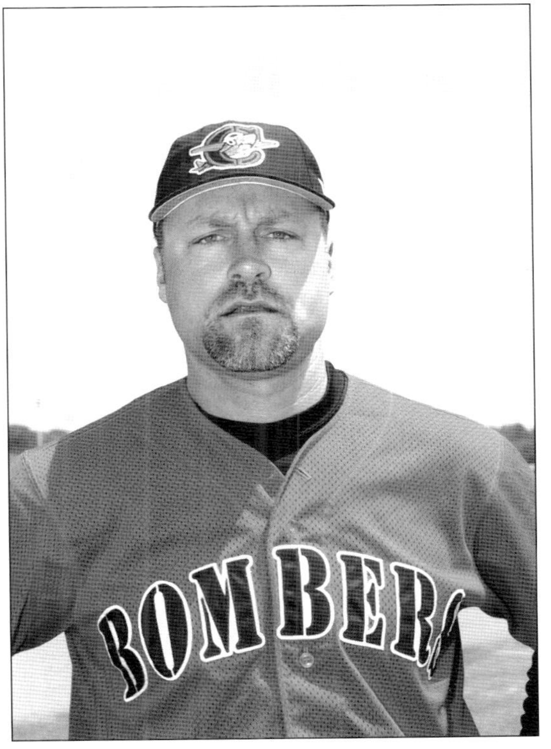

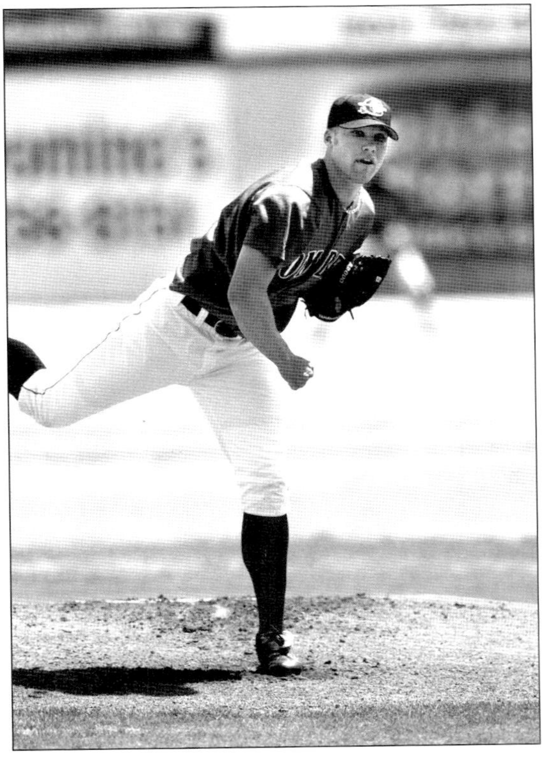

In May 2004, Bombers starting pitcher Matt Lindstrom pitched one of the finest games ever seen in Columbia—a perfect game through seven innings! Lindstrom left the game before it ended, due to pitch restrictions issued by the Mets organization. An injury at the next level opened a roster spot, and Lindstrom got promoted before he could make his next start. Talk about a "perfect" ending. (CCB.)

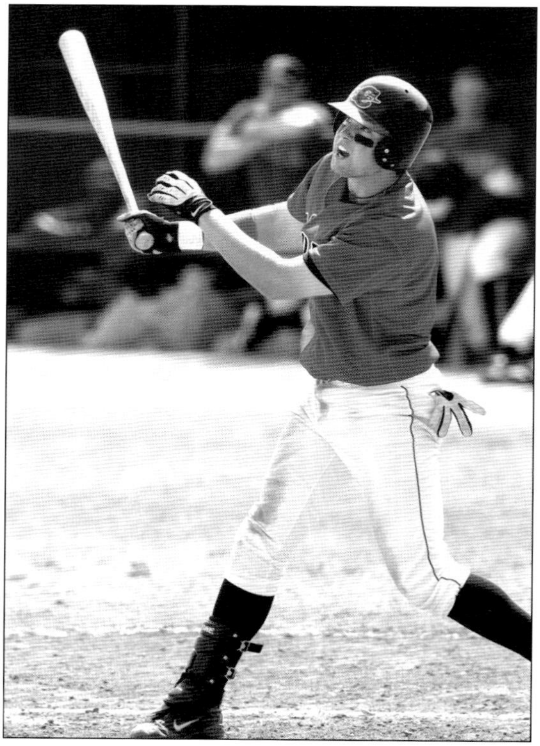

Ian Bladergroen put up offensive numbers in early 2004 that staggered the imagination, earned two SAL Batter of the Week awards, and merited interviews and write-ups on a national scale. The late-round draft pick from New Mexico looked every bit as sharp as his nickname: "Blade." (CCB.)

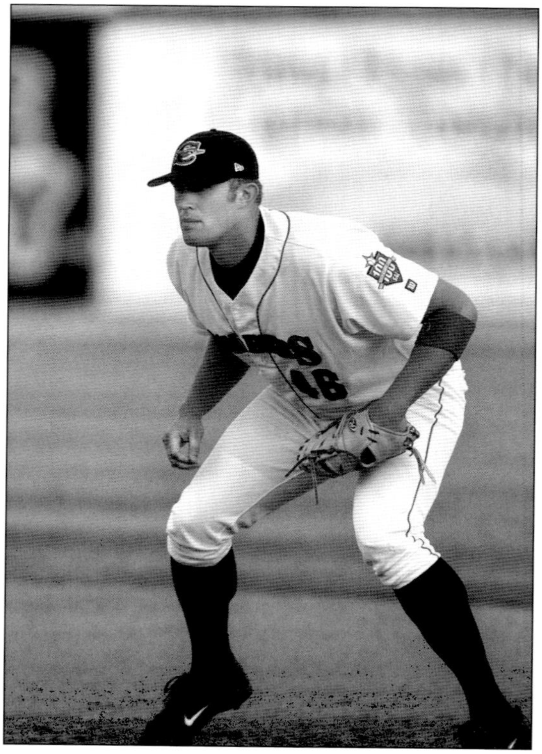

In 2004, Tyler Davidson arrived in Columbia with only one season of professional experience but a career's worth of honors. Davidson's sensational 2003 season in Kingsport made him an Appalachian League All-Star, a *Baseball America* All-Star for short-season leagues, and the Appalachian League Player of the Year. His 6-foot-5-inch frame gives his teammates a great target at first base and his opponents an intimidating foe. (CCB.)

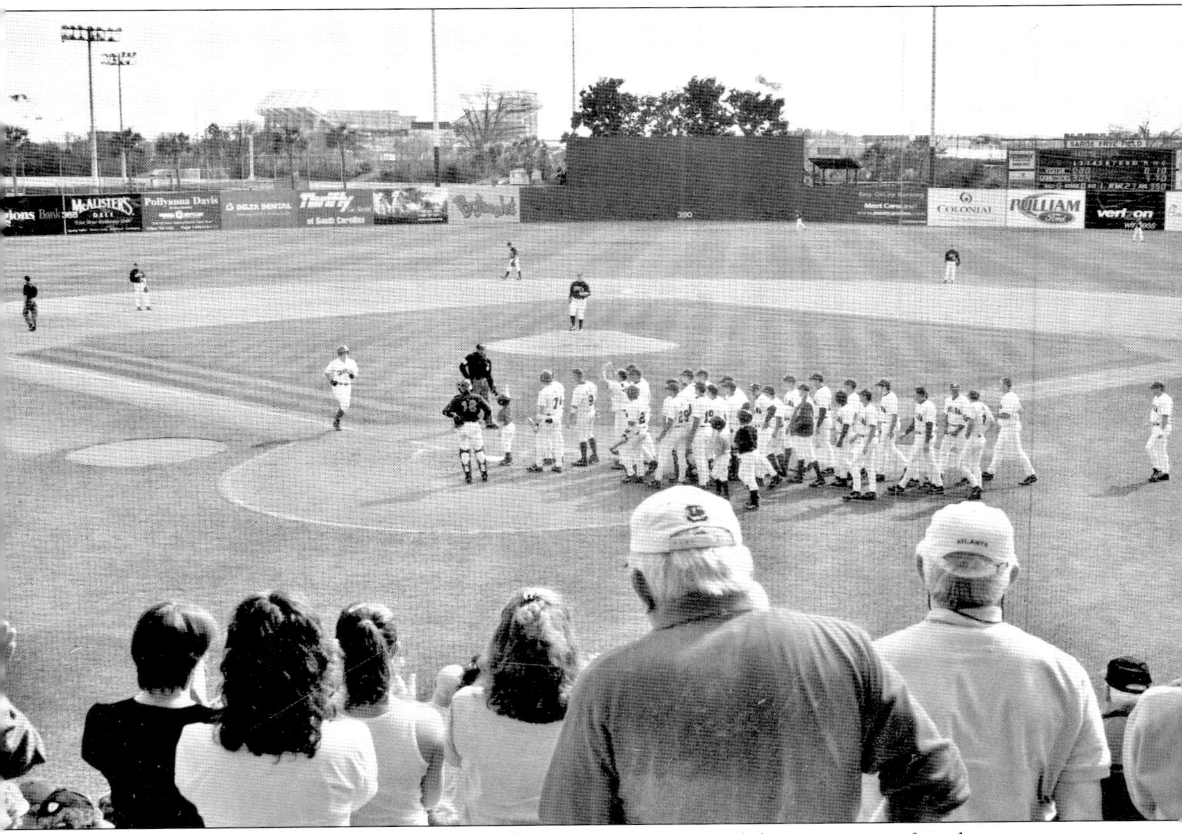

The University of South Carolina baseball team, seen here celebrating one of its home runs against UNC-Wilmington in early 2004, shared its ballpark with Columbia's professional team back in the early 20th century. Some people have suggested that USC and the Bombers try a new cooperative effort. A long series of negotiations between the minor-league owners and university officials produced a working agreement in 2004 for a joint stadium project. Such shared facilities are not unheard of, and one good example sits not far away from the capital city, as the Citadel and the Charleston RiverDogs have successfully shared Joseph P. Riley Jr. Ballpark for several years. Even with a verbal understanding from the school and the pro team, the City of Columbia needed to join as the third member of the partnership to make the new ballpark a reality and to ensure the long and healthy life of baseball in the South Carolina Midlands. That possibility was still in discussion while the Bombers played their 2004 season at Capital City Stadium. The successful South Carolina program has made multiple trips to the College World Series under Coach Ray Tanner. (Author's collection.)

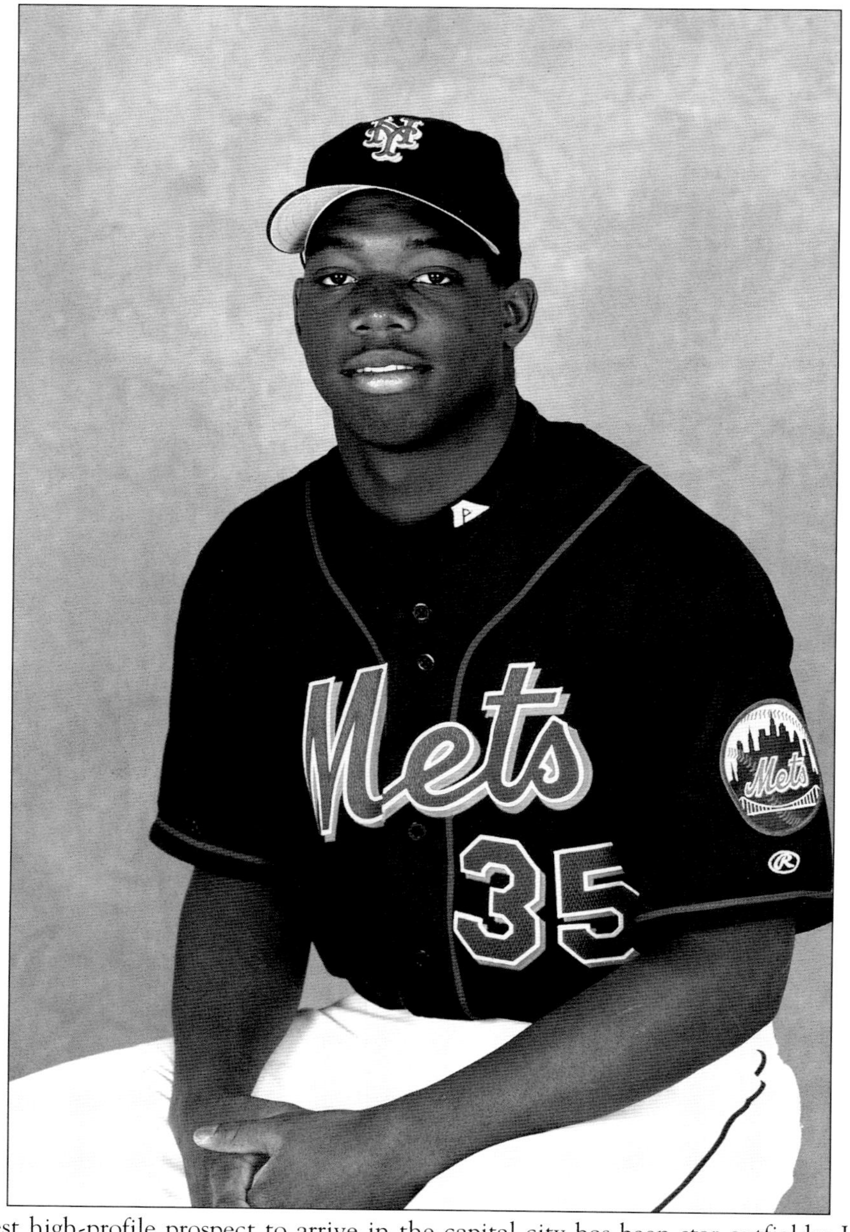

The latest high-profile prospect to arrive in the capital city has been star outfielder Lastings Milledge in 2004. The Mets selected Milledge with the 12th overall pick in the 2003 draft and signed him for more than $2 million. Expectations were high before the teenager even suited up for the Bombers because his talent covered the five tools that scouts study: hitting for average, hitting for power, arm strength, speed, and defense. When Milledge did come to Columbia—delayed a month into the season due to an injury sustained during spring training—he stepped right into the lineup as the leadoff hitter and centerfielder. An aggressive player with good instincts, Milledge is projected as a star of the future. His parents traveled to Columbia from their home in Florida in a new recreational vehicle to watch him play his first full season of professional baseball. (New York Mets.)